ANDROID
Pocket Primer

LICENSE, DISCLAIMER OF LIABILITY, AND LIMITED WARRANTY

ANDROID
Pocket Primer

Oswald Campesato

MERCURY LEARNING AND INFORMATION
Dulles, Virginia
Boston, Massachusetts
New Delhi

Publisher: David Pallai

Mercury Learning and Information
22841 Quicksilver Drive
Dulles, VA 20166
info@merclearning.com
www.merclearning.com
(800) 232-0223

O. Campesato. *Android* Pocket Primer.
ISBN: 978-1-68392-088-5

Library of Congress Control Number: 2017935501
171819321   Printed in the United States of America on acid-free paper.

Our titles are available for adoption, license, or bulk purchase by institutions, corporations, etc. For additional information, please contact the Customer Service Dept. at (800) 232-0223 (toll free). Digital versions of our titles are available at: www.authorcloudware.com and other e-vendors. *Companion files for this title may be requested at info@merclearning.com.*

I'd like to dedicate this book to my parents –
may this bring joy and happiness into their lives.

CONTENTS

Note: Appendices are Companion Files (PDFs) only
Appendix A: Threads and Networking
Appendix B: Performance and Debugging
Appendix C: Miscellaneous Topics

PREFACE

What Is the Goal?

The goal of this book is to provide an introduction and overview of Android mobile development to developers who are relatively new to this platform. The biggest challenge for a book of this length is to provide sufficient detail for the main features of Android, along with suitable code samples that include Android 6 and Android 7. Note that while many code samples will work on older versions of Android (including 2.x and 3.x devices), the market share for mobile devices with Android 4.x or higher exceeds 96%.

This book has an ambitious goal, so it's vitally important to recognize that *this book will not make you an expert in Android*. Some Android topics are covered lightly, and some Android topics are omitted entirely because they do not belong in this type of Android book.

What You Need to Know for This Book

Let's be clear: this book is not for beginners. Even if you are new to Android, you need some development experience in order to benefit from the plethora of topics and the details of the code samples in this book. Most of the material in this book is presented in a sequential manner, and yet sometimes there are "forward references" to topics that are covered later in the book. This situation can create a degree of cognitive dissonance (so to speak), which you will be better equipped to handle if you have a development background.

In particular, you need an understanding of OOP (Object Oriented Programming) and Java. You also need a basic knowledge of XML, because the configuration files in Android applications are XML documents.

Knowledge of another OO programming language instead of Java might be sufficient, but to be on the safe side, glance through the code samples to gauge whether or not you can handle the material.

Wait: Isn't This Book a Pocket Primer?

In fairness to you, the term "Pocket Primer" requires clarification. If you believe that a "Pocket Primer" provides a gentle introduction to some aspects of a technology, then this book might be too advanced for you right now, and perhaps not well-suited to your needs. This book is not a "crash course" in Android: you will get a good overview of various features of Android.

If you read the answer to the previous question, then you already know that this book is not for neophyte developers who consider themselves "absolute beginners." To put things into perspective: if you have graduated from a boot camp that focuses on mobile development, you will be much better prepared than a graduate of a boot camp that focuses on Web development.

The nature of this book is somewhere in the middle: if you perceive a "Pocket Primer" as similar to "jump-starting" your knowledge of a technology, then this book might fit your needs. Be assured that you need to invest some time and effort to master the topics in this book. There are no fluffy chapters that are padded with material that has no actual value. Every chapter (including the first one) justifies its existence solely by its technical content. The technical content of this book strives to ensure that the target audience will get its money's worth, so it's a question of whether or not you are part of the target audience.

If you intend to become an expert in Android, this book will provide a "stepping stone" for your journey.

What about All the Free Code Samples Online?

The value of this book is the convenience of having a set of working code samples available in one location, along with supplemental details. For example, Chapter 7 contains a code sample for displaying processes on an Android device: all processes are displayed on Android 6, but the root processes are not displayed on a Pixel phone. The code in the YouTube video example is simpler than code that's based on the official YouTube Android Player API (though the latter is recommended for production applications), and you will also get information about playing videos on an SD card as well as the res/raw subdirectory of an Android application.

So, while online code samples are obviously useful, you also need to spend time reading them, just as you would for this book. Moreover, you also need to determine which online code samples actually work correctly, which this book has already done for you.

The Target Audience

This book is for advanced beginners, and it's intended to reach an international audience of readers with highly diverse backgrounds in various age groups. While many readers know how to read English, their native spoken language may not be English (which could be their second, third, or even fourth language).

Consequently, this book uses standard English and avoids colloquial expressions that might be confusing to those readers. As you know, many people learn by different types of mimicry, which includes reading, writing, or hearing new material. This book takes these points into consideration in order to provide a comfortable and meaningful learning experience for the intended readers.

Getting the Most from This Book

Some programmers learn well from prose and others learn well from sample code (and lots of it), which means that there's no single style that works perfectly for everyone.

Moreover, some programmers want to run the code first, see what it does, and then return to the code to understand the details (and others use the opposite approach).

Consequently, there is a variety of code samples in this book. Some are short, some are long, and other code samples "build" from earlier code samples.

How Does This Book Help Me?

You will learn about various "core" concepts in Android, and also gain an understanding of how to use many Android APIs. Moreover, the Appendices contain an extensive set of references for extending your knowledge of Android. What you decide to learn about Android after you finish reading this Android Primer depends on your goals and career path. For example, if you are a developer, you will undoubtedly continue learning more about

Android. On the other hand, if you are in management, you will understand enough about Android to interact on a technical level with Android developers.

Why Just Short Code Samples?

As you can see in the title, this book is for people who are new to Android development. The code samples are intended to help you gain an understanding of various Android APIs, and that's why every code sample is at most three pages in length (and often only one or two pages long). The focus is to provide code for Android features (such as buttons, text fields, and media-related APIs) that you are likely to need in your Android applications. The use of shorter code samples allows for more Android APIs to be included in this book.

The code samples are derived in various ways, such as custom code (written by the author), variations of code from the Android documentation, and sections of code from discussions in online forums. In addition, the code samples were developed in Android Studio 2.2 (version 7) on a MacBook Pro with OS X 10.11.6 (El Capitan), and then deployed to a Samsung Galaxy 5 with Android 6.0.1 and a Pixel phone with Android 7.1. However, the code samples should work on all supported platforms.

How Was the Table of Contents Determined?

The decision process was as objective as possible, and it involved several criteria. The first criterion was to include "must have" concepts (such as `Activitys` and `Intents`) and APIs (including basic UI components) that are used in virtually every Android application. The second criterion was to include "nice to have" functionality (such as media-related APIs) that would appeal to Android novices. The third criterion involved Android APIs that could be useful for people who want to write "serious" Android applications. Examples of such APIs include Android sensors. The fourth criterion involved Android APIs that are needed for Android applications in the book.

Which Android Topics Are Excluded and Why?

The Android features that do not meet any of the criteria listed in the previous section are not included in this Primer. Consequently, there is no coverage of AR (Augmented Reality), multitasking, and XML parsers

(SAX and DOM) in this book. Another topic that is not covered is Java Native Interface (JNI), which allows Java code to invoke C/C++ functions. If you are interested in JNI, you need to download and install the Android Native Development Kit (NDK), which contains a set of tools for creating libraries that contain functions that can be called from Java code.

The material in the chapters will familiarize you with the Android APIs, after which you can do further reading to deepen your knowledge. For example, Chapter 4 covers graphics and animation effects, but the code samples in that chapter will not make you a game expert.

Doesn't the Companion Disc Obviate the Need for This Book?

The inclusion of a companion disc with code samples provides an important service: you will save both time and effort, and you will be spared the error-prone process of manually typing code into Android Studio. Yet, there are situations in which you might not have easy Internet access, whereas this book would be accessible to you. Another point to remember is that the code samples in the book contain explanations and details that are omitted from the "pure" code samples on the companion disc.

What Other Books Should I Read after Finishing This Book?

The answer to this question varies widely, mainly because the answer depends heavily on your objectives. Specifically, you need to decide how much effort you are prepared to invest in furthering your knowledge. The amount of time that you need to make significant advances in your technical expertise also depends your current level of technical knowledge and experience. For instance, the needs of a manager, a student, and a professional Android developer (among others) are obviously different. The most appropriate answer to this question is a) to ask friends and coworkers for advice and suggestions, and b) to perform an Internet search and spend some time evaluating other resources that are available.

O. Campesato
March 2017

ABOUT THE TECHNICAL REVIEWER

Siamak "Ash" Ashrafi (link to bio at *https://goo.gl/dmkJ0a*) is an experienced programmer and developer in Android and iOS mobile apps. His frequent code-a-thon wins have become published apps, and he holds several patents related to popular video games. He is the CTO at ZoeWave, building physiologically intelligent clothing called *ZoeWear*. He also has over fifteen years of experience as a biotech researcher in the fields of human physiology and biotechnology. In his spare time, you can find him DJing or competing in snowboarding, surfboarding, and kite boarding.

CHAPTER 1

A QUICK INTRODUCTION TO ANDROID

This introductory chapter discusses how to develop Android applications, as well as their structure, various XML-based configuration files, and some basic features of Android. You will learn how to create mobile applications in Android Studio, which is the recommended IDE for Android development. Two important features of Android are `Activitys` and `Intents`, which you see throughout this book.

The first part of this chapter discusses the structure of Android projects in Android Studio and some of the important files in Android projects. Moreover, this section discusses the "Android way" of providing values for properties that determine the position and size of Android components in Android applications. Note that additional details about positional attributes, different screen densities, and different screen sizes are available in Chapter 2.

The second part of this chapter switches focus to describe Android-specific concepts and features. Specifically, this section quickly introduces you to Android `Activitys` and `Intents`, which are key features of Android. Almost every Android application in this book uses an Android Activity, and several examples use Android Intents.

As you will see, this chapter contains a combination of a "hands on" approach and a conceptual overview of Android. Additional "hands on" material is presented in Chapter 2 so that you will learn techniques and concepts for creating Android applications on an as-needed basis. However, feel free to read this chapter (as well as other chapters) in the order that best fits your learning style.

In some cases you might need to read subsections more than once in order to "synchronize" your understanding of Android applications, which is typical when you learn a new technology. In fact, Android `Intents` will require longer study (compared to Android `Activitys`) because they involve subtle points that you will understand better through practice. Fortunately, subsequent chapters contain code samples that illustrate how to use Intents and how to incorporate various UI components in Android applications.

One final comment: at some point (now would be a good time) please read the Preface for information regarding the goal of this book and assumptions about your technical background.

Major Versions of Android

Android is an open-source toolkit for developing Android mobile applications that was publicly launched in late 2007. Let's barrel through the dates for some of the major releases. Android 4.0 ("Ice Cream Sandwich") was released in late 2011, followed by Android 4.4 in October 2013. Android 5.0 ("Lollipop") was released in November 2014, then Android 6 in October 2015, and finally Android 7 in August 2016. More information about the history of Android versions is here:

http://en.wikipedia.org/wiki/Android_version_history.

The Stack

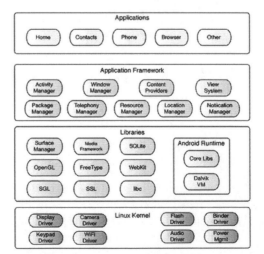

FIGURE 1.1 Android versions and percentage of devices (12/2016).

The features of Android are cumulative (though there are new classes that replace deprecated classes), so each version of Android supports the preceding versions (see Figure 1.1). Keep in mind that sometimes there are changes in the signature of APIs between consecutive Android versions. This progression of features will help you plan your Android applications in terms of which versions you can target with specific features.

Figure 1.1 displays the percentage of devices that operate different versions of Android.

Navigate to the following link to see more recent percentages:

https://developer.android.com/about/dashboards/index.html.

Developing Android Mobile Applications

Until 2014 many Android mobile applications were developed in the open-source Eclipse IDE, and then Google announced that there would be no additional Android support for Eclipse. Android Studio became the official IDE for Android, which is how all the Android applications in this book were created. If necessary, you can export Android applications from Eclipse for the purpose of importing them into Android Studio. In fact, one of the options in the main menu of Android Studio enables you to import an Eclipse-based project.

The code samples in this book were developed in Android Studio 2.2 and deployed to two devices: a Samsung Galaxy S5 smart phone with Android 6.0.1 and a Pixel phone with Android 7.1. Since the companion disc contains the source code for the samples in this book, you can modify them for different (i.e., higher or lower) versions of Android and deploy them to Android devices with different versions of Android.

Android Studio

Navigate to this website in order to install Android Studio on your machine:

https://developer.android.com/sdk/index.html.

If you use the Simulator instead of an Android device, you must create an AVD (Android Virtual Device), which is described in great detail here:

https://developer.android.com/tools/devices/index.html.

You can launch Android applications in the Simulator, but it's often significantly faster to deploy Android applications to a device. You can deploy Android applications from Android Studio as well as from a command line via the `adb` utility (as you will see later). Android devices include (but are not limited to) smart phones in the Nexus series and the Pixel series, tablets, Google Auto, Google TV, Google Things (IoT), and Google VR. In addition, there are several Android application types, including foreground, background, intermittent, widgets, and wallpaper applications.

Dalvik versus ART

Earlier versions of Android used the Dalvik VM, which is an Android implementation of the Java VM. Dalvik runs `.dex` files whereas Java runs `.class` files. A Dalvik executable has an `apk` suffix, and it contains the various resources to launch an Android application. More recent versions of Android use the ART (Android Runtime) VM that uses AOT (ahead of time) compilation. After you create, compile, and run Android applications, Android creates a binary file with an `apk` suffix for each application, which you can deploy to Android devices.

Jack is a newer toolchain for the compilation of Android applications, and if you want to delve into the details (which are beyond the scope of this chapter), navigate to this link:

https://source.android.com/source/jack.html.

Creating Applications in Android Studio

This section describes how to create an application in Android Studio, and a subsequent section shows you the directory structure of an Android application, followed by a discussion of the main files that are created in every Android application.

Launch Android Studio (version 2.2 or higher is required) and perform the following sequence of steps in order to create a new Android application called `HelloWorld`:

Step 1: Click on "Start a new Android Studio project"
Step 2: Enter `HelloWorld` for the Application name
Step 3: Enter a Company Domain (e.g., `yourcompany.com`)
Step 4: Change the Project location or accept the default
Step 5: Click the Next button
Step 6: Click the Phone and Tablet checkbox and click Next
Step 7: Select an Empty Activity
Step 8: Click the "Finish" button

The values in Steps 2 through 8 are for the typical "Hello World" Android application, whereas your values will be adjusted to suit your application.

Later you can create applications with different configurations (such as Basic Activity, Master/Detail, and so forth) or for different platforms (such as Android TV).

After you complete Step 8, Android Studio will generate a new Android project whose structure is described later in this chapter (after you learn how to launch an application from Android Studio).

OTE   *The* `HelloWorld` *project is available on the companion disc.*

Launching Android Apps from Android Studio

Launch the `HelloWorld` Android application in the previous section by right-clicking on the project name `HelloWorld` (in Android Studio) and then selecting `Run as > Android Application`.

If you are using an Android emulator, wait until the emulator completes its initialization steps, which can require a minute or so (but each subsequent launching of your application should be faster).

If you have an Android device attached to your machine via a USB port, make sure that debug mode is enabled on your device. Android Studio will render a pop-up window that displays that mobile device and also the available AVDs. Select your device where you want to launch your application, and in a few moments you will see the `HelloWorld` application displayed on your device. One of the Appendices describes how to use the `adb` command from the command line in order to deploy an Android APK to an Android device.

HelloWorld

Hello World!

Figure 1.2 displays the output of the "Hello World" application in a Samsung Galaxy 5 that is launched from Android Studio.

FIGURE 1.2 "Hello World" on a Samsung Galaxy 5 with Android 6.0.1.

The Structure of an Android Application

The previous section shows you how to launch an application in Android Studio, and in this section let's take a look at the structure of the previously created `HelloWorld` project and the contents of the main files of this application.

Now launch Android Studio, navigate to the HelloWorld project, and right-click on the project name in order to display the expanded directory structure.

NOTE *Earlier versions of Android projects have the XML file* main.xml *instead of* activity_main.xml *as the default UI configuration file.*

Listing 1.1 displays the directory structure of the Android project HelloWorld.

LISTING 1.1 Structure of an Android Project

```
HelloWorld
  app
  app.iml
  build.gradle
  HelloWorld.iml
  libs
  proguard-rules.pro
  src
    main
      AndroidManifest.xml
      java
        com
          iquarkt
            helloworld
              MainActivity.java
      res
        drawable
        layout
          activity_main.xml
        menu
          menu_main.xml
        mipmap-hdpi
          ic_launcher.png
        mipmap-mdpi
          ic_launcher.png
        mipmap-xhdpi
          ic_launcher.png
        mipmap-xxhdpi
          ic_launcher.png
        values
          dimens.xml
          strings.xml
          styles.xml
        values-w820dp
          dimens.xml
  gradle
  gradle.properties
  gradlew
  gradlew.bat
  local.properties
  settings.gradle
```

This Android application contains various Gradle-related files and PNG resource files (which are not discussed here), the `HelloWorld.java` file, and several XML files that are automatically generated for you. The main XML files that you need to understand are `activity_main.xml`, `strings.xml`, and `AndroidManifest.xml`. Later you will learn how to create additional resource-related XML files for Android projects.

The Main Files in a Default Android Application

The files in the `HelloWorld` Android application that we will discuss in this section are listed here, all of which are located relative to the project root directory:

- `app/src/main/java/com/iquarkt/hello/HelloWorld.java`
- `app/src/main/AndroidManifest.xml`
- `app/src/main/res/layout/activity_main.xml`
- `app/src/main/res/values/strings.xml`

In brief, `HelloWorld.java` is the Java class where you put your custom code (typically in the `onCreate()` method). The auto-generated Java class `R.java`, located in the build-related portion of the Android project, is essentially a Java-based "binding" class with static constants that reference the UI components that are defined (by you) in the XML file `activity_main.xml`. As you will soon see, a one-line snippet of Java code enables you to "point" to this XML configuration file, as well as any other configuration files in your Android application.

Here is a brief description of important XML files in Android applications:

1) the `AndroidManifest.xml` file is like a "master control" file that defines Java-based resources (`Activitys`, `Intent   Filters`, `Services`, etc.) and permissions for your Android application
2) the `activity_main.xml` file (which is just the default name) is a configuration file containing the UI components (if any) that are displayed in the main screen
3) the `strings.xml` file contains the text strings that are referenced in the XML file `activity_main.xml`
4) the `dimens.xml` file contains dimension values (e.g., 16dp)

XML files such as `strings.xml` and `dimens.xml` provide a level of indirection that supports a separation between the definition of UI components and the text strings that are used in those UI components.

Notice that the `app/src/main/res/values` subdirectory can also contain other files, such as `styles.xml`, `color.xml`, as well as custom files that you need for your Android application. The contents of these files will be discussed in later chapters.

The HelloWorld.java File

Listing 1.2 displays the contents of HelloWorld.java, which contains all the custom Java code that is required for this Android application.

LISTING 1.2 HelloWorld.java

```
package com.iquarkt.hello;

import android.app.Activity;
import android.os.Bundle;

public class HelloWorld extends Activity
{
    // Called when the activity is first created
    @Override
    public void onCreate(Bundle savedInstanceState)
    {
        super.onCreate(savedInstanceState);
        setContentView(R.layout.activity_main);

        // your custom code goes here
    }
}
```

Listing 1.2 contains "boilerplate" code that is automatically generated during project creation, based on the user-supplied values for the package name and the class name. Your custom code is included immediately after this statement:

```
setContentView(R.layout.activity_main);
```

The preceding code snippet references activity_main.xml in order to make its contents available to the HelloWorld class. However, you can specify a different XML file in the res/layout subdirectory, or from a custom class that is defined elsewhere in your Android project. For example, if you want to specify the XML file new_view.xml that contains UI components to render in the current view, use the following snippet:

```
setContentView(R.layout.new_view);
```

The R.java File (optional)

Although you do not need to understand the contents of R.java right now, you might be interested in its structure (or you can read it later).

Listing 1.3 displays the contents of the resources file R.java that is automatically generated whenever you create an Android application in Android Studio.

LISTING 1.3 R.java

```
/* AUTO-GENERATED FILE. DO NOT MODIFY.

 *
 * This class was automatically generated by the
 * aapt tool from the resource data it found. It
 * should not be modified by hand.
 */

package com.iquarkt.hello;

public final class R {
    public static final class attr {
    }
    public static final class drawable {
        public static final int icon=0x7f020000;
    }
    public static final class layout {
        public static final int activity_main=0x7f030000;
    }
    public static final class string {
        public static final int app_name=0x7f040001;
        public static final int hello=0x7f040000;
    }
}
```

The integer values in Listing 1.3 are essentially references that correspond to assets of an Android application. For example, the variable icon is a reference to the icon.png file that is located in one of the drawable subdirectories of the res directory. The variable activity_main in the Java layout class is a reference to the XML file activity_main.xml (shown later in this section) that is in the res/layout subdirectory. The variables app_name and hello are references to the XML <app_name> element and XML <hello> element that are in the XML file strings.xml (shown earlier in this section) that is in the res/values subdirectory.

Now that you have seen the contents of some Java-based project files, let's turn our attention to some of the other XML-based files, starting with the primary "control file" in our Android project.

The AndroidManifest.xml File

Listing 1.4 displays the entire contents of AndroidManifest.xml for the HelloWorld Android application.

LISTING 1.4 AndroidManifest.xml

```
<?xml version="1.0" encoding="utf-8"?>
<manifest
     xmlns:android="http://schemas.android.com/apk/res/android"
     package="com.iquarkt.hello"
     android:versionCode="1"
     android:versionName="1.0">
     <application android:icon="@drawable/icon"
                  android:label="@string/app_name">
        <activity android:name=".HelloWorld"
                    android:label="@string/app_name">
           <intent-filter>
            <action android:name="android.intent.
                                            action.MAIN" />
            <category android:name="android.intent.
                                        category.LAUNCHER" />
           </intent-filter>
        </activity>

     </application>
     <uses-sdk android:minSdkVersion="9" />
</manifest>
```

Listing 1.4 starts with an XML declaration, followed by an XML `<manifest>` element that contains several XML child elements that provide information about your Android application. Notice that the XML `<manifest>` element contains an attribute with the package name of your Android application: in this example the package name is `com.iquarkt.hello`.

The XML `<application>` element in Listing 1.4 contains an `android:icon` attribute whose value is `@drawable/icon`, which refers to the image file `icon.png` that is located in the `res/drawable` subdirectory. Android supports several types of image files: high density, medium density, and low density. The corresponding directories are `drawable-hdpi`, `drawable-mdpi`, and `drawable-ldpi`, all of which are subdirectories of the `res` directory that appears under the root directory of every Android application.

The XML application element in Listing 1.4 also contains an `android:-label` attribute whose value is `@string/app_name`, which refers to an XML element in the file `strings.xml` (which is in the `res/values` subdirectory).

Listing 1.4 contains an XML `<intent-filter>` element, which is discussed later in this chapter.

The final part of Listing 1.4 specifies the minimum Android version number that is required for this application, as shown here:

```
<uses-sdk android:minSdkVersion="9" />
```

In our current example, the minimum version is 9, which is also the number that we specified during the creation step of this Android application. However, this value can be overridden by the values in the `build.gradle` file, as discussed in the next section.

The Build Values in the Gradle File

The final snippet in Listing 1.4 is used when there is no `build.gradle` file available. However, if a `build.gradle` file is present (which is the case for applications generated in Android Studio), then the values in `build.gradle` override the corresponding entries in the manifest file, which is advantageous for generating multiple APKs for different versions of Android. Additional information regarding the relationship among the various version numbers is here:

https://developer.android.com/studio/build/index.html.

The `strings.xml` File

Listing 1.5 displays the contents of the XML file `strings.xml`, which consists of XML elements that are referenced in other parts of the application.

LISTING 1.5 strings.xml

```
<?xml version="1.0" encoding="utf-8"?>
<resources>
    <string name="hello">Hello World, HelloWorld!</string>
    <string name="app_name">HelloWorld</string>
</resources>
```

Listing 1.5 is very simple: it contains an XML `<resources>` element with two XML child elements that are used to display the string `"Hello World, HelloWorld!"` when you launch this Android application. Note that the XML `<application>` element in the XML document `AndroidManifest.xml` also references the second XML `<string>` element whose `name` attribute has value `app_name`, as shown here:

```
<application android:icon="@drawable/icon"
             android:label="@string/app_name">
```

The `activity_main.xml` File

Listing 1.6 displays the contents of the XML document `activity_main. xml` that contains view-related information about this Android application.

LISTING 1.6 activity_main.xml

```
<?xml version="1.0" encoding="utf-8"?>
<RelativeLayout
    xmlns:android="http://schemas.android.com/apk/res/android"
    android:orientation="vertical"
    android:layout_width="fill_parent"
    android:layout_height="fill_parent"
    >

<TextView
    android:layout_width="fill_parent"
    android:layout_height="wrap_content"
    android:text="@string/hello"
    />
</RelativeLayout>
```

Listing 1.6 contains an XML `<RelativeLayout>` element that is the default layout for an Android application. The `<RelativeLayout>` element and other layout elements (such as `AbsoluteLayout`, `FrameLayout`, and `TableLayout`) are discussed in Chapter 2. We'll delve into the common prefix-plus-attribute combinations in the next section (so you might need to return to this section after reading the next one).

The `<RelativeLayout>` element contains a `fill_parent` attribute that indicates that the current element will be as large as the parent element (minus padding). The attributes `layout_width` and `layout_height` specify the basic values for the width and height of the view.

Working with Layout-Related Attributes

Android applications that contain a `View` component will usually specify various attributes of that `View` component. There are many such attributes, and the following subsections cover some of the more common attributes (and their allowable values) that you are likely to encounter when you create Android mobile applications.

Keep in mind that although the attributes and their purpose is often intuitive, there are nuances involved (such as horizontal and vertical alignment) when you use multiple controls in an Android application. In addition, if you require nested `Layout` components with multiple `View` components, the UI design of your Android application can become quite complex. The following subsections will familiarize you with some basic attributes.

Constraint-based layouts are available in a library that is backward compatible with Android 2.3 (API level 9), and is also available in Android Studio 2.2 or higher. The distinguishing characteristic of constraint-based layouts is that UI components are only one-level deep, thereby reducing the complexity of the UI and improving performance.

The designer functionality in Android Studio can display the layout of your UI on multiple screen sizes during design time, which is significantly faster than checking the accuracy of the layout on different devices by deploying an Android application to those devices (and besides, you might not have all those Android devices in your possession). If you need code samples for your UI, the samples in the Android SDK contain an assortment of layouts with various UI components (or search *www.stackoverflow.com* for solutions).

Working with `width` and `height` Attributes

The width of a `View` component is specified via the `android:layout_width` attribute, whose value can be `wrap_content` or `match_parent` (early versions of Android use `fill_parent` instead of `match_parent`). Similarly, the height of a `View` component is specified via the `android:layout_height` attribute, whose values are the same as those for the `width` property.

Layout Rules for `wrap_content` and `match_parent` Attributes

The `wrap_content` and `match_parent` (which was called `fill_parent` before API Level 8) attributes work as follows:

> `wrap_content`: this value will render the width or the height of a `View` according to the space that is *required* to accommodate its own content
>
> `match_parent`: this value will render the width or the height of a `View` according to the space that is occupied by the enclosing parent

Keep in mind that the "available space" for `match_parent` involves two situations:

1) If a `View` component is the *only* `View` component in the parent element, that `View` component will occupy the entire width/height of the parent (just like `match_parent`)

2) If there are other `View` components which have fixed size or simply wrap their content (that is, they do not occupy all the available space), then the current `View` will occupy the rest of the available width/height. Note that there can be only one `View` set to fill up the remaining space.

Thus, the `match_parent` attribute forces a `View` to expand to take up as much space as is available within the layout element in which it's been placed, whereas the attribute `wrap_content` means "expand enough to display the view (and no more)."

To paraphrase the preceding paragraph: a value of `wrap_content` performs a "minimalistic" match, whereas a value of `fill_parent` or `match_parent` performs a "maximal" or "greedy" match with respect to available space on a screen in an Android device.

Looking back at Listing 1.2, the `TextView` component contains the attributes `layout_width` and `layout_height`, whose values are `fill_parent` and `wrap_content`, respectively. The `wrap_content` attribute specifies that the size of the view will be just big enough to enclose its content (plus padding). The attribute `text` refers to the XML `<hello>` element that is specified in the `strings.xml` file (located in the `res/values` subdirectory), whose definition is shown here:

```
<string name="hello">Hello World, HelloWorld!</string>
```

The string `"Hello World, HelloWorld!"` is displayed when you launch the `HelloWorld` Android application in the Android Emulator or in an Android device.

Meta-Characters in `activity_main.xml`

As you already saw, Listing 1.4 contains some common prefix-plus-attribute combinations in `AndroidManifest.xml`, and there are *many* such combinations that you can specify in `activity_main.xml` (or whatever you decide to name this XML document). For now you need to learn about the @ symbol and the + symbol.

The @ meta-character indicates that the string that follows is the name of an XML file (which implies a `.xml` suffix for the filename). For example, the following attribute appears in Listing 1.4:

```
android:text="@string/hello"
```

The preceding code snippet contains a lot of information, and it is interpreted by Android as follows: `android:text` specifies a text string, and the value of that text string is located in the `<hello>` element in the XML document `strings.xml`. As a reminder, the file `strings.xml` is located in the `$TOP/app/src/main/res/values` subdirectory of your Android application.

This type of "indirection" enables you to localize (called `L10n`) and also internationalize (called `i18n`) Android applications. Localization refers to displaying text in different languages, whereas internationalization refers to displaying the correct formatting and symbols, such as currency, date/time, symbols for numbers (decimal points and commas have different meanings in different languages), zip codes, and telephone numbers.

In general `L10n` also involves `i18n`. For instance, if you switch from American English to French then the symbols for currency, date/time, and symbols in numbers change (and other symbols as well). While `i18n` can also involve `L10n`, sometimes the changes are "smaller." For example, the difference between American English and Australian English is regional, with relatively minor differences (obviously far less than the differences between American English and French).

The default language on an Android device (as well as laptops and desktops) depends on the country in which the device is used (e.g., American English in the United States and British English in the United Kingdom). Fortunately, users can easily change the default language via a menu option.

Appendix A contains an example of `L10n` (the `L10NLanguages` directory on the companion disc), and more information about localization is here:

https://developer.android.com/guide/topics/resources/localization. html.

Assigning a Value to the `id` Attribute

Another use for the @ symbol is shown here (notice the combination of the @ symbol and the + symbol):

```
android:id="@+id/my_button"
```

In the preceding code snippet, the @ symbol instructs the XML parser to parse and expand the rest of the `id` string and identify it as an `id` resource. The string "+id" indicates that the string that follows the slash ("/") will appear as a constant in the auto-generated Java class R.java.

Other Common Attributes

Although we'll defer details until the next section, here are some common combinations involving android and various attributes:

```
android:id              (sample value of "@+id/button1")
android:orientation     (value of "vertical")
android:layout_width    (value of "fill_parent")
android:layout_height   (value of "fill_parent" or
                         "wrap_content")
android:text            (value of "@string/hello")
```

NOTE *There is a learning curve associated with understanding the various combinations of attributes that appear in the UI-related XML files in Android applications.*

The android prefix is a namespace prefix (sort of like an "abbreviation") that is declared in the <manifest> element in AndroidManifest.xml, as shown here:

```
<manifest xmlns:android=http://schemas.android.com/apk/
                                               res/android.
```

Conceptually, namespace prefixes provide a convenient way to "disambiguate" items with the same name that have different sources. For instance, a <customer> element might exist in two different products, and different prefixes ensure that the correct <customer> is referenced. The counterpart (so to speak) of a namespace in Java is a package, which enables you to define classes with the same name in different packages.

The android prefix is used for attributes from Android SDK itself, whereas the app prefix (not defined here) is often associated with the support library. You can even define your own custom namespace, which is discussed in detail in the online documentation.

One starting point for learning more about properties with an android prefix is here:

http://developer.android.com/guide/topics/ui/declaring-layout.html.

At this point you can create basic Android applications, and you can even understand some of the code samples in Chapter 2. However, it's advisable for you first to learn about some of the key concepts in Android that will help you not only for the code samples in Chapter 2, but also the code samples in most of this book.

Android Resource Types

Android allows you to include custom assets in Android applications by placing those assets in the appropriate subdirectory of the `res` directory that is part of every Android application.

Most of the subdirectories are intuitively named (`res/color` is for color resources), but in some cases their purpose is not obvious. For your convenience, the list of allowable subdirectories is shown here:

The `res/anim` subdirectory contains tween animations
The `res/drawable` subdirectory contains frame animations
The `res/drawable` subdirectory also contains bitmaps
The `res/color` subdirectory contains color resources
The `res/layout` subdirectory contains layout files
The `res/menu` subdirectory contains application menus
The `res/raw` subdirectory contains audio/video files
The `res/values` subdirectory contains string definitions
The `res/xml` subdirectory contains XML-based assets

Note that the `res` directory is a subdirectory of `$TOP/app/src/main`, where `$TOP` refers to the top-level directory of an Android Studio project. If you create subdirectories of `res` whose names are not in the preceding list (such as `animation` instead of `anim`), you will get an "invalid directory" error message in your Android project. Always make sure that you have the correct names, which will ensure that your Android project will compile successfully.

In Chapter 4 you will see an animation example that places files in the `res/anim` subdirectory in order to create Android applications with animation effects. You can find code snippets as well as detailed information about all the available Android resource types here:

http://developer.android.com/guide/topics/resources/ available-resources.html.

You can define even more resources in Android, such as `integer`, `integer arrays`, `Boolean`, and so forth. These resources are defined inside an XML `<resources>` element in an XML document. For example, the XML file `integers.xml` (in the `res/values` subdirectory) defines two integers `max_speed` and `min_speed`, whose values are `100` and `10`, respectively, as shown here:

```
<?xml version="1.0" encoding="utf-8"?>
<resources>
  <integer name="max_speed">100</integer>
  <integer name="min_speed">10</integer>
</resources>
```

More information and examples are available here:

http://developer.android.com/guide/topics/resources/more-resources.html.

The next several sections provide an overview of key concepts in Android, starting with an Android `Activity`.

Key Android Concept: `Activitys`

An Android `Activity` is somewhat analogous to a screen on a device, and an `Activity` is active when its contents are made visible on the device's screen. Android applications require at least one `Activity` (additional `Activitys` depend on your requirements). An Android `Activity` has a lifecycle, which is covered in Chapter 2.

Keep in mind that `Activitys` operate on a single thread (the UI thread), which means that long-running tasks in an Android application can block the UI thread. One solution is to "offload" such tasks on a separate thread (which can be part of an Android `Service`). Note that only one `Activity` is active at any given moment, and the creation of additional `Activitys` does not create new threads.

During the project-creation step for Android applications, you manually specify the package name and the class name; the rest of the generated code is the same for every Android project.

Android applications that are created in Android Studio have a main `Activity` whose default name is `MainActivity`, which is the class name as well as the filename (with a "java" extension). You can specify a different main `Activity` during project creation, or later you can change the name in the `AndroidManifest.xml` file. The main `Activity` contains the methods and properties of an `Activity`, which includes three generated

methods: onCreate(), onCreateOptionsMenu(), and onOptions-
ItemSelected(). The onCreate() method is mandatory and the other
two methods are optional (but are required when an Activity contains
a menu).

The onCreate() Method

Jumping ahead slightly, this section describes the onCreate() method,
which will become clearer after you read about the Android lifecycle in Chapter 2. The main entry point of an Android application is the
onCreate() method, which is essentially an event handler. Notice that
HelloWorld.java in Listing 1.2 extends android.app.Activity, and
it also overrides the onCreate() method. In Listing 1.2 the onCreate()
method is passed a Bundle object called savedInstanceState, which
enables you to maintain state information (more details later) between
invocations of an Android application. No data was saved in Listing 1.2,
and therefore savedInstanceState is null.

The Android Activity lifecycle is discussed in Chapter 2.

The onCreate() method invokes its corresponding method in its superclass, followed by the setContentView() method that references an
XML file that contains layout details for the view. This method is passed
an integer value (automatically generated for you) called R.layout.
activity_main ("R" is an abbreviation for "resources") that is associated
with the XML layout file.

An Activity contains one or more views that belong to an Android
application. An Android View is what users see on the screen, which
includes the UI widgets of the Android application. The HelloWorld
Android application contains the Android class HelloWorld.java that
extends the Android Activity class and also overrides the onCreate()
method with custom code (written by you). Android applications can also
extend other Android classes (such as the Service class), and they can
also create threads.

*Every Android Activity in an Android application must be defined in
the XML document AndroidManifest.xml that belongs to the Android
application.*

Many Android applications support interaction with users, so you need
to learn how to handle various types of events, which is discussed in the
next section.

Handling Events in the Android Studio Designer

Android supports various events for its UI components. As you saw earlier, the Android Studio designer enables you to add many UI components. In addition, you can add click event handlers to <button> components. One way involves defining a method in the main activity that will contain event-handling code, and another way is to include an onClick attribute (whose value specifies a method in the Java code) in the XML element itself. The second technique is the recommended solution (but you will encounter both techniques in online code samples). A nice discussion is here:

> *http://stackoverflow.com/questions/21319996/android-onclick-in-xml-vs-onclicklistener.*

The first technique is illustrated via the following method that you add to MainActivity.java:

```
public void buttonOnClick(View v)
{
  // item #1
  Button button=(Button) v;
  button.setText("Button Clicked");

  // item #2
  TextView myTextView=(TextView) findViewById(R.id.textView);
  myTextView.setText("Clicked Button");
}
```

In the preceding code block, item #1 refers to the argument v, which is a View. In particular, it's also the Button component that was added to the application, so you can safely cast v to a Button.

On the other hand, item #2 refers to the TextView component on the screen, which is unknown to the buttonOnClick() method. However, you can still invoke the findViewById() method because every UI component is a subclass of the View component. Notice that the returned component is cast to a TextView component.

Importing Classes in Android Applications

The code block in the preceding section produces an error because the import statements for the Button class and the TextView class do not appear in the list of import statements. You can resolve this issue in several ways. One way is to manually enter the following statements:

```
import android.widget.Button;
import android.widget.TextView;
```

A better way is to ensure that Android Studio includes required `import` statements on-the-fly, which you can set up in Android Studio as follows:

```
Preferences > Editor > General > Auto Import.
```

Return to the designer and you will see `buttonOnClick()` in the drop-down list for the `Button` component.

API Level 23 and Default Layout Files

API level 23 differs from earlier versions when you create an Android project by selecting "Basic Activity" instead of "Empty Activity." The difference involves the automatic creation of a new XML file called `content_main.xml` in addition to `activity_main.xml`.

The file `content_main.xml` is for the things that you want to display to users.

Open the file `activity_main.xml` in Android Studio and you will see an "include" for `content_main.xml`, as shown here:

```
include layout="@layout/content_main"
```

XML Elements and Their Attributes

There are several other things to notice in Listing 1.4. First, attributes of XML elements have the string `android:` as a prefix. You will see this prefix throughout the XML documents that are part of Android applications, and you will also see many different attribute names (especially in UI-related XML documents).

The most common prefix-plus-attribute combinations (with self-explanatory names) in `AndroidManifest.xml` are:

```
android:versionCode
android:versionName
android:icon
android:label
android:name
android:resource
```

Second, there is a period (".") that precedes the Android `Activity` `HelloWorld` in Listing 1.4 (shown in bold). This period is mandatory because the string `.HelloWorld` is appended to the package name `com.iquarkt.hello` (which is specified in Listing 1.4). Therefore, the fully qualified name of `HelloWorld.java` in this Android project is `com.iquarkt.hello.HelloWorld.java`.

Bypassing the Default Configuration File

You can also bypass the default XML configuration file in the onCre-
ate() method. For example, Listing 1.7 illustrates how to import and
instantiate a TextView component and then set its contents.

LISTING 1.7 MainActivity.java

```
package com.iquarkt.helloworldnoxml;

import android.app.Activity;
import android.os.Bundle;
import android.widget.TextView;

public class MainActivity extends Activity
{
    @Override
    public void onCreate(Bundle savedInstanceState)
    {
        super.onCreate(savedInstanceState);

        TextView text = new TextView(this);
        text.setText("Hello World!");
        setContentView(text);
    }
}
```

Notice that Listing 1.7 does *not* contain this code snippet:

```
setContentView(R.layout.activity_main);
```

Usually you define the UI components in an XML configuration file,
especially for complex Android applications.

Multiple Activity Classes

Android applications often contain multiple Activity classes, all of
which must be declared in AndroidManifest.xml.

In very simplified terms, an Android Activity (in the android.
app package) is comparable to a screen or a view in an application. An Android application can contain multiple Android
Activitys, and each Android Activity can contain multiple Intents and IntentFilters (which are part of the android.
content package).

Working in the Android Designer

The code samples in this book are based on Android Studio 2.2, which introduced the Constraint Layout to replace the RelativeLayout (the default layout). However, most Android applications and online code samples that exist today still use RelativeLayout, so it's a good idea to learn about RelativeLayout as well as the Constraint Layout.

As you might surmise by its name, the positions of RelativeLayout components are relative to other components. When you create an Android Application and you remove the default Textfield component, there is only the layout component: consequently, the first component that you add will be relative to the layout container (which is the entire screen). The following subsections briefly discuss the RelativeLayout and property names in Android applications.

The RelativeLayout in Android

Many existing code samples use RelativeLayout, so it's a good idea to learn this layout. In Chapter 2 you will learn about the RecyclerView, which is a very powerful (and more complex) layout.

The RelativeLayout (which can be nested) supports nine positions for any component, which can be described by the paired combination of three horizontal positions and three vertical positions, as shown here:

```
Top:    left, center and right
Center: left, center and right
Bottom: left, center and right
```

For example, the lower-right position is the combination of (bottom, right), and the upper-left position is the combination of (top, left). All components are positioned at one of these nine locations. Fortunately, you are not limited to these nine positions. You can also specify an offset in terms of a margin for a finer-grained position.

For example, a component that is located at the top-left corner of the screen can be shifted 10 pixels to the right and 20 pixels downward by specifying a left margin of 10 and a top margin of 20. Thus, you can place components anywhere you want on the screen.

The Names of Layout Properties

All layout properties have the format `layout_name`, where "name" is replaced with the type of position. For instance, the `Properties` window supports the following properties (which can be true or false):

```
layout_alignParentTop
layout_alignParentLeft
layout_alignParentRight
layout_alignParentBottom
layout_centerInParent
layout_centerVertical
layout_centerHorizontal
```

Hence, a combination of these and `layout_margin` provide all the positioning possibilities that are available in the Android Studio Designer. As an example: if you specify `alignParentLeft` and `alignParentRight`, then the left side of the control is aligned with the left side of the container, and the right side of the control is aligned with the right side of the container.

You can set properties in three ways. One way is to manually place the XML code for a given UI component in the layout file (hardest). Another way is to do so in the property window, where a "tick" sets the property to true, a blank is false, and a minus removes the property from the XML file (simpler). A third way is to simply drag a component around the screen in the Android Studio Designer until it's in the position that you want (easiest). The layout of a screen with many UI components can become complex, and through trial and error you will learn how to create such layouts with greater speed and efficiency.

As a side comment, the `StackView` layout (which can also be nested) is also useful, and it's worth spending a few minutes to look at some of its characteristics:

> *https://developer.android.com/reference/android/widget/StackView.html.*

Key Android Concept: `Intents`

Earlier in this chapter you learned that an Android application can contain multiple `Activity` classes. `Activitys` are independent of each other, which is to say that one activity cannot directly access instance data of another activity. You can use an `Intent` in order to navigate between `Activitys`.

An Android `Intent` is essentially a "messaging" object that can request an action from another component. For example, you can use an `Intent` to start an `Activity`, a `Service`, or a `Broadcast Receiver`. An Android `Intent` acts as a notification between components in Android applications, along with the ability to send and receive data.

In abstract terms, an Android `Intent` represents the details regarding an action (often described by a verb) to perform in an Android application. In concrete terms, you can use an `Intent` to detect changes in the battery level of a mobile device.

Although it's not apparent, even the Android UI (User Interface) consists of `Intent`s and Views.

The `android.content` package contains the `Intent` class, which is for an event or an action. An `Intent` can be either implicit, explicit, or directed. As you will see, an Android `Intent` can do a variety of things (such as launching an Android `Activity`).

An Android `Intent` is similar to an event handler, but Android provides additional functionality for handling multiple `Intent`s and also options for using existing `Intent`s versus starting a new `Intent`. Android `Intent`s can start a new Android `Activity`, and they can also broadcast messages (which are processed by Android `Broadcast Receivers`).

You can also broadcast `Intent`s in order to send messages between components, which provides greater flexibility and "openness" for Android applications.

Creating Android `Intents`

The following snippet illustrates how to create an `Intent` and then start a new `Activity` via that `Intent`:

```
Intent intent = new Intent(action, data);
startActivity(intent);
```

Another way to start an Android `Activity` is shown here:

```
Intent intent = new Intent(FirstActivity.this,SecondActivity.class);
startActivity(intent);
```

In the preceding code snippet, `FirstActivity` is the "main" `Activity` class and `SecondActivity` is another Java class in the same Android application. Recall that all `Activity`s *must* be specified in the associated `AndroidManifest.xml` file.

As a convenience, Android Studio creates an `Intent` for you when you add a new Android `Activity` in a project, as discussed here:

http://abhiandroid.com/androidstudio/create-new-activity-android-studio.

You can send additional data to another `Activity` by specifying "extra" data in an Android `Intent`, as shown in this code block:

```
Intent intent = new Intent(Intent.ACTION_SEND);
intent.setType("text/plain");
intent.putExtra(android.content.Intent.EXTRA_TEXT,
               "Extra Information is Here");
startActivity(intent);
```

The component which receives the `Intent` can extract the extra data (if any) by using the `getIntent().getExtras()` method call, as shown in the following code block:

```
Bundle extras = getIntent().getExtras();
if (extras == null) { return; }

// Get data via the key
String value1 = extras.getString(Intent.EXTRA_TEXT);

if(value1 != null) {
   // Do something with the extra data
}
```

Types of Android `Intents`

There are several types of Android `Intents`, each of which provides slightly different functionality. A *directed* `Intent` is an `Intent` with one recipient, whereas a broadcast `Intent` can be received by any process.

An *explicit* `Intent` specifies the Java class that needs to be invoked. In general, an explicit `Intent` is used between two `Activitys` in the same Android application. A less common scenario involves explicit `Intent` to communicate between two `Activitys` in different Android applications.

An *implicit* `Intent` is an `Intent` that does not specify a Java class, which means that the Android system will determine which application will process the implicit `Intent`. If there are several applications available that can respond to an implicit `Intent`, the Android system gives users the ability to select one of those applications. For instance, if you want to access the Internet from your mobile device and you have multiple browsers installed, Android will prompt you to select a browser from the available browsers (and also ask how often you want to use the browser you have selected). This scenario is an example of an Android `Intent` in action. Similarly, if you want to send email and you have multiple email clients installed on your mobile device, Android will prompt you with a list of the installed email clients.

The `<intent-filter>` Attribute of Android `Activitys`

Android supports something called an `Intent Filter`, which specifies the capabilities of a component in an Android application. Look at Listing 1.4 and notice the `<intent-filter>` element that is automatically generated.

In case you haven't noticed yet, you do not declare the `Intents` of your project in `AndroidManifest.xml`; however, an `<intent-filter>` element *must* be declared for every type of functionality that you want to make available for external applications.

An `Intent Filter` is used for `Intent` resolution. An `Intent Filter` indicates the `Intents` that an Android `Activity` (or Service) can "consume," and the details are specified in the XML `<intent-filter>` element. Note that if an application does not provide an `Intent Filter`, then it can only be invoked by an explicit `Intent` (and not by an implicit `Intent`).

An `Intent Filter` is specified as part of the declaration of an Android `Activity` in `AndroidManifest.xml`, as shown in Listing 1.4, and is reproduced here:

```
<intent-filter>
  <action android:name="android.intent.action.MAIN" />
    <category android:name="android.intent.category.LAUNCHER" />
</intent-filter>
```

The XML `<action>` element in the preceding code snippet specifies the default value `android.intent.action.MAIN` and the XML `<category>` element specifies `android.intent.category.LAUNCHER` (also a default value), which means that the parent `Activity` will be displayed in the application launcher.

An `Intent Filter` must contain an XML `<action>` element, and optionally contain an XML `<category>` element or an XML `<data>` element. As you can see, the `<intent-filter>` element in Listing 1.4 contains the mandatory XML `<action>` element that specifies the default action, and an optional XML `<category>` element, but not the optional XML `<data>` element.

An `Intent Filter` is a set of information that defines a specific action; the XML `<data>` element specifies the data to be acted upon, and the XML `<category>` element specifies the component that will perform the action.

There are various combinations of these three XML elements that can be specified in an `Intent Filter`, because two of these elements are optional.

NOTE *Android uses a priority-based algorithm to determine what will be executed for each `Intent Filter` that you define in `AndroidManifest.xml`.*

If you want more information regarding Intent Filters, consult the Android documentation for additional details.

Intents with Action, Category, Data, and Extra

This section contains a significant amount of information, and if you are unfamiliar with these concepts, you can expect to read this section more than once.

In brief, the type of Intents that an Activity can accept involves specifying one or more of the elements described in this section.

The `<action>` element declares the intent action that is accepted in the name attribute. The value must be the literal string value of an action (not the class constant), an example of which is here:

```
<intent-filter>
    <action android:name="android.intent.action.MAIN" />
    <category android:name="android.intent.category.LAUNCHER" />
</intent-filter>
```

The `<category>` element declares the intent category accepted in the name attribute. The value must be the literal string value of an action (not the class constant). An example is shown in the preceding code block.

The `<data>` element declares the type of data accepted, using one or more attributes that specify various aspects of the data URI (such as `scheme`, `host`, `port`, and `path`) and `MIME` type. The general syntax is here:

```
<data android:scheme="string"
      android:host="string"
      android:port="string"
      android:path="string"
```

```
android:pathPattern="string"
android:pathPrefix="string"
android:mimeType="string" />
```

A simple example is here:

```
<intent-filter . . . >
 <data android:scheme="something"
      android:host="project.example.com" />
 . . .
</intent-filter>
The preceding code snippet is equivalent to the following:
<intent-filter . . . >
  <data android:scheme="something" />
  <data android:host="project.example.com" />
  . . .
</intent-filter>
```

There are many combinations that are possible (sometimes involving interdependencies), and more details are available in the online documentation.

Another scenario involves detecting whether or not an Intent actually exists on the system. The following code block shows you how to check for the existence of an Intent:

```
public static boolean isAvailable(Context ctx, Intent intent)
{
    final PackageManager mgr = ctx.getPackageManager();

    List<ResolveInfo> list =
        mgr.queryIntentActivities(intent,
            PackageManager.MATCH_DEFAULT_ONLY);

    return list.size() > 0;
}
```

You will see code samples with Intents in subsequent chapters, and in Chapter 8 you will learn how to use an Intent to start a Service or a BroadcastReceiver.

Summary

This chapter contains a great deal of information that you will probably read more than once as you progress through the chapters in this book. You first learned about the major versions of Android. Next you learned how to create a "Hello World" Android application and how to deploy the application to an Android device from Android Studio. You also learned about the structure of an Android project, as well as some important XML files and their relevance in an Android application.

In addition, you learned about some of the core concepts in Android, including `Activity`s and various types of Intents that you can create in Android applications.

Now that you have an overview of how Android applications work, you are ready for Chapter 2, which contains code samples of basic UI components in Android applications.

Two other websites containing useful information are here:

https://androiddevsummit.withgoogle.com/
https://android-arsenal.com/?sort=rating

CHAPTER 2

DESIGN AND UI CONTROLS

his chapter contains Android mobile applications with some common UI controls that are available in Android. For simplicity, the code samples typically contain a single UI component, and after reading this chapter you can easily combine multiple UI components in Android applications.

The first half of this chapter contains a summary of some UI controls, attributes, and layouts, whereas the actual code samples are in the second half of the chapter. However, it's not necessary to read everything in the first half before delving into the code samples. So, feel free to alternate between sections in both halves of this chapter.

The first part of this chapter provides an overview of resolution and density independence, UI controls and design, as well as a brief description of layouts, events, and adapters.

The second part discusses different types of constraint-based layouts, padding-related attributes and positional attributes, orientation, weight, and gravity. This section shows you how to maintain values of variables during device rotation (and explains why it's necessary to do so).

The third part of this chapter contains an example of an event listener that can respond to specific events, such as button clicks. This section also explains why computed values are not retained when users rotate their Android devices, along with an example of the type of code that solves this problem.

The final part of this chapter contains information about memory leaks that can occur with event listeners, annotations, and various types of permissions.

There are at least two important topics that you need to be aware of as you become more proficient in Android development: UI Guidelines, and Resolution and Density Independence. At some point you need to acquire a basic understanding of these topics (before you submit Android applications to the Android Play Store). Online classes are available as links on this website:

http://developer.android.com/training/best-ux.html.

One final point pertains to terminology: "UI component" and "UI control" have the same meaning in this book; in addition, "Android Application" is used interchangeably with "Android Mobile Application."

UI Controls in XML Files versus Dynamic Creation

Although you can create UI controls programmatically with Java code in an Android application, best practices encourage you to place UI controls in XML configuration files. Hence, the code examples in this chapter and Chapter 3 demonstrate how to define UI controls in an XML configuration file (whose name is something like `activity_main.xml`). In addition, event listeners in this book are defined programmatically in the method `onCreate()` of the main `Activity` class of our Android applications.

Android also enables you to define custom components. After you learn how to create Android applications with standard UI components, you can learn about custom components here:

http://developer.android.com/guide/topics/ui/custom-components.html.

UI Design for Smart Phones versus Tablets

Android 3.0 was the first version of Android to support Android tablets as well as smart phones. Android 4.0 was a "unifying" version (and a significant improvement over Android 3.0) in the sense that it became possible to create an Android application that rendered appropriately on Android devices with different screen sizes.

The release of Android Studio during Google IO 2013 provided a design-time view of the layout of the UI of an Android application on a variety of screens with different dimensions. This functionality is very convenient and it reduces the development cycle (you can see results almost immediately) and you do not need to purchase/rent/borrow multiple devices to test the UI part of your Android applications.

With the preceding points in mind, the next section gives you an overview of how to manage views, adapters, and events in Android applications.

Working with Android UI Controls

Android provides many UI controls, including buttons, checkboxes, dialogs, dropdown lists, forms, input fields, menus, and spinners (to name just a few). As you learned in Chapter 1, you can develop the UI portion of an Android application using Java code or by including XML fragments that represent UI controls (which are subclasses of the View class) in an XML document. Some Android applications use a combination of both techniques, which you can explore after you have learned the basic concepts.

The following subsections provide a fast-paced description of some UI components that are frequently used in Android applications.

What Are Android Views?

Every UI component is a subclass of the Android View class, which means that every UI component is also a view. You will often see the findView-ById() method invoked in the onCreate() method in order to reference UI components via the value of their id attribute, as shown in a later section. Note that you must cast the result of invoking findViewById() to the specific type of component (e.g., TextView, Button, etc.) that is specified in the XML layout file, as you will see later in this chapter.

After you become comfortable working with views, you can delve into creating custom views, as discussed here:

https://medium.com/@romandanylyk96/android-draw-a-custom-view-ef79fe2ff54b#.ihnygu17z.

Chapter 4 shows you how to create subviews for rendering graphics, which is simpler than the custom views discussed in the preceding link.

What Are Some Common Display Views?

Android supports TextView and ImageView for displaying text and images, respectively. The EditText component is a subview of TextView that supports editable input text. In addition, Android supports ListView, GridView, and Spinner for displaying multiple items, all of which involve an Adapter (discussed later) for managing the displayable items.

What Are ViewGroups?

A ViewGroup is essentially a non-visible container that contains one or more View objects, which includes other ViewGroup objects. A ViewGroup enables you to create a hierarchy of View objects in order to create complex layouts. Android provides various ViewGroups, such as LinearLayout, RelativeLayout, FrameLayout, ScrollView (a subclass of FrameLayout), ViewPager, RecyclerView, StackView, and CoordinatorLayout. You will learn more about some of these ViewGroups in code samples that appear later in this book.

Other Android ViewGroup classes include GridView, ListView, Spinner, SurfaceView, TabHost, ViewFlipper, and ViewSwitcher. Only the ListView class is covered in Chapter 3, but you can consult the Android documentation for information about the other Android ViewGroups listed in this section.

What are Android Layouts?

The XML document activity_main.xml (which is the default XML layout file) contains the UI components—and their layout—in an Android application. Recall from Chapter 1 that the default contents of this file consist of one top-level layout element called RelativeLayout (which is one of several possible layout types) and zero or more XML child elements, one for each corresponding UI component, and possibly other container-related non-visible components.

UI components can also be nested. For example, the top-level layout element can contain a combination of one or more additional layout elements, each of which can contain one or more "simple" UI controls and one or more View elements. These elements are often called widgets (not to be confused with the Android Widgets class).

What Are Android Events?

An event is something that is generated by users or from the system. Android supports the following types of user-generated events:

- Event listeners
- Event handlers
- Touch mode
- Handling focus

In general, the Android applications in this book show you how to handle click events for buttons and scrolling events for lists.

What Are Android Adapters?

Android Adapters are connected to data sources (such as a database or an Array), and UI components access the adapter instead of directly accessing the data source. Thus, `Adapter` classes act as a "buffer" and they manage the data access in order to provide a smoother user experience. Specifically, an adapter is an instance of a class that implements the `Adapter` interface, whereas an adapter view is an instance of a class that extends the abstract `AdapterView` class. In essence, an adapter is a "link" between a data set and an adapter view. Common data sets include `Arrays`, `List` objects, and `Cursor` objects.

The purpose of an adapter is twofold: to retrieve data from the data set and to generate `View` objects based on that data. After the data is retrieved, the adapter view (that is bound to the adapter) is populated with those generated `View` objects. Consider using the Android adapter classes, such as `ArrayAdapter` and `SimpleCursorAdapter`, and also look at open-source alternatives prior to writing custom adapter classes.

A `<button>` Component

Android supports a `Button` component (discussed later in this chapter) for displaying text and an `ImageButton` component for displaying a binary image via its `src` property. After you have read the material and code in this section, you can replace the `<Button>` component with an `ImageButton` component (keeping in mind the `src` property) to create a similar code sample.

You can include multiple XML-based layout files with UI components for an Android application by creating those XML documents in Android Studio and then referencing those XML documents in your Java code. You can also create the XML documents outside of Android Studio and then explicitly import them into the Android applications that you create in Android Studio.

For example, if you create an XML configuration file called `fun_stuff.xml` in the same directory as `activity_main.xml`, you can "point" to this configuration file with the following code snippet in the `onCreate()` method:

```
setContentView(R.layout.fun_stuff);
```

Whenever you need to refer to a UI component in a different XML
OTE *document, use the preceding type of code snippet to "point" to the desired XML document.*

All the Android code samples in this book use `activity_main.xml` for the definition of the UI elements. However, Android applications can contain multiple XML configuration files, and you can find many examples that do so in the Android SDK.

Units of Measure in Android

The Android Studio designer allows you to place view objects in the user interface via drag-and-drop operations. You can modify the properties of those view objects in the designer. For example, you can modify the width of a `TextView` via a right-click operation over that `TextView`, and then select `Layout Width -> Other ...` from the context menu. Enter a new value, which must include a unit of measure from the following list: `in` (inches), `mm` (millimeters), `pt` (points), `dp` (density), `sp` (scale pixels), and `px` (pixels).

Keep in mind the following points regarding the various units of measure. First, one `pt` is 1/72 of an inch. The `dp` unit of measure refers to density-independent pixels, which is sometimes abbreviated as `dip`. This unit of measurement is based on a "baseline" of `160dpi`. For example, `1dp` on a `320dpi` device is actually two pixels.

The `sp` unit of measure is an abbreviation for scale-independent pixels. Use the `sp` unit of measure for font sizes. The `px` unit of measure is the actual screen pixels.

A good point about resolution and density independence is here:

> There are many devices where resolution is not an aspect ratio preserving scaling of a G1 screen. The Motorola Droid is 480x854 and many other HDPI screens are 480x800. This is at the core of why AbsoluteLayout is deprecated—density and resolution are not necessarily linked. Do not use absolute positioning. Use smarter layouts that can handle these cases instead.

The preceding quote is from this link:

> *http://stackoverflow.com/questions/5058310/android-density-independent-pixels-and-the-samsung-galaxy-tab.*

Padding-Related Attributes

Android provides many padding-related attributes. For example, the following attributes set the padding (in pixels) of the left, top, right, and bottom of a `View` component:

```
android:paddingLeft
android:paddingTop
```

```
android:paddingRight
android:paddingBottom
```

The value of these attributes must be a dimension value, which is a floating-point number appended with a unit such as 14.5sp. The permissible units are px (pixels), dp (density-independent pixels), sp (scaled pixels based on preferred font size), in (inches), and mm (millimeters). An example of setting the left padding is here:

```
android:paddingLeft="20dp"
```

You can also specify the padding value as an XML element that is defined in the XML document dimens.xml that is located in the res/values subdirectory. For example, suppose that dimens.xml contains this snippet:

```
<resources>
  <dimen name="my_left_padding">20dp</dimen>
</resources>
```

Then the following snippet will also set the left padding to 20dp:

```
android:paddingLeft="@dimen/my_left_padding"
```

If you want to specify the same padding for all four attributes, you can do so with the following type of code snippet:

```
android:padding="20px"
```

 As an illustration, copy the Android project called LayoutAttributes from the companion disc to a convenient location. Next, replace the default contents of activity_main.xml with the contents of Listing 2.1.

LISTING 2.1 activity_main.xml

```
<RelativeLayout
    xmlns:android="http://schemas.android.com/apk/res/android"
    xmlns:tools="http://schemas.android.com/tools"
    android:layout_width="match_parent"
    android:layout_height="match_parent"
    android:padding="16dp"
    tools:context=".MainActivity" >

    <LinearLayout
        android:layout_width="match_parent"
        android:layout_height="wrap_content"
        android:layout_alignParentBottom="false"
        android:layout_alignParentLeft="false" >
        <Button
            android:id="@+id/Button01"
            android:layout_width="match_parent"
            android:layout_height="wrap_content"
```

```
                android:layout_weight="1"
                android:text="Button1" />
            <Button
                android:id="@+id/Button02"
                android:layout_width="match_parent"
                android:layout_height="wrap_content"
                android:layout_weight="1"
                android:text="Button2" />
            <Button
                android:id="@+id/Button03"
                android:layout_width="match_parent"
                android:layout_height="wrap_content"
                android:layout_weight="1"
                android:text="Button3" />
            <TextView
                android:layout_width="fill_parent"
                android:layout_height="wrap_content"
                android:layout_weight="1"
                android:text="Text1" />
    </LinearLayout>
</RelativeLayout>
```

As you can clearly see, Listing 2.1 contains a root-level `RelativeLayout` component with a nested `LinearLayout` component, which in turn contains three `Button` components and one `TextView` component. The UI components in Listing 2.1 use some of the attributes that are discussed earlier in this chapter. You can experiment with these UI components by specifying other attributes that you have seen in this chapter.

As a convenience, Android also provides two padding-related "setters" methods `setPadding(int, int, int, int)` and `setPaddingRelative(int, int, int, int)`. Moreover, Android providers various "getters" for querying padding-related values, such as `getPaddingLeft()`, `getPaddingTop()`, `getPaddingRight()`, `getPaddingBottom()`, `getPaddingStart()`, and `getPaddingEnd()`. These methods are useful when you need to programmatically modify the values of attributes.

Figure 2.1 is a screenshot from after launching the Android `LayoutAttributes` project on a Samsung Galaxy S5 with Android 6.0.1.

FIGURE 2.1 Three Buttons and One TextView in an Android Application.

Working with Positional Attributes

Android supports the following positional attributes that specify the position of a `View` component in relation to an existing `View` component that is defined in an XML layout file:

```
android:layout_above
android:layout_below
android:layout_toLeftOf
android:layout_toRightOf
```

The attribute `android:layout_above` positions the bottom edge of a `View` component above another `View` component. An example of placing a `TextView` component above a `Button` component is here:

```
<Button android:id="@+id/clickme"
    android:layout_width="fill_parent"
    android:layout_height="wrap_content"
    android:layout_alignParentBottom="true"
    android:text="@string/clickme" />

<TextView android:id="@+id/text1"
    android:layout_width="fill_parent"
    android:layout_height="wrap_content"
    android:text="@string/hellot"
    android:layout_above="@id/clickme"
    />
```

If you want to position a `View` component below, to the left of, or to the right of another `View` component, you can use the corresponding attribute that is displayed in the beginning of this section.

While it's helpful to read about how to render UI components, a good way to learn how to change the layout of UI components is to experiment with the various attributes that are available. Here are some examples that you can try in Android applications. Note that some samples use layout managers (such as `FrameLayout`) that have not been discussed yet, so you need to defer those samples until later if you do not already know how to use those layout managers.

Sample #1: Create a new layout file with a top-level `RelativeLayout` component and position `Button` #1 so that it is displayed below `Button` #2 (and both are on the top-right portion of the screen), as shown here:

```
<Button
    android:id="@+id/button1"
```

```
    android:layout_below="@id/button2"
    android:layout_alignParentRight="true"
    android:layout_width="wrap_content"
    android:layout_height="wrap_content"
    android:text="Button1" />
<Button
    android:id="@+id/button2"
    android:layout_above="@id/button1"
    android:layout_toLeftOf="@id/button1"
    android:layout_width="wrap_content"
    android:layout_height="wrap_content"
    android:text="Button2" />
```

Sample #2: You can shift the preceding two buttons to the bottom of the screen by adding this property to both `Button` elements:

```
android:layout_alignParentBottom="true"
```

Sample #3: Create a new layout file with a top-level `FrameLayout` component, center the second `TextView` component and place it on top of the first `TextView` component (which is also centered on the screen):

```
<TextView
    android:layout_width="100dp"
    android:layout_height="100dp"
    android:layout_gravity="center"
    android:text="First"
    android:background="#00f" />
  <TextView
    android:layout_width="50dp"
    android:layout_height="50dp"
    android:layout_gravity="center"
    android:text="Second"
    android:background="#f00" />
```

Sample #4: Experiment with the following gravity-related values in the preceding code block:

```
android:layout_gravity="right"
android:gravity="center_horizontal|bottom"
```

Sample #5: Create a new layout file with a top-level `LinearLayout` component, and display three `TextView` elements vertically:

```
<LinearLayout
    xmlns:android="http://schemas.android.com/apk/res/android"
    xmlns:tools="http://schemas.android.com/tools"
    android:layout_width="match_parent"
    android:layout_height="match_parent"
    android:orientation="vertical"
```

```
    tools:context=".LinearLayout" >
    <!-- specify three TextView elements here -->
</LinearLayout>
```

Sample #6: Change the line in bold in the preceding code block to this line:

```
android:orientation="horizontal"
```

Sample #7: create a new layout file with a top-level `LinearLayout` component, and display a pair of `TextView` elements horizontally, and then display another pair of `TextView` elements vertically:

```
<LinearLayout xmlns:android="http://schemas.android.com/
                                            apk/res/android"
              xmlns:tools="http://schemas.android.com/tools"
              android:layout_width="match_parent"
              android:layout_height="match_parent"
              android:orientation="vertical"
              tools:context=".LinearLayout" >

    <LinearLayout android:orientation="horizontal" ...>
        <!-- specify two TextView Elements -->
    </LinearLayout>
    <!-- specify three TextView Elements -->
</LinearLayout>
```

The sample layouts in this section give you enough information to create a variety of layouts. You can also experiment with the effects of moving UI components around the Android Studio Designer, and then inspect the values of the attributes in the XML layout file.

Other Display-Related Attributes and Direction

You can specify the orientation of an Android mobile application with the attribute `android:orientation`, which can be either `portrait` or `landscape`. The attribute `android:weight` in a linear layout assigns a "weight" property to its children. Layout weight is essentially a percentage of width that a `View` component is assigned in its linear layout parent.

Some additional attributes (with sample values in parentheses) include:

- android:columnWidth (250dp)
- android:gravity (center)
- android:layout_marginTop (2px)
- android:numColumns (auto_fit)
- android:stretchMode (columnWidth)
- android:textSize (20px)

Additional information about Android attributes and their values is here:

http://developer.android.com/reference/android/view/View.html.

Specifying Text and Component Direction

Android 4.1 introduced some support for RTL (right-to-left) text in the `TextView` and `EditText` components, and then Android 4.2 introduced full support for RTL. This functionality involves the following attributes:

- android:layoutDirection sets the direction of a component's layout
- android:textDirection sets the direction of a component's text
- android:textAlignment sets the alignment of a component's text
- getLayoutDirectionFromLocale() gets the locale-specified direction

Working with Different Densities and Screen Sizes

If you define the dimensions of a PNG file in terms of the unit `px`, that PNG file will be displayed as a small image on screens with higher densities. However, if you define the dimensions of a PNG file in terms of the unit `dp` ("device independent pixels") that PNG file will be displayed in the same size, regardless of the density or the physical dimensions of a screen on a mobile device.

Android supports `small`, `normal`, `large`, and `xlarge` screen sizes as follows:

```
xlarge screens are at least 960dp x 720dp
large screens are at least 640dp x 480dp
normal screens are at least 470dp x 320dp
small screens are at least 426dp x 320dp
```

Android also supports the following densities: `ldpi` (~120dpi), `mdpi` (~160dpi), `hdpi` (~240dpi), and `xhdpi` (~320dpi).

You can ensure that your Android application renders appropriately on mobile devices with different screen sizes in the following ways:

- include a `<supports-screens>` element in the manifest
- specify the screen sizes that your application supports
- provide different layouts for different screen sizes
- provide different bitmap drawables for different screen densities

An example of the `<supports-screens>` element is here:

```
<manifest ...>
  <supports-screens
    android:largeScreens="true"
    android:requiresSmallestWidthDp="600" />
  ...
</manifest>
```

Also keep in mind that Android 3.2 introduced the following attributes:

- `android:requiresSmallestWidthDp`
- `android:compatibleWidthLimitDp`
- `android:largestWidthLimitDp`

If you're developing your application for Android 3.2 and higher, you should use these attributes to declare your screen size support, instead of the attributes based on generalized screen sizes.

The general format (note that `android:resizeable` is deprecated) is shown here:

```
<supports-screens
    android:resizeable=["true"| "false"]
    android:smallScreens=["true" | "false"]
    android:normalScreens=["true" | "false"]
    android:largeScreens=["true" | "false"]
    android:xlargeScreens=["true" | "false"]
    android:anyDensity=["true" | "false"]
    android:requiresSmallestWidthDp="integer"
    android:compatibleWidthLimitDp="integer"
    android:largestWidthLimitDp="integer"
/>
```

More information regarding support for multiple screen sizes is here:

http://developer.android.com/guide/practices/ screens_support.html.

Now that you have a basic understanding about Android resources, layout-related Android attributes, and different screen sizes, the code samples in this book will make more sense to you.

Before we start working with Android UI components, the next section shows you how to detect a change in orientation of an Android mobile device, which can be performed by adding a mere two lines of code in a Java class. This will be the first useful Android application that you have encountered in this book.

Detecting Changes in Device Orientation

A change in orientation of an Android device is very simple to detect because of the following fact: the main `Activity` in an Android application is destroyed and recreated *each time* that users rotate their mobile device from portrait to landscape and vice versa. The proof is simple. Create an Android application and include the following `import` statement in the main `Activity` class:

```
import android.util.Log;
```

Next, include the following statement in the `onCreate()` method:

```
Log.d("onCreate", "inside onCreate");
```

Deploy the Android application to a mobile device and observe that the previous string is displayed in `LogCat` each time that you rotate your mobile device. Moreover, computed values (such as the click count for a button) that are displayed on the screen are reset to their initial values when users rotate their device. Later in this chapter you will learn how to retain computed values and to display their correct values.

The next section shows you how to create an Android application that consists of an Android `Button` component, followed by a code sample that shows you how to handle a `Button` click event.

Working with Buttons

The Android package `android.widget` contains the class `Button` that provides button-like functionality.

 Copy the directory called `SimpleButton` from the companion disc to a convenient location. This sample application contains a `Button` control and a `TextView` control.

Listing 2.2 displays the contents of `SimpleButtonActivity.java`, which illustrates how to use a `Button` class in an Android application.

LISTING 2.2 SimpleButtonActivity.java

```
package com.example.oswaldcampesato2.simplebutton;

import android.app.Activity;
import android.os.Bundle;
import android.widget.Button;

public class SimpleButtonActivity extends Activity
```

```
{
    private Button myButton = null;

    @Override
    public void onCreate(Bundle savedInstanceState)
    {
        super.onCreate(savedInstanceState);

        this.setContentView(R.layout.activity_main);
        this.myButton = (Button)this.findViewById(R.id.button1);
    }
}
```

Listing 2.3 displays the contents of `activity_main.xml`, which contains the definition of the Android `Button` that is referenced in Listing 2.2.

LISTING 2.3 activity_main.xml

```
<?xml version="1.0" encoding="utf-8"?>
<RelativeLayout
xmlns:android=http://schemas.android.com/apk/res/android
    android:id="@+id/layout1"
    android:orientation="vertical"
    android:layout_width="fill_parent"
    android:layout_height="fill_parent"
    >

  <Button android:id="@+id/button1"
    android:layout_width="fill_parent"
    android:layout_height="wrap_content"
    android:text="@string/hellob"
    android:layout alignParentBottom="true" />

  <TextView
    android:layout_width="fill_parent"
    android:layout_height="wrap_content"
    android:text="@string/hellot"
    />
</RelativeLayout>
```

Listing 2.3 is straightforward: the root element is a `RelativeLayout` that contains a `Button` control and a `TextView` control as its child elements. The text that is displayed in the `Button` element is specified as `@string/button1` and the text for the `TextView` element is specified as `@string/hello`. Whenever you see this type of expression, check the XML document `strings.xml` for the actual strings that are substituted for this expression.

As a side comment, if you display a grid-like pattern with two or more columns of <button> elements that have text strings of different lengths, sometimes the columns will have different widths. However, you can insert the string
 in the middle of the longest text string so that its contents will span multiple lines, which will decrease the width of the column that contains this `<button>` element. This technique will resize all the `<button>` elements that occupy the same column so that they have the same width. Moreover, both columns will be resized accordingly, which can result in a more pleasing interface. You can generalize this technique for multiple columns and also for text strings that require multiple inserts of the string `&#10;`.

NOTE   *The string `&#10;` splits a text string into multiple lines.*

Listing 2.4 displays the contents of `strings.xml`, which contains the definition of the strings that are used in the `SimpleButton` Android application.

FIGURE 2.2 A `Button` in an Android Application.

LISTING 2.4 strings.xml

```
<resources>
    <string name="app_name">SimpleButton</string>
    <string name="hellot">Hello Textfield</string>
    <string name="hellob">Hello Button</string>
</resources>
```

The key point to observe in Listing 2.4 is the first XML `<string>` element contains the actual text that is displayed in the `TextView` element. In addition, the second XML `<string>` element contains the text that is displayed as the `Button` label.

Figure 2.2 displays the rendering of the `SimpleButton` project on a Samsung Galaxy S5 with Android 6.0.1.

Click Events in Android

Since there is no mouse connected to a smart phone, you might be wondering about the rationale for discussing click events. The reason is simple: Android provides an `onClick()` method (shown later in this chapter) and an `onLongClick()` method, both of which are described in the Android documentation as follows:

`onClick()`

From View.OnClickListener. This is called when the user either touches the item (when in touch mode), or focuses upon the item with the navigation-keys or trackball and presses the suitable "enter" key or presses down on the trackball.

`onLongClick()`

From View.OnLongClickListener. This is called when the user either touches and holds the item (when in touch mode), or focuses upon the item with the navigation-keys or trackball and presses and holds the suitable "enter" key or presses and holds down on the trackball (for one second).

The preceding information (along with details regarding other touch-related events) is here:

http://developer.android.com/guide/topics/ui/ui-events.html.

Now let's look at an Android application that handles button click events. Despite the conceptual simplicity of this functionality, you might be surprised by the Android-specific details that you will learn in this section.

An event listener in Android is an interface that contains a single callback method. The Android interface `android.view.View.OnClickListener` declares the `onClick()` method that you must implement in your code in order to handle button clicks.

This example shows you how to handle click events, and the example in the next section shows you how to handle click events *and* rotating an Android device. Copy the directory called `ClickButton` from the companion disc to a convenient location.

Listing 2.5 displays the contents of the Java class `MainActivity.java` that illustrates how to use a `Button` class with an event handler in an Android application.

LISTING 2.5 MainActivity.java

```
package com.example.oswaldcampesato2.clickbutton;

import android.os.Bundle;
import android.support.v7.app.AppCompatActivity;
import android.view.View;
import android.view.View.OnClickListener;
import android.widget.Button;
import android.widget.RelativeLayout;

public class MainActivity extends AppCompatActivity
```

```
{
    private RelativeLayout relLayout = null;
    private Button myButton = null;
    private int clickCount  = 0;
    private String TAG      = "ClickMe";

    @Override
    public void onCreate(Bundle savedInstanceState)
    {
        super.onCreate(savedInstanceState);
        this.setContentView(R.layout.activity_main);

// uncomment this code block later (section #1)
/*
        if(savedInstanceState != null)
        {
            clickCount = savedInstanceState.getInt("clickCount");
        }
*/

        this.myButton  = (Button)this.findViewById(R.id.button1);
        this.relLayout = (RelativeLayout)this.findViewById(R.id.layout1);

        myButton.setText("Click Me: "+clickCount);

        this.myButton.setOnClickListener(new OnClickListener() {
            @Override
            public void onClick(View v) {
                ++clickCount;
                myButton.setText("Click Me: "+clickCount);

                // toggle the background color
                if (clickCount % 2 == 0) {
                    relLayout.setBackgroundColor(0xFFFF0000);
                } else {
                    relLayout.setBackgroundColor(0xFF0000FF);
                }
            }
        });
    }

// uncomment this code block later (section #2)
/*
@Override
protected void onSaveInstanceState(Bundle outState)
{
    outState.putInt("clickCount", clickCount);
    super.onSaveInstanceState(outState);
}
*/
}
```

The code in boldface in Listing 2.5 is the new Java code that has been added to `MainActivity.java` in Listing 2.2 in order to add an event listener that responds to button click events.

The first section of new code contains view-related `import` statements, and the second section of new code contains event-handling statements, as shown here:

```
this.myButton.setOnClickListener(new OnClickListener() {
    @Override
    public void onClick(View v) {
        ++clickCount;
        myButton.setText("Click Me: "+clickCount);

        // toggle background color code omitted
    }
});
```

The preceding code block contains an `onClick()` method that is invoked whenever users click on the button, after which the `clickCount` variable is incremented and the new click count is displayed as a label for the `Button` control.

The second part of the `onClick()` method toggles the background color of the screen, and alternates between `RED` and `BLUE`. Although best practices encourages you to place `onClick()` methods in XML configuration files, many code samples use this technique, so it's probably worth your while to learn this style.

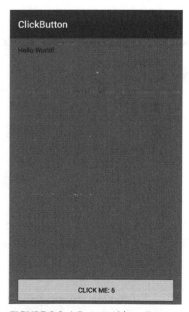

Best practices suggest placing `onClick()` methods in XML configuration files.

Launch the application, click the button several times, and notice how the label of the `Button` control is updated each time you click on that button.

Figure 2.3 displays the rendering of `ButtonClick` on a Samsung Galaxy S5 with Android 6.0.1.

FIGURE 2.3 A Button with an Event Listener in an Android Application.

Handling Android Device Rotation

Whenever users rotate an Android device, Android destroys and then recreates the `Activity` class, which causes the `onCreate()` method to be executed again. Hence, the values of variables are reinitialized, and so intermediate values are lost.

 Copy the directory `RotateClickButton` from the companion disc to a convenient location. This application modifies the project `ClickButton` by "uncommenting" the two sections of code in Listing 2.5.

Launch the application, click the button several times, and rotate your Android device: notice that the program does not crash with a null pointer exception. However, the value of `clickCount` is set to zero because the `MainActivity` class is destroyed and recreated, which results in `click-Count` being initialized to zero.

The solution involves two new blocks of code. The first code block involves storing the value of `clickCount` in the `savedInstanceState` variable, as shown here:

```
@Override
protected void onSaveInstanceState(Bundle outState)
{
    outState.putInt("clickCount", clickCount);
    super.onSaveInstanceState(outState);
}
```

The second code block needs to be inserted in the `onCreate()` method after the `super()` invocation in order to retrieve the saved value for `clickCount`:

```
if(savedInstanceState != null)
{
    clickCount = savedInstanceState.getInt("clickCount");
}
```

Uncomment the two new code blocks in Listing 2.2 and launch the application. When you click the button and then rotate your Android device, you will see that the correct value for `clickCount` is displayed.

Using a Different File for Landscape Mode (optional)

This section contains information about Android applications that use one layout file for portrait mode and one layout file for landscape mode (otherwise consider this section optional).

The following post describes how to create a layout file for landscape mode:

http://abhiandroid.com/androidstudio/add-create-landscape-layout-android-studio.html.

If you add a different layout file for landscape mode in the RotateClickButton code sample, users will encounter a null pointer exception when they rotate an Android device. The solution is to place the appropriate UI controls in both files.

Specifically, if the file for landscape mode does not contain a Button control, the following code snippet returns a null pointer:

```
this.myButton = (Button)this.findViewById(R.id.button1);
```

Consequently, the following code snippet crashes the application:

```
myButton.setText("Click Me: "+clickCount);
```

Copy the Button control from activity_main.xml into the contents of the file for landscape mode. The application will work correctly now because the code will find the Button control in both layout files.

One other detail: screen orientation (landscape or portrait) is considered a variation of screen size, which is a topic that is covered in more detail here:

https://developer.android.com/training/basics/supporting-devices/screens.html.

Other Event Listener Techniques

There are two other ways to define an event listener for a Button control. One way is specify the click listener in code (in the onCreate() method), and the other way is to specify the click listener method in the XML file.

Method #1: Include the following code block in Listing 2.2:

```
// reference a button from layout
Button myButton = (Button)findViewById(R.id.button1);

// register an onClick listener with the implementation below
button.setOnClickListener(myButtonListener);

private OnClickListener myButtonListener = new OnClickListener() {
    public void onClick(View v) {
      // handle the button click
    }
};
```

Method #2: Include the following code block in the <Button> definition:

```
<Button android:id="@+id/button1"
    android:layout_width="fill_parent"
    android:layout_height="wrap_content"
    android:layout_alignParentBottom="true"
    android:text="@string/clickme"
    android:onClick="handleButtonClick" />
```

Next, in the `MainActivity` class define the `handleButtonClick()` method and replace the click handling code in Method #1 in Listing 2.2 with this code block:

```
public void handleButtonClick(View v)
{
    ++clickCount;
    myButton.setText("Click Me: "+clickCount);

    // toggle the background color
    if (clickCount % 2 == 0) {
      relLayout.setBackgroundColor(0xFFFF0000);
    } else {
      relLayout.setBackgroundColor(0xFF0000FF);
    }
}
```

The following link provides additional information regarding the manner in which Android invokes the `onSaveInstanceState()` method:

http://developer.android.com/guide/components/activities.html.

Finding the `id` of a UI Component

Insert the following code inside the `handleButtonClick()` method:

```
int id = view.getId(); // a number that appears in R.java
String idStr = view.getResources().getResourceEntryName(id);
Log.i("Button Tap idStr = ",idStr);
```

```
int resourceId = getResources().getIdentifier(idStr, "raw",
                                 "this.package.name");
Log.i("Button Tap resourceId = ",resourceId);

// play an audio file
MediaPlayer mPlayer = MediaPlayer.create(this, resourceId);
mPlayer.start();
```

The preceding technique is useful for Android applications with multiple elements that have the same click handler, and you need to determine which element has been clicked. Another approach is to define a unique event listener for each UI component in the layout file, which can be simpler to debug (but more code is required).

Differences between OnClickListener and OnClick

The following stackoverflow post contains a very good summary and comparison of the two techniques for handling click events:

> http://stackoverflow.com/questions/21319996/android-onclick-in-xml-vs-onclicklistener.

The details are given below:

OnClickListener is the interface you need to implement and can be set to a view in Java code. On one hand, OnClickListener is what waits for someone to actually click, whereas onClick determines what happens when someone clicks.

Android added an XML attribute to views called android:onClick that can be used to handle clicks directly in the view's activity without the need to implement any interface.

You could easily swap one listener implementation with another if you need to do so. An OnClickListener enables you to separate the action/behavior of the click event from the View that triggers the event. Although this is a minor detail for simple cases, the situation might differ for complex event handling in terms of improved readability and maintainability of the code. Since OnClickListener is an interface, the class that implements this interface has some flexibility regarding instance variables and methods for handling the event.

The onClick event with function binding in XML Layout is a binding between onClick and the function that it will call. The function must have one argument (the View) in order for onClick to function correctly.

Although one technique involves "pure" Java code and another technique involves specifying an event listener via an XML attribute, the result is the same.

Now that you know how to define `Button` and `TextView` components and event listeners in Android, you might also be interested in reading the code in the Java class `SimpleEditText.java` on the companion disc that illustrates how to enable users to enter text in an editable input field.

Event Listeners and Return Values

You probably noticed that some event listeners in Android (such as `onClick()`) do not return a value. However, some event listeners, such as `onLongClick()`, `onKey()`, and `onTouch()` return a `Boolean` value. This `Boolean` value indicates whether or not the event has been consumed. In the case of the `onTouch()` event listener, it's possible to have multiple consecutive touch-related actions, and therefore a return value is required in order to indicate whether or not an action was taken in the code.

Android Annotations

Every Android project with an `Activity` class in this book uses the `@Override` annotation that precedes the `onCreate()` method in the main `Activity` class. This annotation indicates that your code is overriding *a method with the same name* in the parent class. Hence, if you misspell the name of the method that you intend to override, a compilation error will alert you about the misspelled method name.

Other annotations are available that can reduce the amount of code in your Android applications, as described here:

http://tools.android.com/tech-docs/support-annotations.

In addition, there are various open source projects that provide additional annotations for Android applications. For instance, the `excilys` project provides Android annotations, and its home page is here:

https://github.com/excilys/androidannotations/tree/master.

As a simple example, Listing 2.5 contains this code block for handling a click event on an Android `Button` control:

```
this.myButton = (Button)this.findViewById(R.id.button1);

this.myButton.setOnClickListener(new OnClickListener() {
  @Override
  public void onClick(View v) {
     myButton.setText("Click Me: "+clickCount);
  }
});
```

The `excilys` project enables you to replace the preceding code block with the following code that contains an `@Click` annotation:

```
@Click(R.id.button1)
void button1Clicked() {
  myButton.setText("Click Me: "+clickCount);
}
```

As you can see, the preceding code block with the annotation is much simpler to understand, shorter in length, and less error-prone than the original code block.

In addition to reducing the lines of code, Android annotations can make your code more readable and also simplify maintenance in larger Android applications.

Another open source project that provides Android annotations is here:

http://jakewharton.github.io/butterknife.

Perform an Internet search to find various other open source projects for Android annotations and evaluate them to determine which one best suits your needs.

Android Application Lifecycle

Although the information in this section is important, it's not essential for creating simple Android applications in Android Studio. If you prefer, skim through its contents and then return to this section after you feel more comfortable creating Android applications.

Figure 2.4 displays the Android `Activity` lifecycle diagram that is from this website:

https://developer.android.com/reference/android/app/Activity.html.

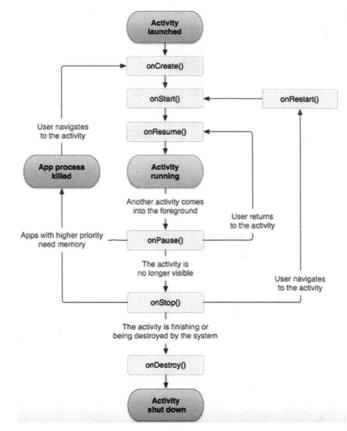

FIGURE 2.4 The Android `Activity` lifecycle.

Earlier in this chapter you saw the contents of `HelloWorld.java` that contains a method called `onCreate()` that overrides the same method in the superclass. In case you are wondering, the `onCreate()` method is one of the seven Android methods that comprise the Android application lifecycle that is described (very briefly) in this section.

An Android application executes the following methods (in the following order) during the lifecycle of the application: `onCreate()`, `onRestart()`, `onStart()`, `onResume()`, `onPause()`, `onStop()`, and `onResume()`.

The `onCreate()` method is invoked when an `Activity` is created, and its role is similar to `init()` methods in other languages. The `onDestroy()` method is invoked when an `Activity` is removed from memory, and its role is essentially that of a destructor method in C++.

The onPause() method is invoked when an Activity must be paused (such as reclaiming resources). Include custom code for persisting data and values of variables (if any) in this method. For example, since Activitys are destroyed and recreated when users rotate their Android device, you can save data values in this method, which is an alternative to the technique that you saw in Chapter 2. Another point to remember is that Android invokes the onPause() method before terminating an application, so the onPause() method is the logical place to include data-saving code.

The onRestart() method is invoked when an Activity is being restarted. By comparison, the onResume() method is invoked when an Activity interacts with a user, whereas the onStart() method is invoked when an Activity becomes visible on the screen. Finally, the onStop() method is invoked in order to stop an Activity.

The methods onRestart(), onStart(), and onStop() are in the visible phase; on the other hand, the methods onResume() and onPause() are in the foreground phase. An Android application can pause and resume many times during the execution of that application; the details are specific to the functionality of the application (and possibly the type of user interaction as well).

Finally, each Android application runs in a Unix process on an Android device and each application maintains its own lifecycle. Android applications rely on the virtual machine in order to interact with the operating system of an Android device in accordance with the lifecycle described in this section.

Android Memory Leaks

This section provides a brief summary of how memory leaks can occur in Android applications, along with links that provide additional information.

The main culprits for potential memory leaks are listed here:

- Inner classes
- Anonymous classes
- Static activities or views
- Subclasses of AsyncTask
- Handlers
- Threads
- Timer tasks
- Sensor manager

Two articles that contain code samples that illustrate memory leaks and how to address them are here (make sure you read the comments in these posts as well):

https://medium.com/freenet-engineering/memory-leaks-in-android-identify-treat-and-avoid-d0b1233acc8#.y2duxl6dw

http://blog.nimbledroid.com/2016/05/23/memory-leaks.html

You won't encounter some of these topics (such as the sensor manager) until the second half of this book, or in an appendix (such as Threads), so you don't need to worry about dealing with memory leaks right now.

Fortunately, Android provides various tools to help you detect memory leaks in Android applications, some of which are described in one of the appendices for this book. In addition, Square provides a memory leak detection library for Android as well as Java, and it's downloadable here:

https://github.com/square/leakcanary.

Summary

This chapter showed you how to develop native Android applications with simple UI controls, including buttons and text fields. You also learned how to create event listeners so that your Android application can respond to specific events, such as button clicks.

In addition, you learned about different types of constraint-based layouts, padding-related attributes and positional attributes, orientation, weight, and gravity. You saw how to maintain values of variables during device rotation. Finally, you learned about the lifecycle methods for an Android Activity and different types of memory leaks.

CHAPTER 3

ADDITIONAL *UI* CONTROLS

This chapter contains code samples with an assortment of Android
UI components. Please read Chapter 2 (if you have not already
done so) because it contains useful information regarding UI components, event handlers, and so forth. Unless otherwise noted, the UI
components in this chapter are supported from Android version 2.0 and
higher.

The first part of this chapter briefly discusses UI components that provide
container-like functionality, followed by Android Alerts and TimePickers.
The second part of this chapter discusses Android Fragments (which are
essentially submodules of an Android Activity) that were introduced in
Android 3.x.

The third part of this chapter discusses some Android layout managers,
including LinearLayout and RelativeLayout (you saw the latter in
Chapter 2). This section also discusses briefly the Android RecyclerView,
which is a powerful and more efficient "successor" to the LinearLayout
manager and GridLayout manager. Note that Android provides other
layout managers (such as AbsoluteLayout, FrameLayout, and
TableLayout) that are not discussed in this chapter.

Many Android applications support user interaction, often consisting of
one or more buttons, perhaps a scroll list for displaying items, and also
input fields for data entry (or some combination). The Android application with radio buttons introduces the Android Toast class that displays a
brief message whenever users click or tap on a radio button. The Android
code sample with an Android Spinner component also contains an

Android `Toast` class. This approach of combining functionality in a single application provides more value to you than just a simple copy/paste from the Android SDK or from a website. For your convenience, the Android code samples are presented alphabetically so that you can locate them quickly, but feel free to read them in the order that interests you.

Alerts

Android Alerts enable your Android application to display a message when a particular event has occurred.

 Copy the directory `MyAlert` from the companion disc to a convenient location. Listing 3.1 displays the contents of `MainActivity.java`, which illustrates how to display an `Alert` in an Android application.

LISTING 3.1 MainActivity.java

```
package com.example.oswaldcampesato2.myalert;

import android.app.AlertDialog;
import android.content.DialogInterface;
import android.os.Bundle;
import android.support.v7.app.AppCompatActivity;

public class MainActivity extends AppCompatActivity
{
    @Override
    public void onCreate(Bundle savedInstanceState)
    {
        super.onCreate(savedInstanceState);
        setContentView(R.layout.activity_main);

        AlertDialog.Builder builder = new AlertDialog.
                                           Builder(this);

        builder
          .setMessage("Are you sure you want to exit?")
          .setCancelable(false)
          .setPositiveButton("Yes",
              new DialogInterface.OnClickListener() {
                  public void onClick(DialogInterface dialog,int id){
                      MainActivity.this.finish();
                  }
              })
          .setNegativeButton("No",
              new DialogInterface.OnClickListener() {
                  public void onClick(DialogInterface dialog,int id){
```

```
                    dialog.cancel();
               }
          });

     AlertDialog alert = builder.create();

     // now display the alert
     alert.show();
   }
}
```

Listing 3.1 starts with the usual boilerplate Java code, and the `onCreate()` method instantiates an `AlertDialog.Builder` object called `builder` that uses method chaining in order to set three properties. These properties are the `cancel`, `yes`, and `no` options that users can select in an `Alert` dialog.

If you are unfamiliar with the `Builder` pattern, read item #2 of this link:

https://github.com/mgp/book-notes/blob/master/effective-java-2nd-edition.markdown.

After creating ("building") an instance of `AlertDialog.Builder`, you need to obtain an instance of the `AlertDialog` class and then invoke the `show()` method to launch the alert, as shown here:

```
AlertDialog alert = builder.
               create();

// now display the alert
alert.show();
```

Figure 3.1 displays the result of launching the `MyAlert` project on a Pixel Phone with Android 7.1.

FIGURE 3.1 An Alert in an Android Application.

Time Pickers

The Android package `android.widget` contains the class `TimePicker` that provides date-related functionality. In addition, Android supports a date picker widget that enables users to select a date based on the year,

month, and day. The example in this section shows you how to use the
`TimePicker` component.

 Copy the directory `MyTimePicker` from the companion disc to a convenient location. Listing 3.2 displays the contents of `MainActivity.java`, which illustrates how to use a time picker control in an Android application. Each time that you change the current time in the `TimePicker` component, its value is displayed as a string in a `TextView` component.

LISTING 3.2 MainActivity.java

```
package com.example.oswaldcampesato2.mytimepicker;

import android.app.AppCompatActivity;
import android.os.Bundle;
import android.widget.TextView;
import android.widget.TimePicker;

public class MainActivity extends AppCompatActivity
{
    // a text field to display the selected date and time
    private TextView mTimeDisplay;

    @Override
    protected void onCreate(Bundle savedInstanceState)
    {
        super.onCreate(savedInstanceState);
        setContentView(R.layout.activity_main);

        // instantiate a TimePicker class and set hours/
                                                   minutes
        TimePicker timePicker =
                (TimePicker) findViewById(R.id.timePicker);
        timePicker.setHour(12);
        timePicker.setMinute(15);

        mTimeDisplay = (TextView) findViewById(R.id.timeDisplay);

        timePicker.setOnTimeChangedListener(
                new TimePicker.OnTimeChangedListener() {
                    public void onTimeChanged(
                            TimePicker view, int
                                    hourOfDay, int minute) {
                            updateTimeDisplay(hourOfDay, minute);
                    }
                });
    }
```

```
private void updateTimeDisplay(int hour, int minute)
{
    String padHour = pad(hour);
    String padMin  = pad(minute);

    mTimeDisplay.setText(padHour+":"+padMin);
}

private static String pad(int c)
{
    if (c >= 10) {
        return String.valueOf(c);
    } else {
        return "0" + String.valueOf(c);
    }
}
}
```

The onCreate() method in Listing 3.2 creates an instance of the Android TimePicker class and then sets the hour and minute with this block of code:

```
TimePicker timePicker =
            (TimePicker) findViewById(R.id.timePicker);
timePicker.setHour(12);
timePicker.setMinute(15);
```

The next portion of Listing 3.2 displays a string with the hour and minute values in a TextView component after prepending a 0 (if necessary) to this string. The last block of code in onCreate() adds an event listener to the TimePicker component: whenever the time is changed, the method updateTimeValue() is invoked with the new hour and minute values.

The updateTimeValue() method invokes the pad() method that (if necessary) prepends a "0" to the hour and minute values, after which the contents of the TextView component are updated with the concatenation of the hour and minute values, as shown here:

```
mTimeDisplay.setText(padHour+":"+padMin);
```

The code sample in this section is a "bare bones" example of using the TimePicker component. Regarding the DatePicker component: additional options are available, such as setting the mode to "spinner," as well as a CalenderView option. Consult the Android documentation for details about the DatePicker component.

What Are Android Fragments?

Android Fragments were added to the Android API in Honeycomb (API 11) and they are even supported in Android 1.6 (API 4) via the Compatibility Package. This section discusses Fragments for Android 3.0 or higher, and online documentation describes the differences for earlier versions of Android.

Fragments are reusable components, and they allow for better UI designs such as cards and floating action buttons. Fragments are well-suited for a Master-Detail UI design, as well as dynamic layouts to accommodate various screen sizes and configurations, for phones as well as tablets. Another important point: the instantiation of a new Activity can be time-consuming compared to a Fragment. (Comparing an Activity to a Fragment is somewhat analogous to comparing a process to a thread.)

Think of a Fragment as a piece of an application's user interface or behavior that can be placed in an Activity. Interaction with Fragments is done through FragmentManager, which is available via the Activity.get-FragmentManager() method and also the Fragment.getFragment-Manager() method.

In essence, the Fragment class represents a particular operation or interface that is running within a larger Activity. A Fragment is closely tied to its "enclosing" Activity, and cannot be used apart from an Activity. Although a Fragment defines its own lifecycle, that lifecycle is dependent on its Activity: if the Activity is stopped, no Fragments inside of it can be started; when the Activity is destroyed, all Fragments will be destroyed.

All subclasses of Fragment must include a public empty constructor, which is needed whenever the framework re-instantiates a Fragment class (such as during state restore). If the empty constructor is unavailable, a runtime exception will occur in some cases during state restore.

A Fragment *can only* be used inside an Activity, and if the parent Activity is stopped, no Fragments inside that Activity can be started. As you might surmise, whenever an Activity is destroyed, all its Fragments are also destroyed.

Activitys and Fragments have a one-to-many relationship: a best practice is to use at most four or five fragments in an Activity (but nothing will stop you from using many more). In general, use an Activity to launch existing Android resources (video player, browser, and so forth), and use a Fragment to modify the UI components of application.

Fragment subclasses must include a public empty constructor, otherwise a runtime exception will occur.

Fragment-Related Classes

The Android package `android.app` contains the `Fragment` class. A `Fragment` has its own lifecycle (discussed later), with its own input events that you can add or remove while the "parent" `Activity` is active.

The Android `android.app` package contains several `Fragment` subclasses, including `DialogFragment`, `ListFragment`, `PreferenceFragment`, and `WebViewFragment`.

The Android package `android.sup-port.v4.app` *provides a* `Fragment` *class for Android mobile applications prior to Android 3.0 (API Level 11).*

The package `android.sup-port.v4.app` contains not only the `Fragment` base class, but also the `Fragment`-related classes `ListFragment`, `FragmentActivity`, and `FragmentTransaction`.

The Fragment Lifecycle Methods

Just to give you an idea (but without delving into their details), the following methods are associated with a `Fragment` lifecycle:

```
onAttach(Activity)
onCreate(Bundle)
onCreateView(LayoutInflater,
            ViewGroup, Bundle)
onActivityCreated(Bundle)
onViewStateRestored(Bundle)
onStart()
onResume()
```

An Android Fragment is conceptually like a modular section of an Activity that also has its own lifecycle. A Fragment also receives its own input events, and

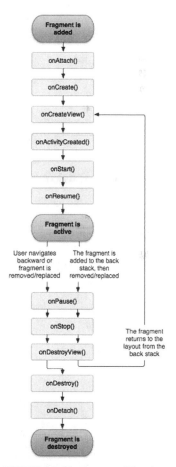

FIGURE 3.2 The Fragment lifecycle.

you can add or remove while the "main" activity is running. More information about Fragments is here:

http://developer.android.com/guide/components/fragments.html.

Figure 3.2 displays the `Fragment` lifecycle, which is also displayed in the preceding link.

Google recommends the use of Fragments, which can be used as "containers" for `Activitys`. Fragments make it easier to reuse components in different layouts.

Since Android 4 (ICS) supports both smart phones and tablets, you can deploy the same Android application in both devices. However, the visual display will probably be different on these two devices, and Fragments provide a nice solution. Although Fragments are not mandatory, they do make it easier to support multiple screen sizes.

NOTE *If you intend to work extensively with Fragments, then you also need to learn about the `Fragment` lifecycle, which is available in the online Android documentation.*

Working with Android Fragments

You can instantiate a Fragment as a whole-screen activity on a smart phone or as a partial screen. You can distinguish between mobile phones and tablets with conditional logic involving a few lines of code.

Types of Android Fragments

There are three main types of Fragments:

1) Static Fragments, which are placed in an Activity layout and never change
2) Dynamic framework Fragments
3) Dynamic support Fragments from the v4 support library, which work with `AppCompatActivities`

Later in this chapter you will see an example of a static `Fragment`.

Android Classes for Fragments

Android applications use one of the following classes for Fragments:

- `android.app.Fragment`: The base class for all fragment definitions

- `android.app.FragmentManager`: The class for interacting with fragment objects inside an `activity`
- `android.app.FragmentTransaction`: The class for performing an atomic set of `fragment` operations

You can create a `Fragment` programmatically or you can define a `Fragment` in an XML layout file (which is also true of other UI components). If a `Fragment` component is defined in an XML layout file, the `android:name` attribute specifies the corresponding class. In the former case, you define a `Fragment` by extending one of the following classes that are in the package `android.app`:

- Fragment
- ListFragment
- DialogFragment
- PreferenceFragment
- WebViewFragment

Note that the `Fragment` class is the base class for the other classes in the preceding list.

Creating Custom Fragments

Create a `Fragment` custom class by extending the `Fragment` class and overriding lifecycle methods with your application-specific logic, in much the same way that you override methods in an Android `Activity` class.

However, an Android `Fragment` must use the `onCreateView()` callback to define the layout. This callback method is the only method that you need to implement in order to run an Android Fragment.

As you can probably guess, an `Activity` can communicate with each of its `Fragments` (and vice versa). This approach is better than having `Fragments` communicate directly with each other, because the former approach increases the reusability of your custom `Fragment` classes.

An Android Fragment Example

This section contains a very simple example of creating a custom `Fragment` class. Copy the Android project `MyFragment` from the companion disc into a convenient location. Open the project in Android Studio and then deploy the application to an Android device.

The main files of interest are listed here:

```
./java/com/example/oswaldcampesato2/myfragment/
                                       Fragment1.java
./java/com/example/oswaldcampesato2/myfragment/
                                       Fragment2.java
./java/com/example/oswaldcampesato2/myfragment/
                                       MyFragment.java
./res/layout/activity_my_fragment.xml
./res/layout/fragment1.xml
./res/layout/fragment2.xml
```

The main `Activity` is defined in `MyFragment.java` and its associated layout file is `activity_main.xml`. Fragment one and fragment two are defined in `Fragment1.java` and `Fragment2.java`, respectively, and their corresponding layout files are `fragment1.xml` and `fragment2.xml`.

Listing 3.3 displays the contents of `activity_my_fragment.xml` with the contents of the main layout file. As you will see later, one fragment is displayed in portrait mode and the other fragment is displayed in land-scape mode (not both of them).

LISTING 3.3 activity_my_fragment.xml

```
<?xml version="1.0" encoding="utf-8"?>
<android.support.constraint.ConstraintLayout
    xmlns:android="http://schemas.android.com/apk/res/android"
    xmlns:app="http://schemas.android.com/apk/res-auto"
    xmlns:tools="http://schemas.android.com/tools"
    android:id="@+id/activity_my_fragment"
    android:layout_width="match_parent"
    android:layout_height="match_parent"
    tools:context="com.example.oswaldcampesato2.
                                myfragment.MyFragment">

    <LinearLayout
        xmlns:android="http://schemas.android.com/apk/
                                res/android"
        android:layout_width="fill_parent"
        android:layout_height="fill_parent" >

        <fragment
            android:id="@+id/fragment2"
            android:name="com.example.oswaldcampesato2.
                                myfragment.Fragment2"
            android:layout_width="0px"
```

```
            android:layout_height="match_parent"
            android:layout_weight="1"
            />

    <fragment
            android:id="@+id/fragment1"
            android:name="com.example.oswaldcampesato2.
                        myfragment.Fragment1"
            android:layout_width="0px"
            android:layout_height="match_parent"
            android:layout_weight="1"
            />
    </LinearLayout>
</android.support.constraint.ConstraintLayout>
```

Listing 3.3 contains a `<LinearLayout>` element that in turn contains two XML `<fragment>` elements. The two fragments are bound to the Java files `Fragment1.java` and `Fragment2.java` (shown later).

Listing 3.4 displays the contents of `MyFragment.java`, which is the main `Activity` class for this code sample.

LISTING 3.4 MyFragment.java

```
package com.example.oswaldcampesato2.myfragment;

import android.support.v7.app.AppCompatActivity;
import android.os.Bundle;

public class MyFragment extends AppCompatActivity
{
    @Override
    protected void onCreate(Bundle savedInstanceState)
    {
        super.onCreate(savedInstanceState);
      //setContentView(R.layout.activity_my_fragment);

        Configuration config = getResources().getConfiguration();

        FragmentManager fragmentManager = getFragmentManager();
        FragmentTransaction fragmentTransaction =
                        fragmentManager.beginTransaction();

        // Check the device orientation
        if (config.orientation == Configuration.
                                ORIENTATION_LANDSCAPE)
        {
          // Landscape mode of the device
          Fragment1 fragment1 = new Fragment1();
          fragmentTransaction.replace(android.R.id.
                                content, fragment1);
```

```
        }
        else
        {
            // Portrait mode of the device
            Fragment fragment2 = new Fragment2();
            fragmentTransaction.replace(android.R.id.
                                     content, fragment2);
        }

        fragmentTransaction.commit();
    }
}
```

Listing 3.4 contains boilerplate code followed by the onCre-
ate() method that contains several sections of code. The first
section initializes the variable config (which is an instance of the
Configuration class) that is used later for determining the orientation of the Android device. The second section contains two lines of
code that initialize the variable fragmentTransaction that is used
for transaction-related purposes. The third section uses the config
variable and simple conditional logic to render content associated
with Fragment1 in landscape mode, and content associated with
Fragment2 in portrait mode.

Listing 3.5 displays the contents of Fragment1.java, which contains the
code for the first fragment.

LISTING 3.5 Fragment1.java

```
package com.example.oswaldcampesato2.myfragment;

import android.app.Fragment;
import android.os.Bundle;
import android.view.LayoutInflater;
import android.view.View;
import android.view.ViewGroup;

public class Fragment1 extends Fragment
{
    @Override
    public View onCreateView(LayoutInflater inflater,
                             ViewGroup container,
                             Bundle savedInstanceState)
    {
        return inflater.inflate(R.layout.
                             fragment1,container, false);
    }
}
```

Listing 3.5 contains an onCre-
ateView() method that inflates
the XML layout file fragment1.
xml into the main container (i.e.,
the <LinearLayout> element in
Listing 3.3).

Similarly, Fragment2.java contains an onCreateView() method
that also inflates the XML layout
file fragment2.xml into the main
container.

As you probably surmised, the contents of Fragment2.java are almost
identical to Fragment1.java: simply
replace Fragment1 and fragment1
with Fragment2 and fragment2,
respectively.

Listing 3.6 displays the contents of
fragment1.xml with the contents of
the layout file for the first fragment.

FIGURE 3.3 An Android Fragment in portrait mode.

LISTING 3.6 fragment1.xml

```
<?xml version="1.0" encoding="utf-8"?>
<LinearLayout xmlns:android="http://schemas.android.
                                    com/apk/res/android"
        android:orientation="vertical"
        android:layout_width="match_parent"
        android:layout_height="match_parent">
    <TextView
        android:id="@+id/textView1"
        android:layout_width="match_parent"
        android:layout_height="wrap_content"
        android:text="This is Fragment One View1"
        android:textAppearance="?android:attr/textAppearanceLarge" />

    <CalendarView
            android:layout_width="match_parent"
            android:layout_height="wrap_content"
            android:id="@+id/calendarView" />
</LinearLayout>
```

Listing 3.6 consists of a <LinearLayout> element that contains a
<TextView> element followed by a <CalendarView> element.

Listing 3.7 displays the contents of `fragment2.xml` with the contents of the layout file for the second fragment.

LISTING 3.7 fragment2.xml

```xml
<?xml version="1.0" encoding="utf-8"?>
<LinearLayout xmlns:android="http://schemas.android.
                                    com/apk/res/android"
    android:orientation="vertical"
    android:layout_width="match_parent"
    android:layout_height="match_parent">
    <TextView
        android:id="@+id/textView1"
        android:layout_width="match_parent"
        android:layout_height="wrap_content"
        android:text="This is Fragment Two View1"
        android:textAppearance="?android:attr/
                                    textAppearanceLarge" />

    <TimePicker
        android:layout_width="match_parent"
        android:layout_height="wrap_content"
        android:id="@+id/timePicker" />

    <TextView
        android:id="@+id/textView2"
        android:layout_width="match_parent"
        android:layout_height="wrap_content"
        android:text="This is Fragment Two View2"
        android:textAppearance="?android:attr/
                                    textAppearanceLarge" />

</LinearLayout>
```

FIGURE 3.4 An Android Fragment in landscape mode.

Listing 3.7 consists of a <LinearLayout> element that in turn contains three child elements: a <TextView> element, followed by a <CalendarView> element, and then another <TextView> element.

Figure 3.3 displays the rendering of MyFragment in portrait mode on a Pixel phone with Android 7.1.

Figure 3.4 displays the rendering of MyFragment in landscape mode on a Pixel phone with Android 7.1.

There are various uses for Android Fragments, such as using a clickable list of thumbnail images in a carousel, and then displaying the clicked image in a "main" fragment. Similarly, Fragments can be used for playing audio files or video files. In fact, Android TV applications (discussed in Chapter 9) make significant use of Android Fragments.

This concludes the overview of Android Fragments. If you want to obtain a deeper understanding of Fragments, additional information is available in the Android documentation.

Lists and Array Adapters

Displaying a list is common in many mobile applications. Android provides a ListView in the android.widget package that works well for many situations. However, if your application enables users to scroll through hundreds of items (such as a list of Twitter tweets), you need to use an Android Adapter class and an ArrayAdapter (also in the android. widget package) to improve performance, thereby creating a better user experience. Keep in mind that you will not see a discernible performance improvement with the Android Adapter class when the number of list items is small (fewer than 100 items).

 Copy the directory MyList from the companion disc to a convenient location. Listing 3.8 displays the contents of MainActivity.java, which illustrates how to render a list of strings in an Android application.

LISTING 3.8 MainActivity.java

```
package com.example.oswaldcampesato2.mylist1;

import android.app.ListActivity;
import android.os.Bundle;
import android.view.View;
import android.widget.ArrayAdapter;
```

```
import android.widget.ListView;
import android.widget.Toast;

public class MainActivity extends ListActivity
{
    @Override
    protected void onCreate(Bundle savedInstanceState) {
        super.onCreate(savedInstanceState);
        setContentView(R.layout.activity_main);

        // Create an array of Strings for the ListActivity
        String[] names = new String[] {
                "San Francisco", "New York", "Los Angeles",
                "Tokyo", "Berlin", "Paris", "Istanbul",
                "Delhi", "Rio de Janeiro", "Rome"};

        // Create an ArrayAdapter that makes the Strings above
        // appear in the ListView
        this.setListAdapter(new
                ArrayAdapter<String>(this,
                android.R.layout.simple_list_item_checked,
                                                    names)));
    }

    @Override
    protected void onListItemClick(ListView l, View v,
                                int position, long id) {
        super.onListItemClick(l, v, position, id);

        // Get the item that was clicked
        Object obj = this.getListAdapter().getItem(position);
        String keyword = obj.toString();

        Toast.makeText(this, "You selected: " + keyword,
                Toast.LENGTH_LONG).show();
    }
}
```

Listing 3.8 declares the variable names that references an array of strings, which is used to instantiate an Android Adapter class, as shown here:

```
this.setListAdapter(new ArrayAdapter<String>(this,
    android.R.layout.simple_list_item_checked, names));
```

Whenever users check an item in the list of names, the onListItem-Click() method is invoked. This method uses the position of the selected item in the array in order to retrieve the actual item string and then display a toast with that item string:

```
Toast.makeText(this, "You selected: " + keyword,
                Toast.LENGTH_LONG).show();
```

Listing 3.9 displays the contents of `activity_main.xml`, which contains a `<List>` element for rendering a list of items.

LISTING 3.9 activity_main.xml

```
<?xml version="1.0" encoding="utf-8"?>
<RelativeLayout
    xmlns:android="http://schemas.android.com/apk/res/android"
    xmlns:tools="http://schemas.android.com/tools"
    android:id="@+id/activity_main"
    android:layout_width="match_parent"
    android:layout_height="match_parent"
    android:paddingBottom="@dimen/activity_vertical_margin"
    android:paddingLeft="@dimen/activity_horizontal_margin"
    android:paddingRight="@dimen/activity_horizontal_margin"
    android:paddingTop="@dimen/activity_vertical_margin"
    tools:context="com.example.oswaldcampesato2.
                              simplelist1.MainActivity">

    <TextView
        android:text="TextView"
        android:layout_width="wrap_content"
        android:layout_height="wrap_content"
        android:layout_alignParentTop="true"
        android:layout_centerHorizontal="true"
        android:layout_marginTop="33dp"
        android:id="@+id/textView" />

    <ListView
        android:layout_width="match_parent"
        android:layout_height="match_parent"
        android:layout_below="@+id/textView"
        android:layout_centerHorizontal="true"
        android:layout_marginTop="147dp"
        android:id="@android:id/list" />
</RelativeLayout>
```

Listing 3.9 has a `RelativeLayout` component as the root component, which in turn contains a `TextView` component and a `ListView` component.

Notice the different syntax for the `id` attribute of the `<ListView>` element, which is shown in bold in Listing 3.9. If you use the "regular" syntax for the `id` attribute, you will get the following runtime error:

```
RuntimeException: Your content must have a ListView whose id
attribute is 'android.R.id.list'
```

Listing 3.10 displays the contents of the `simple_list_item_checked.xml` layout file that specifies the layout details of a single item in the list, which is simply one `<TextView>` element.

LISTING 3.10 simple_list_item_checked.xml

```
<?xml version="1.0"
            encoding="utf-8"?>
<TextView
    xmlns:android="http://
    schemas.android.com/apk/res/
                        android"
    android:id="@+id/
                rowTextView"
    android:layout_width="fill_
                    parent"
    android:layout_height="wrap_
                    content"
    android:padding="10dp"
    android:textSize="16sp" >
</TextView>
```

Figure 3.5 displays the rendering of
SimpleList on a Samsung Galaxy S5
with Android 6.0.1.

TextView

San Francisco	✓
New York	✓
Los Angeles	✓
Tokyo	✓
Berlin	✓
Paris	✓
Istanbul	✓
Delhi	✓
Rio de Janeiro	✓

FIGURE 3.5 A List in an Android Application.

Android Layout Managers

First, let's review the following points: Android Layout Managers are sub-classes of the ViewGroup subclass, and the ViewGroup class is a sub-class of the View class. Android Layout Managers are container views whose purpose is to control the screen layout of their child views (hence their name). Android supports several Layout Managers, including RelativeLayout that you saw in Chapter 2.

Some properties, such as Text, can be set directly on a View object. There are other properties that you must set on an appropriate LayoutParam object, after which the latter object is set at the View object's LayoutParam property.

One point to keep in mind: each Layout type has an associated class whose name is the concatenation of the Layout type and the LayoutParam class. As an example, LinearLayout has an associated class called LinearLayout.LayoutParam (and similarly for the other Layout managers). The LinearLayout.LayoutParam class is sort of like a "definition class" that defines the layout properties that are available to any View object that is added to a LinearLayout object.

Instantiate the LinearLayout.LayoutParam class as follows:

```
LinearLayout.LayoutParam linLayoutParams =
          new LinearLayout.LayoutParam(200,200);
```

Set the preceding class in `View` objects that you add to the `LinearLayout` as follows:

```
btn.setLayoutParams(linLayoutParams);
linLayout.addView(b3);
```

After executing the preceding code block, the `Button` `btn` will be 200x200 pixels. However, keep in mind that the pixels are *not* device-independent pixels. In addition, more complex `Layout` objects have more complex `LayoutParams` that must be initialized.

The `LayoutParams` class can also provide a constructor to set some properties (such as the weight), whereas other properties are set by invoking the `setProperty()` methods after the constructor has been invoked, where you need to replace `Property` with the property in question. The details depend on the specific `Layout` manager.

For example, you can replace `Property` with `Margins`, an example of which is here:

```
linLayout.setMargins(10,10,10,10);
```

The next section introduces you to the `RecyclerView`, which is a powerful and flexible component that provides performance-related advantages. In particular, the `RecyclerView` is well-suited for Android applications that use constraint-based layouts.

The RecyclerView

Android 5.x introduced the `RecyclerView`, which is an improvement over the `ListView` component. The `RecyclerView` "recycles" `View` elements more efficiently in order to improve performance. The `RecyclerView` simplifies the display and handling of large data sets by providing layout managers (such as the `CardView LayoutManager`) for positioning items.

A list of some supported built-in layout managers is here:

- LinearLayoutManager (vertical or horizontal scrolling list)
- GridLayoutManager (items in a grid)
- StaggeredGridLayoutManager (items in a staggered grid)

The `RecyclerView` also supports custom layout managers: do so by extending the `RecyclerView.LayoutManager` class.

Setting Up a RecyclerView

In order to use a `RecyclerView`, you must do two things: specify an adapter and a layout manager. You create an adapter by extending the `RecyclerView.Adapter` class: the actual details of the implementation depend on the specifics of your dataset and the type of views in your application.

The reason for specifying a layout manager is straightforward: the layout manager positions item views inside a `RecyclerView` and determines when to reuse item views that are no longer visible to the user. Moreover, when a view is reused (or recycled), the layout manager may instruct the adapter to replace the contents of such a view with a different element from the dataset. This recycling technique improves performance by avoiding the creation of unnecessary views or performing expensive `find-ViewById()` lookups.

A RecyclerView Code Sample

The code sample in this section shows you how to use the basic features of the `RecyclerView` with a list of items.

 Copy the directory `RecyclerViewTextView` from the companion disc to a convenient location. Listing 3.11 displays the contents of `MainActivity.java`, which illustrates how to set up a `RecyclerView` in an Android application.

LISTING 3.11 MainActivity.java

```
package com.android_examples.recyclerview_android_examplescom;

import android.content.Context;
import android.support.v7.app.AppCompatActivity;
import android.os.Bundle;
import android.support.v7.widget.LinearLayoutManager;
import android.support.v7.widget.RecyclerView;
import android.view.Window;
import android.widget.RelativeLayout;

public class MainActivity extends AppCompatActivity
{
```

```
Context context;
RecyclerView recyclerView;
RelativeLayout relativeLayout;
RecyclerView.Adapter recyclerViewAdapter;
RecyclerView.LayoutManager recylerViewLayoutManager;

String[] wineList = {
  "Merlot", "Barolo", "Cremona", "Tokai",
  "Retsina", "Pinot Noir", "Cabernet",
  "Merlot", "Barolo", "Cremona", "Tokai",
  "Retsina", "Pinot Noir", "Cabernet",
  "Merlot", "Barolo", "Cremona", "Tokai",
  "Retsina", "Pinot Noir", "Cabernet",
  "Merlot", "Barolo", "Cremona", "Tokai",
  "Retsina", "Pinot Noir", "Cabernet",
  "Merlot", "Barolo", "Cremona", "Tokai",
  "Retsina", "Pinot Noir", "Cabernet"
};

@Override
protected void onCreate(Bundle savedInstanceState)
{
    super.onCreate(savedInstanceState);
    requestWindowFeature(Window.FEATURE_ACTION_BAR);
    setContentView(R.layout.activity_main);

    context = getApplicationContext();

    // find the RelativeLayout component
    relativeLayout =
      (RelativeLayout) findViewById(R.id.relativeLayout);

    // find the RecyclerView component
    recyclerView = (RecyclerView) findViewById
                                (R.id.recyclerView);

    recylerViewLayoutManager =
                    new LinearLayoutManager(context);

    // #1: set layout manager component in recyclerView
    recyclerView. setLayoutManager(recylerViewLayoutManager);

    // #2: set adapter component in recyclerView
    recyclerViewAdapter =
      new RecyclerViewAdapter(context, wineList);

    recyclerView.setAdapter(recyclerViewAdapter);
  }
}
```

Listing 3.11 contains boilerplate code, followed by the context variable, which is used later when an instance of the RecyclerView manager is initialized as an instance of the `LinearLayoutManager`. The comments that start with #1 and #2 involve setting the layout manager and the view adapter, respectively, for the `RecyclerView`.

Listing 3.12 displays the contents of `RecycleViewAdapter.java`, which contains the code for the adapter that is required for a `RecyclerView` component.

LISTING 3.12 RecyclerViewAdapter.java

```
package com.android_examples.recyclerview_android_examplescom;

import android.content.Context;
import android.support.v7.widget.RecyclerView;
import android.view.LayoutInflater;
import android.view.View;
import android.view.ViewGroup;
import android.widget.TextView;

public class RecyclerViewAdapter extends
        RecyclerView.Adapter<RecyclerViewAdapter.ViewHolder>
{
    String[] wineList;
    Context context;
    View view;
    ViewHolder viewHolder;
    TextView textView;

    public RecyclerViewAdapter(Context context,
                                        String[] wineList)
    {
        this.wineList = wineList;
        this.context = context;
    }

    public static class ViewHolder extends
                                RecyclerView.ViewHolder
    {
        public TextView textView;

        public ViewHolder(View v){
            super(v);
            textView =
              (TextView)v.findViewById(R.id.item_textview);
        }
    }

    @Override
    public RecyclerViewAdapter.ViewHolder
            onCreateViewHolder(ViewGroup parent, int viewType)
```

```
    {
        view = LayoutInflater.from(context)
                .inflate(R.layout.
                        recyclerview_items,parent,false);

        viewHolder = new ViewHolder(view);

        return viewHolder;
    }

    @Override
    public void onBindViewHolder(ViewHolder holder,
                                        int position){
        holder.textView.setText(wineList[position]);
    }

    @Override
    public int getItemCount(){
        return wineList.length;
    }
}
```

Listing 3.12 contains boilerplate code, a simple constructor to initialize the variables `wineList` and `context`, followed by the custom `ViewHolder` class that extends the Android class `RecyclerView.ViewHolder`. The `ViewHolder` class contains the method that sets the variable `textView` as a reference to the `TextView` component defined in the `recyclerview_items.xml` layout file.

The `onCreateViewHolder` method associates an instance of the `ViewHolder` class that is based on inflating the `recyclerview_items.xml` layout file. Finally, the `onBindViewHolder` method coordinates an instance of the `ViewHolder` class with an item in the `wineList` array.

Listing 3.13 displays the contents of `activity_main.xml`, which contains a top-level `RelativeLayout` component and a `RecyclerView` component.

LISTING 3.13 *activity_main.xml*

```
<?xml version="1.0" encoding="utf-8"?>
<RelativeLayout
    xmlns:android="http://schemas.android.com/apk/res/android"
    xmlns:tools="http://schemas.android.com/tools"
    android:layout_width="match_parent"
    android:layout_height="match_parent"
    android:paddingBottom="@dimen/activity_vertical_margin"
    android:paddingLeft="@dimen/activity_horizontal_margin"
    android:paddingRight="@dimen/activity_horizontal_margin"
```

```
android:paddingTop="@dimen/activity_vertical_margin"
tools:context="com.android_examples.recyclerview_
                        android_examplescom.MainActivity"
android:id="@+id/relativeLayout">

    <android.support.v7.widget.RecyclerView
        android:id="@+id/recyclerView"
        android:scrollbars="vertical"
        android:layout_width="fill_parent"
        android:layout_
height="fill_parent"
        />
</RelativeLayout>
```

Figure 3.6 displays the rendering of RecyclerViewTextView on a Pixel phone with Android 7.1.

As you can see, this section contains a minimalistic code sample whose purpose is to help you understand the components of a RecyclerView. However, the RecyclerView is much more powerful than the example in this section, and can become correspondingly more complex. One option for managing some of that complexity is the epoxy toolkit from Airbnb, whose home page is here

https://github.com/airbnb/epoxy.

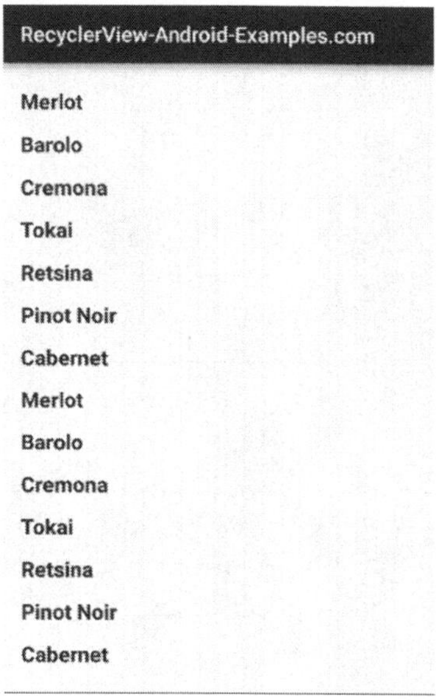

RecyclerView-Android-Examples.com

Merlot

Barolo

Cremona

Tokai

Retsina

Pinot Noir

Cabernet

Merlot

Barolo

Cremona

Tokai

Retsina

Pinot Noir

Cabernet

FIGURE 3.6 A RecyclerView in an Android Application.

Constraint-Based Layouts

This section discusses the constraint-based layout for Android applications that was introduced in Android Studio 2.2.

The ConstraintLayout is the Android layout type (introduced in Android Studio 2.2) that provides several new features, along with a sophisticated built-in Layout Editor. The ConstraintLayout decreases the depth and complexity of the view hierarchy in Android applications. ConstraintLayout helps you optimize the UI rendering phase of Android applications. In particular, ConstraintLayout is well-suited for use with the RecyclerView. ConstraintLayout is contained in the Android Support Library, it is compatible with all currently available Views and ViewGroups, and it works down to API level 9.

Android Studio enables you to convert existing Android applications to the new constraint-based layout. Simply navigate to an existing layout resource file, open the visual editor and right-click on a `RelativeLayout` (for example), and then click the option to convert to a constraint layout. The remainder of this section delves into some of the details of the constraint-based layout, along with an example.

What Is `ConstraintLayout`?

`ConstraintLayout` is a more recent type of layout for Android Applications that is backward compatible down to API level 9 and is also part of the support library. The purpose of the `ConstraintLayout` is to reduce the depth of layout hierarchies, to improve performance of layouts, and to reduce the complexity of trying to work with `RelativeLayouts`. Fortunately, this new layout is compatible with other layouts, which means that you are not forced to choose one particular layout.

Converting Existing Android Applications

In case you have not already done so, download the latest version of Android Studio (version 2.2 or higher), which also provides a new layout editor.

Step 1: add the following code snippet to your `build.gradle` dependencies:

```
compile 'com.android.support.
constraint:constraint-layout:1.0.0-beta4'
```

Note that Android Studio automatically adds the `ConstraintLayout` dependency to `build.gradle` when you create a new layout in Android Studio.

Step 2: open `activity_main.xml` and click on the `Design` tab.

Step 3: click on the `Component` panel under the `Palette` panel.

Step 4: right-click and select `Convert LinearLayout to ConstraintLayout`.

If your application uses a `RelativeLayout`, then in Step 4 you will see the `LinearLayout` replaced with `RelativeLayout`.

Constraints and the Constraints System

Think of constraints as rules for the layout and alignment of various UI components in an application. When you use constraint-based layouts, you can resize many components simply by dragging one of the four vertices of the enclosing rectangle, which is a very nice feature that is unavailable in other layout managers (more effort is required). The small round circles on either side of a UI component enable you to add horizontal constraints.

You need to spend time experimenting with the features of the Android Studio Designer in conjunction with constraint-based layouts in order to master its very rich set of features.

The layout engine uses sophisticated heuristics and all the constraints associated with each UI component in order to calculate the positions of the UI components on the screen. The designer provides buttons to clear all the constraints and also to watch the constraints dynamically added to UI components. Check the online documentation for additional details.

Incidentally, sometimes the designer displays confusing (misleading?) error messages, such as this one:

Rendering Problems Preview timed out while rendering the layout. This typically happens when there is an infinite loop or unbounded recursion in one of the custom views. (Details) Tip: Try to refresh the layout.

In general, refreshing the layout solves this error and various other types of errors.

Keep in mind the following point: constraints are calculated based on the top-to-bottom and left-to-right sequence of the UI components on the screen. You can also drag a group of elements as follows:

1) locate the upper-left UI component that you want to move
2) perform a long press on that component
3) right-drag your mouse to encompass the desired group of elements

After Step 3 the group elements are highlighted inside a "dotted" rectangle, which you can move around the screen to the desired location.

Android 6.0 Features (Android M)

The main new features of Android Marshmallow are here:

- Applications permissions
- Application links
- Mobile Payments
- Fingerprint support
- Power and charging

Chapter 6 discusses the new permissions model, whereby users are prompted to accept or deny permissions when a certain feature is used; the web experience for Android will be improved by Chrome custom tabs that open on top of applications; and application links will be more aware of where they should open, whether in an application or a browser.

Google has added native fingerprint scanning support to Mobile payments with Android Pay. Doze for Android will provide smarter power management, which uses motion detection to determine whether or not the device has been used. According to Google, devices can last twice as long when they are in standby mode, and devices will use USB Type-C chargers.

The next section of this chapter briefly mentions some of the new features in Android 7.

Features in Android 7 (Nougat)

The significant new features in Android 7 (Nougat) include Enhanced UI, Multi-Window Capabilities, Daydream VR (discussed in Chapter 9), and the Vulkan API. Android N also supports split-screen mode, which allows you to run two applications simultaneously, either side by side or one above the other in split-screen mode.

In addition, Android applications running on televisions can use picture-in-picture mode to continue video playback while users are interacting with another application. Android N also supports application shortcuts for specific actions in an application.

A short list containing some of the new features of Android Nougat is here:

- App Shortcuts
- Image Keyboard Support

- New Professional Emoji
- Enhanced Live Wallpaper Metadata
- Round Icon Resources
- Storage Manager Intent
- Improved VR Thread Scheduling
- New Screen Densities for Wear Devices

More information about the preceding list of new features in Android N is here:

https://www.android.com/versions/nougat-7-0/.

Note that you will see an example of app shortcuts, which involves an Android `Broadcast Receiver`, and so the code sample is deferred until Chapter 8 in the appropriate section.

Summary

This chapter showed you how to create Android applications that create various UI controls, such as Android Alerts and TimePickers. Then you learned about Android Fragments (which are essentially submodules of an Android `Activity`) that were introduced in Android 3.x.

You also got an overview of some Android layout managers, including `LinearLayout` and `RelativeLayout`. In addition, you saw an example of the Android `RecyclerView`, which is a powerful and more efficient "successor" to the `LinearLayout` manager and `GridLayout` manager. Next you learned about `ConstraintLayout`, which is more powerful and more efficient than other list-based layouts, and it's intended to replace the `RelativeLayout` manager. You got a brief introduction to some Android 6 features, followed by a list of some features of Android 7.

CHAPTER 4

GRAPHICS AND ANIMATION

This chapter contains Android code samples for creating various graphics and animation effects. You will learn how to render 2D shapes (code samples are on the companion disc), create gradient effects and filter effects, how to render binary images, and how to create 2D animation effects in Android applications. Additional open source toolkits, such as Glide and Picasso, are discussed in Appendix A.

The first part of this chapter shows you how to render text strings with gradient colors and how to render nested gradient rectangles. The companion disc contains Android code samples that render other 2D shapes, such as line segments, rectangles, circles, ellipses, and Bezier curves. The second part of this chapter shows you how to apply filter effects to PNG files, such as a Gaussian blur in a code sample. The final part of this chapter discusses animation effects in Android, and also shows you several techniques for creating animation effects.

This chapter contains code samples with graphics or animation effects that are invoked via button clicks. However, you can enhance the code samples in this chapter so that they incorporate various user gestures that are discussed in Chapter 5. For example, after you learn how to render a PNG image, you could add DnD (drag and drop) support so that users can drag PNG images across the screen of an Android mobile device.

Overview of Graphics in Android

Android provides packages and Java classes with extensive feature support, some of which are discussed in the following sections. The graphics library supports optimized 2D graphics and 3D graphics based on the embedded version of OpenGL ES.

The techniques for creating graphics and animation effects in Android vary in terms of their complexity. The point to keep in mind is that the graphics-related Android APIs allow you to write to a View component or directly on the Android Canvas.

Android provides a nice set of animation features through Java classes that are in various Android packages. The main packages for graphics and for processing images in Android are android.graphics and android.graphics.drawable.

The Android package android.graphics provides low-level graphics tools such as canvases, color filters, points, and rectangles that let you handle drawing to the screen directly.

The Android package android.graphics.drawable provides classes to manage a variety of visual elements that are intended for display only, such as bitmaps and gradients. Android provides the android.graphics.Bitmap class for processing images (because images are bitmaps).

The android.graphics.drawable.shapes package supports various shapes, including arcs, ovals, paths, rectangles, and rounded rectangles. You can also define your own custom shape via the PathShape class and the Path class. The latter class supports standard shapes as well as cubic and quadratic Bezier curves, all of which you can include as part of the desired custom path.

Yet another option for graphics and animation is OpenGL, which is the most sophisticated graphics and animation technology. Although it is more complex to learn, OpenGL has the advantage of portability. The choice of techniques obviously depends on your requirements and what you are trying to accomplish in your Android application. A good introduction to OpenGL is here: *https://developer.android.com/guide/topics/graphics/opengl.html*.

The next section introduces you to the (A,R,G,B) color model that is available in Android.

The (A,R,G,B) Color Model

The use of colors is ubiquitous, so you need a basic understanding of how to specify colors in Android. In brief, the (A,R,G,B) model for colors specifies the red, green, blue, and opacity components of a color, where the value for each component is an integer between 0 and 255. These numbers can be expressed as decimal or as hexadecimal numbers.

In Android the opacity is between 0 and 255, but in other systems the opacity can be a decimal number between 0 and 1.

Another point to keep in mind is that the hexadecimal values for colors in many programming languages are of the following form: 0xRRGGBBAA.

However, the hexadecimal values for a color and opacity in Android are of the following form: 0xAARRGGBB.

You can also set colors in an XML document. For example, the following code snippet sets the background to Red:

```
android:background = "#FFFF000000"
```

This extremely brief overview about (A,R,G,B) colors is enough information to work with colors in this chapter. A useful color converter is here: *http://rapidtables.com/web/color/RGB_Color.htm.*

Another color model is (H,S,L), which represents the Hue, Saturation, and Luminosity. This color model is not used in this book, but you can perform an Internet search to find online tutorials with information about the (H,S,L) color model.

Android Built-In Support for Gradients

You have probably seen linear gradients and radial gradients, either from other programming languages or in pictures, and gradients are essentially the same in Android.

The Android package android.graphics contains the LinearGradient class and the RadialGradient class for creating linear and radial gradients, respectively. You can apply gradient effects to text fields by means of an XML configuration that specifies values for gradients. Two useful links with documentation for gradients are here:

> *http://developer.android.com/reference/android/graphics/ LinearGradient.html*

> *http://developer.android.com/reference/android/graphics/ RadialGradient.html*

The next section contains a complete example that shows you how to display text strings with gradients.

Gradient Effects with `TextView` Components

The Android example in this section shows you how to define color gradients in an XML file, which is the simplest way to define color gradient effects in Android. Then you will learn how to apply those gradient effects to a text string. The key idea is to specify an XML file with gradient definitions via the Android `android:background` attribute.

 Copy the directory `MySimpleGradients` from the companion disc to a convenient location. The class `MainActivity.java` contains only the code that was dynamically generated during the creation of the project, so we don't need to review its contents (i.e., pure boilerplate code).

Listing 4.1 displays the contents of `activity_main.xml` that defines gradient effects.

LISTING 4.1 activity_main.xml

```
<?xml version="1.0" encoding="utf-8"?>
<LinearLayout xmlns:android="http://schemas.android.
                                    com/apk/res/android"
android:layout_width="fill_parent"
android:layout_height="fill_parent"
android:orientation="vertical" >

<!-- Use gradient1.xml -->
<LinearLayout
  android:layout_width="match_parent"
  android:layout_height="80dp"
  android:layout_margin="20dp"
  android:background="@drawable/gradient1"
  android:orientation="vertical"
  android:padding="5dp" >

  <TextView
    android:layout_width="fill_parent"
    android:layout_height="wrap_content"
    android:text="@string/hello"
    android:textColor="#000"
    android:textSize="32dp" />
</LinearLayout>

<!-- Use gradient2.xml -->
<LinearLayout
  android:layout_width="match_parent"
```

```
    android:layout_height="80dp"
    android:layout_margin="20dp"
    android:background="@drawable/gradient2"
    android:orientation="vertical"
    android:padding="8dp" >

    <TextView
        android:layout_width="fill_parent"
        android:layout_height="wrap_content"
        android:text="@string/hello"
        android:textColor="#FFF"
        android:textSize="20dp" />
</LinearLayout>
</LinearLayout>
```

Listing 4.1 specifies a top-level `LinearLayout` component that contains two child `LinearLayout` components. The first child `LinearLayout` component references `gradient1.xml` and the second child references `gradient2.xml`, both of which define gradient effects.

Listing 4.2 displays the contents of `gradient1.xml` and Listing 4.3 displays the contents of `gradient2.xml`.

LISTING 4.2 gradient1.xml

```
<?xml version="1.0" encoding="utf-8"?>
<shape xmlns:android="http://schemas.android.com/
                                    apk/res/android"
    android:layout_width="fill_parent"
    android:layout_height="fill_parent"
    ˋ
    <stroke
        android:width="8dp"
        android:color="#FFFFFF" />

    <corners android:radius="15dp" />
    <padding
        android:top="4px"
        android:bottom="4px" />

    <gradient
        android:angle="270"
        android:centerColor="#FFFFFF"
        android:endColor="#FF0000"
        android:startColor="#0000FF" />
</shape>
```

Listing 4.2 contains a top-level XML <shape> element with several XML child elements that are used to define the properties of a radial gradient. The XML <gradient> child element contains attributes whose values specify the start color, center color, and the end color for the radial gradient.

LISTING 4.3 gradient2.xml

```
<?xml version="1.0" encoding="utf-8"?>
<shape xmlns:android="http://schemas.android.com/apk/
                                              res/android"
       android:layout_width="fill_parent"
       android:layout_height="fill_parent"
       >
       <stroke
           android:width="2dp"
           android:color="#FFFFFF" />

       <corners android:radius="5dp" />

       <gradient
           android:angle="90"
           android:centerColor="#FF0000"
           android:endColor="#0000ff"
           android:startColor="#00FF00" />
</shape>
```

Listing 4.3 also defines a radial gradient, and since it is very similar to Listing 4.2 and does not introduce any new concepts, we can skip the details.

Using Custom Subviews for Graphics

You might be surprised to discover that you already know enough about Android to create your own custom views. The key idea involves defining a subclass of the Android View class and then putting your custom code in the onDraw() method of the subclass. In fact, the technique in this section is exactly the same technique that is used in the code samples to create graphics effects.

LISTING 4.4 MyCustomSubviewActivity.java

```
public class MyCustomSubviewActivity
{
    @Override
```

```
public void onCreate(Bundle savedInstanceState)
{
    super.onCreate(savedInstanceState);
  //setContentView(R.layout.activity_main);
    setContentView(new SimpleView(this));
}

private static class SimpleView extends View
{
    public SimpleView(Context context) {
        super(context);
        setFocusable(true);

        doSomethingInteresting();
    }

    public void doSomethingInteresting() {
        // the fun stuff goes here
    }

    // override onDraw() for custom graphics

    @Override
    protected void onDraw(Canvas canvas) {
        super.onDraw(canvas);
        // render your graphics code here
    }
  }
}
```

Listing 4.4 contains a code snippet shown in bold that replaces the default setContentView() method invocation, as shown here:

```
//setContentView(R.layout.activity_main);
  setContentView(new SimpleView(this));
```

The preceding code snippet instantiates the private Java class called SimpleView (whose contents are written by you) that is defined in the same file. The details of the private Java class are omitted from Listing 4.4, but you will see an example shortly.

Graphics Effects in Android Canvas

There are actually two options available: you can write directly on the Android Canvas element via a subview (as outlined in the previous section) in conjunction with graphics APIs, or you can write to a SurfaceView (described later in this chapter). The first approach is the simplest way to render graphics directly in Android Canvas. If you are impatient, you can read the complete code sample in the following section that renders a set of nested rectangles.

The relevant Java classes and available graphics APIs are in Java classes that belong to the Android package android.graphics. This package contains the Canvas class that enables you to render 2D shapes, and also apply transforms and animation effects to those 2D shapes. The list of 2D shapes includes line segments, rectangles, circles, polygons, and Bezier curves.

The Android Canvas class contains an onDraw() method that looks like this:

```
@Override
protected void onDraw(Canvas canvas)
{
    super.onDraw(canvas);
    // render your graphics here
}
```

As you can see from the preceding code block, an instance of the Canvas class is automatically supplied as an argument of the onDraw() method.

Incidentally, you can create a new Canvas object by first defining a bitmap for drawing shapes using the Bitmap class, and then instantiating a Canvas instance with the bitmap instance, as shown here:

```
Bitmap b = Bitmap.createBitmap(0, 0, Bitmap.Config.ARGB_8888);
Canvas c = new Canvas(b);
```

Graphics effects in Android Canvas typically use the Paint class (which also belongs to the android.graphics package) to create color-related effects. For example, the following code block renders a white Canvas:

```
@Override
protected void onDraw(Canvas canvas)
{
    super.onDraw(canvas);

    // instantiate a Paint object:
    Paint paint = new Paint();
    paint.setStyle(Paint.Style.FILL);

    // render a white canvas inside onDraw():
    paint.setColor(Color.WHITE);
    canvas.drawPaint(paint);
}
```

The following code block (which you would place inside the `onDraw()` method) renders a circle and a rectangle:

```
paint.setColor(Color.BLUE);
canvas.drawCircle(100, 50, 20, paint);

paint.setColor(Color.GREEN);
canvas.drawRect(50, 50, 200, 100, paint);
```

The following code snippet renders a text string:

```
canvas.drawText("Hello World", 50, 50, paint);
```

The following code snippet renders a bitmap that is a resource in an Android application:

```
Resources res = this.getResources();
Bitmap bitmap = BitmapFactory.decodeResource(res, R.drawable.
icon);
canvas.drawBitmap(bitmap, 100, 100, paint);
```

The next section contains a complete code sample that creates a gradient effect by rendering a set of nested rectangles.

Android Canvas 2D Transforms

The Android `Canvas` class supports 2D transforms that enable you to rotate, scale, skew, and translate 2D shapes. The APIs for these transforms are here:

```
void   rotate(float degrees)
final void rotate(float degrees, float px, float py)
final void scale(float sx, float sy, float px, float py)
void   skew(float sx, float sy)
void   translate(float dx, float dy)
```

The preceding APIs are straightforward, and the documentation provides examples that use the preceding methods. If you just want an overview of these APIs, some details are here: *http://developer.android.com/reference/android/graphics/Canvas.html*.

The Android package `android.graphics` contains the `Matrix` class, which supports many methods, including the following methods:

- void setRotate(float degrees): sets the matrix to rotate about (0,0) by the specified number of degrees
- void setRotate(float degrees, float px, float py): sets the matrix to rotate by the specified number of degrees, with a pivot point at (px, py)

- void setScale(float sx, float sy, float px, float py): sets the matrix to scale by sx and sy, with a pivot point at (px, py)
- void setSkew(float kx, float ky, float px, float py): sets the matrix to skew by sx and sy, with a pivot point at (px, py)
- void setTranslate(float dx, float dy): sets the matrix to translate by (dx, dy)

There are many other methods available in the `Matrix` class, and you can get additional information about this class here: *http://developer.android. com/reference/android/graphics/Matrix.html.*

The next section shows you how to render a drawable PNG, which is to say that you can display a PNG and then draw other graphics shapes on top of the PNG.

Rendering Binary Images

PNG images are useful in a variety of Android applications. For instance, many game-related Android applications (and also applications for educational purposes) contain various PNG files. Android makes it easy to render PNG files in a mobile application, and the example in this section shows you how this can be accomplished in Android. Later you will see the methods for transforms (such as rotate and reflect) that you can apply to PNG images, and also how to update the pixel values in a PNG image.

The Android package `android.widget` contains the class `ImageView` for rendering PNG files in an Android application.

 Copy the directory `MyDrawablePNG` from the companion disc to a convenient location. Listing 4.5 displays the contents of `MainActivity.java`, which illustrates how to render a drawable PNG file in an Android application.

LISTING 4.5 MyDrawablePNG.java

```
package com.example.oswaldcampesato2.mydrawablepng;

import android.content.Context;
import android.graphics.Bitmap;
import android.graphics.BitmapFactory;
import android.graphics.Canvas;
import android.graphics.Color;
import android.graphics.Paint;
import android.support.v7.app.AppCompatActivity;
import android.os.Bundle;
import android.view.Menu;
```

```
import android.view.View;

public class MyDrawablePNG extends AppCompatActivity
{
    private MyGraphicsView graphicsView;

    @Override
    protected void onCreate(Bundle savedInstanceState)
    {
        super.onCreate(savedInstanceState);

        graphicsView = new MyGraphicsView(this);
        setContentView(graphicsView);
    }

    private class MyGraphicsView extends View
    {
        private boolean initialized = true;
        private Context mContext;
        Paint paint = new Paint();

        public MyGraphicsView(Context context) {
            super(context);
            mContext = context;
        }

        protected void initialize(Canvas canvas)
        {
            paint.setStyle(Paint.Style.FILL);

            // a white canvas
            paint.setColor(Color.WHITE);
            canvas.drawPaint(paint);

            Bitmap b = BitmapFactory.decodeResource(
                            mContext.getResources(),
                            R.mipmap.sample1);

            canvas.drawColor(Color.TRANSPARENT);
            canvas.drawBitmap(b, 0, 0, null);

            canvas.save();
            canvas.scale(0.5f, 0.5f);
            canvas.drawBitmap(b, 600, 100, null);
            canvas.restore();

            canvas.save();
            canvas.skew(0.2f, 0.3f);
            canvas.drawBitmap(b, 500, 300, null);
            canvas.restore();

            canvas.save();
            canvas.rotate(45);
```

```
        canvas.drawBitmap(b, 400, 100, null);
        canvas.restore();

        // blue circle with anti aliasing turned off
        paint.setAntiAlias(false);
        paint.setColor(Color.BLUE);
        canvas.drawCircle(200, 200, 100, paint);

        // green circle with anti aliasing turned on
        paint.setAntiAlias(true);
        paint.setColor(Color.GREEN);
        canvas.drawCircle(500, 200, 100, paint);

        initialized = false;
    }

    @Override
    protected void onDraw(Canvas canvas)
    {
        super.onDraw(canvas);
        if(initialized) { initialize(canvas); }
    }
}

@Override
public boolean onCreateOptionsMenu(Menu menu)
{
    return true;
}
}
```

Listing 4.5 contains boilerplate code and a code snippet that instantiates an instance of the `Bitmap` class, which references the PNG `sample1.png`, as shown here:

```
Bitmap b = BitmapFactory.decodeResource(
                mContext.getResources(),
                R.mipmap.sample1);
```

Keep in mind that filenames of binary files must not contain uppercase letters.

The actual directory names depend on the version of Android, and for Android 4.2 they are as follows:

```
    drawable-hdpi
    drawable-ldpi
    drawable-mdpi
    drawable-xhdpi
    drawable-xxhdpi
```

Figure 4.1 displays the rendering of
MyDrawablePNG on a Pixel phone with
Android 7.1.

If you plan to use graphics extensively in
Android applications, consider the Vulkan
Graphics API that is written specifically
for Android. Vulkan provides a cross-plat-
form API for 3D graphics, and detailed
information is here: *https://developer.
android.com/ndk/guides/graphics/index.
html*.

One other point: large binary images
require a significant amount of memory,
and sometimes you need to reduce them
dynamically (using a toolkit such as Glide,
which is discussed in an Appendix) in order
to make them small enough to load into
memory.

FIGURE 4.1 Rendering a PNG
file in an Android application.

One alternative to binary images is SVG (Scalable Vector Graphics),
which is an XML vocabulary for rendering 2D shapes. SVG is not covered
in this book, so you can perform an online search for examples of using
SVG in Android applications.

The next section contains a code sample that uses the Bitmap class and
the Matrix class to rotate a PNG file.

Rotating PNG Files with the Matrix Class

The Android package android.graphics contains the Bitmap class for
displaying PNG files, after which you can apply methods in the Matrix
class to the PNG file in order to perform transforms (such as scaling and
rotation).

 Copy the directory SimpleRotateImage from the companion disc to a convenient location. Listing 4.6 displays the contents of activity_main.xml,
which displays the UI components in this code sample.

LISTING 4.6 activity_main.xml

```
<?xml version="1.0" encoding="utf-8"?>
<RelativeLayout
```

```
xmlns:android="http://schemas.android.com/apk/res/android"
xmlns:app="http://schemas.android.com/apk/res-auto"
xmlns:tools="http://schemas.android.com/tools"
android:id="@+id/activity_main"
android:layout_width="match_parent"
android:layout_height="match_parent"
android:paddingBottom="@dimen/activity_vertical_margin"
android:paddingLeft="@dimen/activity_horizontal_margin"
android:paddingRight="@dimen/activity_horizontal_margin"
android:paddingTop="@dimen/activity_vertical_margin"
tools:context="com.example.oswaldcampesato2.
                          simplerotateimage.MainActivity">

<ImageView
    android:layout_width="wrap_content"
    android:layout_height="wrap_content"
    app:srcCompat="@android:drawable/alert_dark_frame"
    android:layout_alignParentTop="true"
    android:layout_centerHorizontal="true"
    android:layout_marginTop="204dp"
    android:id="@+id/imageView" />
<Button
    android:text="ClickMe"
    android:layout_width="wrap_content"
    android:layout_height="wrap_content"
    android:layout_below="@+id/imageView"
    android:layout_centerHorizontal="true"
    android:layout_marginTop="79dp"
    android:id="@+id/button" />
</RelativeLayout>
```

As you can see, Listing 4.6 is a simple layout file containing an `ImageView` component and a `Button` component.

Listing 4.7 displays the contents of `MainActivity.java`, which illustrates how to use the `Bitmap` class and the `Matrix` class to rotate a PNG file.

LISTING 4.7 MainActivity.java

```
package com.example.oswaldcampesato2.simplerotateimage;

import android.graphics.Bitmap;
import android.graphics.BitmapFactory;
import android.os.Bundle;
import android.support.v7.app.AppCompatActivity;
import android.widget.Button;
import android.widget.ImageView;

import android.graphics.Matrix;
import android.view.Menu;
import android.view.View;

public class MainActivity extends AppCompatActivity
```

```
{
    private Bitmap image;
    private ImageView imageView;
    private Button button;

    @Override
    protected void onCreate(Bundle savedInstanceState)
    {
        super.onCreate(savedInstanceState);

        setContentView(R.layout.activity_main);

        this.button = (Button) findViewById(R.id.button);
        this.imageView =
                (ImageView) findViewById(R.id.imageView);
        this.imageView.setImageBitmap(image);

        this.button.setOnClickListener(new View.
                                        OnClickListener() {
            private int current = 0;

            @Override
            public void onClick(View view) {
                Bitmap toRemove = image;
                Matrix matrix = new Matrix();
                matrix.setRotate(30, 0.5f, 0.5f);

                image = Bitmap.createBitmap(image, 0, 0,
                        image.getWidth(),
                        image.getHeight(),
                        matrix, true);

                imageView.setImageBitmap(image);

                if(toRemove != null) {
                    toRemove.recycle();
                }
            }
        });
    }

    @Override
    public boolean onCreateOptionsMenu(Menu menu) {
        return true;
    }
}
```

Listing 4.7 contains the usual boilerplate code, followed by the `onCre-ate()` method that references an image file and a `Button` component in the layout file `activity_main.xml`. When users click on this button, the code rotates the PNG by invoking the `createBitmap()` method of the `Bitmap` class. Notice how the `matrix` variable, which is an instance of the

`Matrix` class (that also specifies a rotation of 30 degrees) is used in the following code block:

```
Matrix matrix = new Matrix();
matrix.setRotate(30, 0.5f, 0.5f);

image = Bitmap.createBitmap(image, 0, 0,
                            image.getWidth(),
                            image.getHeight(),
                            matrix, true);
```

You can also crop a rotated image with the following code snippet that defines an instance of the `RectF` class (such as the variable `rectF`), sets the rotation value, and then crops the image:

```
RectF rectF = new RectF(0, 0,
source.getWidth(),

source.getHeight());
Matrix matrix = new Matrix();
matrix.mapRect(rectF);
```

Figure 4.2 displays the rendering of `SimpleRotateImage` on a Pixel phone with Android 7.1.

NOTE *The project* `SimpleRotateImage` *works on an Android device but not in a simulator.*

The next section discusses some other graphics effects that you can apply to binary images.

FIGURE 4.2 A rotated image on a Pixel phone with Android 7.1.

Applying Other Effects to PNG Files

Android provides classes that enable you to apply various filters to PNG files. A list of available Android classes for filter effects is here: *http://developer.android.com/reference/android/graphics/package-summary.html*.

The Android package `android.graphics` contains the class `EmbossMaskFilter` for creating filter effects. You can also manipulate the values of individual pixels in a PNG, an example of which is here: *http://www.developer.com/ws/android/programming/Working-with-Images-in-Googles-Android-3748281-2.htm*.

You might be surprised to discover that it's possible to use JavaScript to manipulate pixel values of a PNG file that is rendered in an HTML5 Web page. Such a code sample is available in this book: *http://www.amazon. com/HTML5-Canvas-CSS3-Graphics-Primer/dp/1936420341*.

You can apply a blur filter effect to a PNG file, and code samples are available through an online search.

One thing to keep in mind is performance, and one optimization technique involves `Fourier` `Transforms` (FT) and `Fast` `Fourier` `Transforms` (FFT). If you really need the performance improvement (or you are highly motivated and you would enjoy the complexity), more information about FFTs is here: *http://en. wikipedia.org/wiki/Fast_Fourier_transform*.

Transforms in Android

Transforms are available in many programming languages, and the semantics are similar in Android graphics. A transform in graphics can involve a change in the shape or location of a graphics image. Common transforms include `translate` (move horizontally and/or vertically), `scale` (contract or expand), `rotate` (spin), or `skew` (a twisting-like effect, and also sometimes called shear).

Each of these transforms can be expressed in a matrix, for 2D as well as 3D effects (skew is not defined for 3D). The Android `Canvas` class provides the following intuitively named methods (and many other graphics-related methods) for performing transforms:

- `void rotate(float degrees);`
- `final void scale(float sx, float sy, float px, float py);`
- `void skew(float sx, float sy)`
- `void translate(float dx, float dy)`

Transforms can be applied sequentially or in parallel. For example, sequentially translating a rectangle 50 units to the right and then doubling size creates an effect that is different from applying both transforms simultaneously.

Plenty of additional information about the `Canvas` class is here: *https:// developer.android.com/reference/android/graphics/Canvas.html*.

One more fine point: sometimes you will see a distinction made between a transform (as discussed above) and a transition: the latter involves a change in an attribute or property. For example, changing the color of a rectangle from white to red would be a transition (not a transform).

Android also provides a transitions framework whereby you can apply transforms to the views in a hierarchy. The transitions framework also provides abstractions for scenes, transitions, and transition managers.

A detailed description of the Android transitions framework is here: *https://developer.android.com/training/transitions/overview.html.*

Overview of Animation in Android

Android added animation-related packages and classes in version 3.0, and also enhanced the functionality in those packages in Android 4.1. Android provides two main packages for creating animation effects: the package `android.animation` and the package `android.view.animation`.

The Android package `android.animation` provides functionality for the property animation system, which allows you to animate object properties of any type (such as `int`, `float`, and `hexadecimal` color values). You can animate any other type by telling the system how to calculate the values for that given type with a custom `TypeEvaluator`.

The Android package `android.view.animation` supports "tweened" animation for simple transformations (such as position, size, and rotation) in the content of a `View`.

The Android class `AnimationDrawable` provides frame-by-frame animation. This effect involves loading a series of `Drawable` resources sequentially. Both tweening and frame-by-frame animation types can be used in any `View` object to provide simple rotating timers, activity icons, and other UI elements.

The Java class `ViewPropertyAnimator` in the Android package `android.view` enables automatic and optimized animation of select properties on `View` objects. This class is well-suited for animating multiple properties simultaneously, whereas an `ObjectAnimator` is available for animating one or two properties of a `View` object.

The `ViewPropertyAnimator` class enables you to animate properties that you set as `android` attributes in the configuration file (such as `activity_main.xml`) for your Android application. For example, the methods `scaleX()` and `scaleY()` animate the attributes specified as `android:scaleX` and `android:scaleY`, respectively. Similar comments apply to the two methods `rotateX()` and `rotateY()` in this Java class.

The next two sections provide additional (albeit brief) details about tweening animation and frame-by-frame animation.

Tweened Animation in Android

The Android package `android.view.animation` contains classes that handle *tweened* animation, which is animation that varies from an initial value to a final value. Intermediate values are called interpolated values, and the formula for calculating the interpolated values determines the type of tweening effect. For example, linear interpolation (the simplest type of interpolation) uses a linear equation to calculate the interpolated values between the initial value and the final value. Other types of interpolation include `Bezier` interpolation, and you can perform an Internet search to find the details of interpolation techniques.

Frame-by-Frame Animation in Android

The second type of animation involves frame-by-frame animation, which is handled by the `AnimationDrawable` class. This class loads a series of `Drawable` resources one after the other. Both animation types can be used in any `View` object to provide simple rotating timers, activity icons, and other UI elements: *http://developer. android.com/guide/topics/graphics/view-animation.html.*

The `Animation` abstract class in the package `android.view.animation` is the "base" class for animation, and the class `AnimationUtils` provides common utility methods for working with animation. Other useful animation-related classes are:

- `TranslateAnimation (move)`
- `RotateAnimation (rotate)`
- `AlphaAnimation (change the transparency)`
- `ScaleAnimation (resize)`
- `AnimationSet (composite animation)`

Android also provides a set of `Interpolator` classes that specify the behavior of animation effects, as shown here:

- `AccelerateDecelerateInterpolator (accelerate, decelerate, then accelerate)`
- `AccelerateInterpolator (accelerate)`
- `DecelerateInterpolator (decelerate)`
- `LinearInterpolator (constant rate)`
- `CycleInterpolator (repeats animation)`

The preceding animation classes can be applied to other animation classes, such as `TranslateAnimation` and other animations in same list shown above.

In addition to defining animation effects programmatically, you can specify animation effects in XML, as shown here:

```
<?xml version="1.0" encoding="utf-8"?>
<alpha xmlns:android="http://schemas.android.com/apk/
                                                res/android"
        android:fromAlpha="1.0"
        android:toAlpha="0.0" />
```

Now that you know about the relevant animation-related classes, let's look at an example of creating a "fade in" effect for a PNG image, which is the topic of the next section.

Fade Animation Effects via XML

The example in this section uses the classes `Animation` and `AnimationUtils` (both belong to the Android package `android.graphics`) in conjunction with the opacity value to create a "fade in" animation effect.

Recall that the section about colors discussed the (`A`, `R`, `G`, `B`) color model in which the component `A` represents the opacity, which can be a number between 0 and 1. When the opacity value of a shape or image is 0, that object is not visible; when the value is 1, the object is fully visible.

The code sample in this section changes the opacity of an image from 0 to 1 during a 5000-millisecond interval, which creates a "fade in" effect.

 Copy the directory `FadeAnimation` from the companion disc to a convenient location. Listing 4.8 displays the contents of `MainActivity.java`, which illustrates how to create a "fade in" effect with a PNG image.

LISTING 4.8 MainActivity.java

```
package com.example.fadeanimation;

import android.app.Activity;
import android.os.Bundle;
import android.view.Menu;
import android.view.animation.Animation;
import android.view.animation.AnimationUtils;
import android.widget.ImageView;

public class MainActivity extends Activity
```

```
{
    ImageView image;

    @Override
    public void onCreate(Bundle savedInstanceState)
    {
        super.onCreate(savedInstanceState);

        setContentView(R.layout.activity_main);
        image = (ImageView)findViewById(R.id.sample1);

        Animation animationFadeIn =
            AnimationUtils.loadAnimation(this, R.anim.fadein);
        image.startAnimation(animationFadeIn);
    }

    @Override
    protected void onPause() {
        super.onPause();
        image.clearAnimation();
    }

    @Override
    public boolean onCreateOptionsMenu(Menu menu) {
        // Inflate the menu; this adds items
        // to the action bar if it is present.
        getMenuInflater().inflate(R.menu.main, menu);
        return true;
    }
}
```

The onCreate() method in Listing 4.8 first obtains a reference to a PNG image that is defined in activity_main.xml, and then defines the animationFadeIn variable, which is an instance of the Animation class. The details of the animation effect are defined in the XML document fadein.xml (shown in Listing 4.9). The animation effect starts as soon as the Android application is launched because of the following code:

```
Animation animationFadeIn =
    AnimationUtils.loadAnimation(this, R.anim.fadein);
image.startAnimation(animationFadeIn);
```

Listing 4.9 displays the contents of fadein.xml with the details of the animation effect.

LISTING 4.9 fadein.xml

```
<?xml version="1.0" encoding="utf-8"?>
<set xmlns:android="http://schemas.android.com/apk/res/android"
```

```
            android:shareInterpolator="false">
<alpha android:fromAlpha="0.0"
       android:toAlpha="1.0"
       android:duration="5000">
</alpha>
</set>
```

Listing 4.9 contains an XML <alpha> element that specifies the values 0.0, 1.0, and 5000 for the attributes fromAlpha, toAlpha, and duration, respectively. These values cause the opacity to vary linearly from 0 to 1 (hence the "fade in" effect) during a period of 5000 milliseconds.

Listing 4.10 displays the contents of activity_main.xml with an ImageView component and a TextView component.

LISTING 4.10 activity_main.xml

```
<?xml version="1.0" encoding="utf-8"?>
<RelativeLayout
    xmlns:android="http://schemas.android.com/apk/res/android"
    xmlns:app="http://schemas.android.com/apk/res-auto"
    xmlns:tools="http://schemas.android.com/tools"
    android:id="@+id/activity_main"
    android:layout_width="match_parent"
    android:layout_height="match_parent"
    android:paddingBottom="@dimen/activity_vertical_margin"
    android:paddingLeft="@dimen/
activity_horizontal_margin"
    android:paddingRight="@dimen/
activity_horizontal_margin"
    android:paddingTop="@dimen/
activity_vertical_margin"
    tools:context="com.example.
oswaldcampesato2.
        fadeanimation.MainActivity">

    <TextView

android:layout_width="wrap_content"

android:layout_height="wrap_content"
        android:text="Hello World!"
        android:id="@+id/textView" />

    <ImageView

android:layout_width="match_parent"

android:layout_height="wrap_content"
```

FIGURE 4.3 A fade-in effect on a Pixel phone with Android 7.1.

```
    app:srcCompat="@android:drawable/alert_light_frame"
    android:layout_below="@+id/textView"
    android:layout_toEndOf="@+id/textView"
    android:layout_marginStart="69dp"
    android:layout_marginTop="133dp"
    android:id="@+id/imageView" />
</RelativeLayout>
```

Figure 4.3 displays a snapshot of a "fade in" on a Pixel phone with Android 7.1.

Transforms via XML

The code sample in the previous section showed you how to create a "fade in" effect with a PNG image in an Android application based on attributes in an XML configuration file.

You can also use an XML configuration file to specify transforms, such as rotate and scale, as well as "tweening" effects. As a simple example, the following XML-based code block shows you how to apply a `scale` transform:

```
<scale android:interpolator="@android:anim/
                           accelerate_decelerate_interpolator"
    android:fromXScale="1.0"
    android:toXScale="1.4"
    android:fromYScale="1.0"
    android:toYScale="0.6"
    android:pivotX="50%"
    android:pivotY="50%"
    android:fillAfter="false"
    android:duration="700" />
```

A good example of applying various transforms is here: *http://developer.android.com/guide/topics/graphics/view-animation.html*.

The preceding link provides the following information about transforms:

The animation XML file belongs in the res/anim/ directory of your Android project. The file must have a single root element: this will be either a single <alpha>, <scale>, <translate>, <rotate>, interpolator element, or <set> element that holds groups of these elements (which may include another <set>). By default, all animation instructions are applied simultaneously. To make them occur sequentially, you must specify the startOffset attribute.

This concludes the graphics and animation techniques for this chapter. Although you could also learn about `RenderScript` for graphics and animation, the graphics and animation techniques in this chapter are suitable for the majority of Android applications that do not involve intensive game-related functionality.

Other Graphics and Animation Techniques

There are several other techniques for creating graphics effects in Android applications, such as `NinePatch`, `SurfaceView`, and `OpenGL`. Starting from Android Lollipop (API level 21), Google supports native support for vector image assets, allowing for images to be represented geometrically as a set of points, lines, and curves, as well as their associated color information.

The following subsections contain very brief descriptions of the preceding techniques (except for SVG). If you are unfamiliar with SVG but are interested in learning about some of its features, here is a modest introduction: *https://www.amazon.com/SVG-Pocket-Primer-Oswald-Campesato/dp/1944534598*.

Nine-Patch

The Android `android.graphics` package contains the `NinePatch` class that enables you to render a bitmap in nine sections (and hence its name). Nine-patch (aka 9-patch) graphics are PNG files whose names have an extended suffix of `.9.png`. These PNG files can be edited in standard graphics tools, and because of their naming convention, Android applies nine-patch rules to their use: *http://developer.android.com/reference/android/graphics/NinePatch.html*.

You can experiment with the `draw9patch` program located in the `tools` subdirectory of your Android SDK installation.

Drawing on an Android `SurfaceView`

The `SurfaceView` class is a subclass of the `View` class that provides a dedicated drawing surface within the `View` hierarchy. Android provides this "alternate" drawing surface so that an application can use it in a separate thread (which is discussed in an Appendix) instead of waiting until the `View` hierarchy is ready to render on its `Canvas`.

This technique uses a `SurfaceHolder` to indirectly manipulate a `Surface` object instead of manipulating the `Surface` directly. In brief, there are two main steps involved:

1) create a custom subclass of `SurfaceView`
2) implement `SurfaceHolder.Callback` in the subclass

More information about SurfaceViews is available in the Android documentation.

OpenGL Animation in Android

Yet another option for graphics and animation is `OpenGL`, which is the most sophisticated graphics and animation technology (but not covered in this book). Although it is more complex to learn, `OpenGL` has the advantage of portability. The choice of techniques obviously depends on your requirements and what you are trying to accomplish in your Android application.

Other Useful Links

The `DevBytes` series of videos are on the Android developers channel on YouTube: *http://www.youtube.com/playlist?list= PLWz5rJ2EKKc_XOgcRukSoKKjewFJZrKV0*.

In addition, it's worth watching other content in that channel, along with the Google IO talks, all of which are also available on YouTube.

A useful tool for managing images is the open source project `fresco`, whose home page is here: *http://frescolib.org/index.html*.

You can download `fresco` here: *https://github.com/facebook/fresco*.

A custom class that supports tinting of images (including Android Material icons) is here: *http://andraskindler.com/blog/2015/tinting_drawables/*.

If you want to delve more deeply into the techniques that are discussed in this chapter, the following links for Android graphics and animation contain more information:

http://developer.android.com/guide/topics/graphics/2d-graphics. html#frame-animation

http://developer.android.com/guide/topics/graphics/prop-animation. html

http://developer.android.com/guide/topics/graphics/view-animation. html

Summary

This chapter showed you various techniques for creating graphics effects. First you learned how to use XML-based configuration files to render gradient effects. Next you learned how to use Java code to programmatically create gradient effects. You also learned about `NinePatch` for creating graphics effects. In addition, you saw how to apply filter effects to PNG files.

In the animation-related portion of this chapter, you learned how to use XML-based configuration files to create "fade in" effects as well as multiple animation effects on PNG files.

CHAPTER 5

USER GESTURES

This chapter shows you how to detect and respond to touch-related events and various user gestures in Android applications. The code samples show you how to handle simple gestures, and links are provided for handling some of the more complex types of gestures in Android. As you will see, the second half of this chapter contains code samples that combine user gestures with graphics, partly because they provide some pleasing visual effects, and also to provide you with "base code" to which you can add your own enhancements.

The first part of this chapter contains an Android code sample that shows you how to detect and process touch events. This section also shows you how to add touch-related event handlers to the Android application `BarChart2D` that is available on the companion disc. The second part of this chapter contains Android code samples that show you how to detect other gestures, such as pinch and swipe events. The final part of this chapter contains code samples that create simple animation effects.

When you have completed this chapter, you will know how to create Android applications that combine graphics and animation effects (discussed in Chapter 4) with user gestures. The basic examples in this chapter will serve as a starting point for you to create richer and more interesting Android applications.

Methods for Handling Touch Events

The code sample with a `Button` component in Chapter 2 showed you that detecting click events in Android is straightforward.

Fortunately, it's also straightforward to detect various touch-related events in Android. The recommended approach is to capture events from the specific `View` object that users interact with. The `View` class provides the means to do so, which works well because every UI component in Android is a subclass of the `View` class.

The `View` class belongs to the Android package `android.view`, and the following list contains some of the touch-related methods in the `View` class:

```
public boolean onTouchEvent(MotionEvent event)
public boolean onDoubleTap(MotionEvent event)
public boolean onDoubleTapEvent(MotionEvent event)
public boolean onSingleTapConfirmed(MotionEvent event)
public boolean onTouch(View v, MotionEvent event)
public void onClick(View v)
public boolean onKey(View v, int keyCode, KeyEvent event)
public boolean onDown(MotionEvent event)
public void onLongPress(MotionEvent event)
public boolean onScroll(MotionEvent e1, MotionEvent e2,...)
public void onShowPress(MotionEvent event)
public boolean onSingleTapUp(MotionEvent event)
```

The next section shows you how to write custom code for the Android method `onTouchEvent()`, which enables you to detect and process a very common event in Android applications.

The onTouchEvent() Method

Android provides APIs for handling touch-related events that correspond to mouse-related events in a browser on a laptop or a desktop. The mouse events `mousedown`, `mousemove`, and `mouseup` correspond to the touch events `touchstart`, `touchmove`, and `touchend`, respectively.

The code sample in this section shows you how to implement the Android `onTouchEvent()` that handles simple touch events. Listing 5.1 displays the contents of this method.

LISTING 5.1 The onTouchEvent() Method

```
@Override
public boolean onTouchEvent(MotionEvent event)
{
    float touchX = event.getX();
    float touchY = event.getY();

    String xyLoc = "("+touchX+","+touchY+")";
```

```
switch (event.getAction()) {
      case MotionEvent.ACTION_DOWN:
            Log.i("ACTION_DOWN (x,y) = " , xyLoc);
            break;

      case MotionEvent.ACTION_MOVE:
            Log.i("ACTION_MOVE (x,y) = " , xyLoc);
            break;

      case MotionEvent.ACTION_UP:
            Log.i("ACTION_MOVE (x,y) = " , xyLoc);
            break;
}

return true;
}
```

The first part of Listing 5.1 shows you that the Event object provides the x coordinate and y coordinate of the location where users have performed a touch event. This code sample merely displays a message containing the coordinates of each touch event in the console via the Log.i() method.

The main section of code in Listing 5.1 is the switch statement that compares the value of event.getAction() with three constants that correspond to touch down, touch move, and touch up events. In this example, the coordinates of the location of the touch event are displayed in the console. Later in this chapter you will see examples where touch-related events trigger other actions, such as redrawing the graphics on the screen.

A Multi-Line Graph with Touch Events

The code sample in this section illustrates how to add touch-related functionality to graphics-related Android applications. This lengthy code sample contains mainly graphics code that is similar to code that you have already seen, so we discuss just the touch-related code.

 Copy the directory MultiLineGraph2D from the companion disc to a convenient location. Listing 5.2 displays portions of the Android class MainActivity.java, which is a multi-line graph with touch-related functionality.

LISTING 5.2 Portions of MainActivity.java

```
package oac.xample.oswaldcampesato2.mutilinegraph2d;

// import statements omitted for brevity
```

```
public class MultiLineGraph2D extends Activity
{
    @Override
    public void onCreate(Bundle savedInstanceState)
    {
        super.onCreate(savedInstanceState);
        setContentView(new SimpleView(this));
    }

    public SimpleView(Context context)
    {
        super(context);
        setFocusable(true);

        // perform other initialization
        // and render the multiple lines
        initialize();
    }

    // details of all the methods in the
    // onDraw() are omitted for brevity

    @Override
    protected void onDraw(Canvas canvas) {
        renderLineSegments(canvas);
        renderHorizontalAxis(canvas);
        renderVerticalAxis(canvas);
        labelHorizontalAxis(canvas);
        labelVerticalAxis(canvas);
    }

    @Override
    public boolean onTouchEvent(MotionEvent event) {
        switch (event.getAction()) {
            case MotionEvent.ACTION_DOWN:
                randomizeMultiLines();
                invalidate();
                break;
            case MotionEvent.ACTION_MOVE:
                break;
            case MotionEvent.ACTION_UP:
                break;
        }

        return true;
    }
}
}
```

The key point to notice in Listing 5.2 is the method onTouchEvent() that contains a switch() statement with several case statements. The first case statement handles a user touch event by first invoking the `randomizeMulti-Lines()` method to compute a new set of randomly generated line segments. Next this `case` statement invokes the built-in `invalidate()` method, which indicates to the application that it's necessary to refresh the screen. In this case, the new line segments are rendered on the screen.

This simple functionality shows you the sequence for handling user gestures: detect the occurrence of a gesture, execute some custom code, and then invoke the Android `invalidate()` method to update the screen.

Figure 5.1 displays the rendering of `MultiLineGraph2D` on a Pixel phone with Android 7.1.

FIGURE 5.1 A Multi-line graph that supports mouse events.

The next portion of this chapter provides an overview of touch-related events and user gestures, followed by some code samples that illustrate how to detect those events in Android mobile applications.

Overview of Touch Events and Gestures

This section provides an encapsulated overview of the Android class, interfaces, and methods that are available for handling gestures. Android supports triple tap and two-finger swipe, both of which require Android 4 or higher. Android also provides support for other gestures, such as fling, pan, pinch, swipe, and zoom.

The next subsections provide details about the `android.gesture` package as well as the `View.OnTouchListener` interface that provide methods for handling an assortment of gestures in Android applications.

The `android.gesture` Package

The Android package `android.view` contains the `GestureDetector` class that detects various gestures and events using the supplied `MotionEvent` instance. The `GestureDetector` class contains the following nested interfaces and class:

- the interface `GestureDetector.OnDoubleTapListener`, which is used to notify the occurrence of a double-tap or a confirmed single-tap
- the interface `GestureDetector.OnGestureListener`, which is used to notify the occurrence of gestures
- the class `GestureDetector.SimpleOnGestureListener` that you can extend when you want to listen for only a subset of all the gestures

You use the `GestureDetector` class as follows:

1) Create an instance of the `GestureDetector` for your `View`
2) In the `onTouchEvent(MotionEvent)` method ensure you call the method `onTouchEvent(MotionEvent)`

The methods defined in your callback will be executed when the events occur. The `GestureDetector` class contains the following public methods:

boolean isLongpressEnabled()

boolean onTouchEvent(MotionEvent me): analyzes the given motion event and if applicable, triggers the appropriate callbacks on the GestureDetector.OnGestureListener supplied.

void setIsLongpressEnabled(boolean isLongpressEnabled): set when longpress is enabled; if this is enabled when a user presses and holds down, you get a longpress event

void setOnDoubleTapListener(GestureDetector.OnDoubleTapListener onDoubleTapListener): sets the listener that is called for double-tap and related gestures

The `android.gesture` package provides a way to create, recognize, load, and save gestures. Alas, this package does not provide support for gestures such as tap and drag, nor support for multi-touch gestures such as pinch zoom.

The `View.OnTouchListener` Interface

The Android package `android.view.View` contains the `OnTouchListener` interface that defines the method `onTouchEvent()` that you must implement in your custom code. This method has two arguments: the first has type `View` (the affected component) and the second has type `MotionEvent` (with information about the user gesture).

The Android class `ZoomButtonsController` implements the interface `View.OnTouchListener`, and you can use this class for showing and hiding the zoom controls and positioning it relative to an owner view. Consult the online documentation for more information about this Android class.

The code sample in the next section shows you how to detect touch-related events and user gestures in an Android mobile application.

Comprehensive Tap/Touch-Related Example

The previous sections provided an overview of handling touch events, and the complete sample in this section shows you the code for handling tap and touch events.

This code sample works on a Samsung Galaxy 5 with Android 6.0.1, but might not work in a simulator.

 Copy the directory `SimpleTouch` from the companion disc to a convenient location. Listing 5.3 displays the contents of `MainActivity.java`, which detects various touch-related events in the `onTouch()` method.

LISTING 5.3 MainActivity.java

```java
package com.example.oswaldcampesato2.simpletouch;

import android.os.Bundle;
import android.support.v7.app.AppCompatActivity;
import android.util.Log;
import android.view.GestureDetector.OnDoubleTapListener;
import android.view.GestureDetector.OnGestureListener;
import android.view.KeyEvent;
import android.view.MotionEvent;
import android.view.View;
import android.view.View.OnClickListener;
import android.view.View.OnKeyListener;
import android.view.View.OnTouchListener;

public class MainActivity extends AppCompatActivity
        implements OnClickListener,
                   OnGestureListener,
                   OnKeyListener,
                   OnDoubleTapListener,
                   OnTouchListener
{
    float touchX = 0;
    float touchY = 0;
    String xyLoc = "";

    @Override
    public void onCreate(Bundle savedInstanceState)
    {
        super.onCreate(savedInstanceState);
        setContentView(R.layout.main);
    }

    @Override
    public boolean onTouchEvent(MotionEvent event)
    {
        touchX = event.getX();
```

```
        touchY = event.getY();
        xyLoc = "("+touchX+","+touchY+")";

        switch (event.getAction()) {
            case MotionEvent.ACTION_DOWN:
                Log.i("ACTION_DOWN (x,y) = " , xyLoc);
                break;

            case MotionEvent.ACTION_MOVE:
                Log.i("ACTION_MOVE (x,y) = " , xyLoc);
                break;

            case MotionEvent.ACTION_UP:
                Log.i("ACTION_UP (x,y) = " , xyLoc);
                break;
        }

        return true;
    }

    // override three methods for double-tap events...
    @Override
    public boolean onDoubleTap(MotionEvent event)
    {
        touchX = event.getX();
        touchY = event.getY();

        xyLoc = "("+touchX+","+touchY+")";
        Log.i("DOUBLE_TAP (x,y) = " , xyLoc);

        return false;
    }

    @Override
    public boolean onDoubleTapEvent(MotionEvent event)
    {
        touchX = event.getX();
        touchY = event.getY();

        xyLoc = "("+touchX+","+touchY+")";
        Log.i("DOUBLE_TAP E (x,y) = " , xyLoc);

        return false;
    }

    @Override
    public boolean onSingleTapConfirmed(MotionEvent event)
    {
        touchX = event.getX();
        touchY = event.getY();

        xyLoc = "("+touchX+","+touchY+")";
        Log.i("SINGLE_TAP C (x,y) = " , xyLoc);
```

```java
        return false;
}

// implement method for OnTouchListener...
@Override
public boolean onTouch(View v, MotionEvent event)
{
    touchX = event.getX();
    touchY = event.getY();

    xyLoc = "("+touchX+","+touchY+")";
    Log.i("ON_TOUCH (x,y) = " , xyLoc);

    return false;
}

// implement method for OnClickListener...
@Override
public void onClick(View v)
{
    // TODO
}

// implement method for OnKeyListener...
@Override
public boolean onKey(View v, int keyCode, KeyEvent event)
{
    // TODO
    return false;
}

// implement method for OnGestureListener...
@Override
public boolean onDown(MotionEvent event)
{
    // TODO Auto-generated method stub
    return false;
}

@Override
public boolean onFling(MotionEvent e1, MotionEvent e2,
                       float velocityX, float velocityY)
{
    touchX = e1.getX();
    touchY = e2.getY();

    xyLoc = "("+touchX+","+touchY+")";
    Log.i("ON_FLING (x,y) = " , xyLoc);

    return false;
}

@Override
```

```
public void onLongPress(MotionEvent event)
{
    touchX = event.getX();
    touchY = event.getY();

    xyLoc = "("+touchX+","+touchY+")";
    Log.i("LONG_PRESS (x,y) = " , xyLoc);
}

@Override
public boolean onScroll(MotionEvent e1, MotionEvent
                    e2, float distanceX, float distanceY)
{
    return false;
}

@Override
public void onShowPress(MotionEvent event)
{
    touchX = event.getX();
    touchY = event.getY();

    xyLoc = "("+touchX+","+touchY+")";
    Log.i("SHOW_PRESS (x,y) = " , xyLoc);
}

@Override
public boolean onSingleTapUp(MotionEvent event)
{
    touchX = event.getX();
    touchY = event.getY();

    xyLoc = "("+touchX+","+touchY+")";
    Log.i("SINGLE_TAP_UP (x,y) = " , xyLoc);

    return false;
}
}
```

The Java class in Listing 5.3 implements a number of touch-related listeners, which means that the methods in those listeners must also be implemented in Listing 5.3. The list of methods in Listing 5.3 is shown here:

```
public boolean onTouchEvent(MotionEvent event)
    public boolean onDoubleTap(MotionEvent event)
    public boolean onSingleTapConfirmed(MotionEvent event)
    public boolean onTouch(View v, MotionEvent event)
    public void onClick(View v)
    public boolean onKey(View v, int keyCode, KeyEvent event)
    public boolean onDown(MotionEvent event)
    public boolean onFling(MotionEvent e1, MotionEvent e2,
                        float velocityX, float velocityY)
```

```
public void onLongPress(MotionEvent event)
public boolean onScroll(MotionEvent e1, MotionEvent e2,
                        float distanceX, float distanceY)
    public void onShowPress(MotionEvent event)
public boolean onSingleTapUp(MotionEvent event)
```

As you can see in the preceding list, the onClick() method takes a View argument and the onKey() method takes a KeyEvent argument. All the other methods take a MotionEvent argument (and sometimes other arguments as well). Moreover, all the touch-related methods obtain the coordinates of the touch point with the following two lines of code:

```
touchX = event.getX();
touchY = event.getY();
```

Notice that the name of each method in Listing 5.3 indicates the type of gesture. For example, when the method onTouchEvent() is being executed, you know that the gesture is a touch event, whereas when you are inside the onDoubleTap() method, you know that the gesture is a double tap, and so forth for the other intuitively named methods in the preceding list.

Listing 5.3 also contains the method onFling() that is executed whenever a fling event is detected (and it displays information about that event).

A Sketching Program

The Android SDK contains a sketching program called FingerPaint. java that enables users to create freestyle sketching or "finger painting" on the screen. This Java class is three pages in length and you can find it in the samples subdirectory of the Android SDK that you installed on your machine. Listing 5.4 displays the contents of the onCreate() method that illustrates how to initialize some variables (such as mPaint) and also specify values of various attributes.

LISTING 5.4 The onCreate() Method of FingerPaint.java

```
@Override
protected void onCreate(Bundle savedInstanceState) {
    super.onCreate(savedInstanceState);
    setContentView(new MyView(this));

    mPaint = new Paint();
    mPaint.setAntiAlias(true);
    mPaint.setDither(true);
```

```
mPaint.setColor(0xFFFF0000);
mPaint.setStyle(Paint.Style.STROKE);
mPaint.setStrokeJoin(Paint.Join.ROUND);
mPaint.setStrokeCap(Paint.Cap.ROUND);
mPaint.setStrokeWidth(12);

mEmboss = new EmbossMaskFilter(
            new float[] {1, 1, 1 }, 0.4f, 6, 3.5f);

mBlur = new BlurMaskFilter(8,BlurMaskFilter.Blur.NORMAL);
}
```

The onCreate() method in Listing 5.4 instantiates three variables that are used during the rendering process in order to create a richer visual effect. The first part of the code instantiates the mPaint variable, which is an instance of the Paint class. The next seven lines of code set various attributes in the mPaint variable. The remaining code in the onCreate() method instantiates the mEmboss variable (an instance of the EmbossMarkFilter class) as well as the mBlur variable (which is an instance of the BlurMaskFilter class).

The FingerPaint class also contains the following touch-related methods that keep track of users' movements on the screen:

```
private void touch_start(float x, float y)
private void touch_move(float x, float y)
private void touch_up()
```

The onDraw() method is very short, and it renders users' finger movements that are tracked in a path element, as shown here:

```
@Override
protected void onDraw(Canvas canvas) {
    canvas.drawColor(0xFFAAAAAA);
    canvas.drawBitmap(mBitmap, 0, 0, mBitmapPaint);
    canvas.drawPath(mPath, mPaint);
}
```

Another example of drawing is the Java class TouchPaint.java (roughly eight pages long) that "demonstrates the handling of touch screen, stylus, mouse and trackball events." This Java class is also available in the SDK in the same directory as FingerPaint.java. Both of these code samples contain useful information and techniques for rendering freestyle graphics.

The next portion of this chapter contains some information about detecting other gestures in Android mobile applications.

Handling Other Types of Gestures

From a high-level perspective, there are essentially three steps required in order to handle a pinch/zoom gesture in an Android mobile application. Examples of handling this type of gesture are here:

http://javapapers.com/android/android-pinch-zoom/

http://www.theappguruz.com/blog/android-pinch-zoom

A pan gesture is common for maps and panels, where the pan gesture is often accompanied by a scroll event. An example of handling this type of gesture is here: *http://blahti.wordpress.com/2013/01/07/pan-zoom-examples-for-android/*.

A fling/swipe gesture can occur in many mobile applications. A detailed code sample of handling a fling/swipe gesture is here:

http://www.eridem.net/android-tip-010-left-and-right-swipe-gesture-events

http://findnerd.com/list/view/how-to-detect-swipe-left-or-right-function-on-listview-item-in-android/785/

The Android package `android.view` contains classes for handling Drag-and-Drop (DnD) functionality. Code samples for handling a DnD gesture are here:

http://developer.android.com/guide/topics/ui/drag-drop.html

http://www.vogella.com/articles/AndroidDragAndDrop/article.html

Multiple Animation Effects via XML

This section uses the `AnimationDrawable` class that belongs to the Android package `android.graphics` to create an animation effect.

 Copy the directory `DrawableAnimation` from the companion disc to a convenient location. Listing 5.5 displays the contents of `MainActivity.java`, which illustrates how to create multiple animation effects with PNG images.

LISTING 5.5 MainActivity.java

```
package com.example.oswaldcampesato2.drawableanimation;

import android.graphics.drawable.AnimationDrawable;
```

```java
import android.os.Bundle;
import android.support.v7.app.AppCompatActivity;
import android.view.Menu;
import android.view.MotionEvent;
import android.widget.ImageView;

public class MainActivity extends AppCompatActivity
{
    AnimationDrawable imageAnimation;

    public void onCreate(Bundle savedInstanceState)
    {
        super.onCreate(savedInstanceState);

        setContentView(R.layout.activity_main);

        ImageView imageView = (ImageView) findViewById
                                        (R.id.imageView);
        imageView.setBackgroundResource(R.drawable.
                                        spin_animation);
        imageAnimation = (AnimationDrawable) imageView.
                                        getBackground();
    }

    public boolean onTouchEvent(MotionEvent event)
    {
        if (event.getAction() == MotionEvent.ACTION_DOWN)
        {
            imageAnimation.start();
            return true;
        }
    }

    @Override
    public boolean onCreateOptionsMenu(Menu menu) {
        return true;
    }

    @Override
    public void onStart() {
        super.onStart();
    }

    @Override
    public void onStop() {
        super.onStop();
    }
}
```

Listing 5.5 contains an `onCreate()` method that references an image resource in the `drawableAnimation.xml` configuration file (shown in

Listing 5.6). Listing 5.5 also defines an `onTouchEvent()` that starts the animation effect whenever users touch the screen.

LISTING 5.6 spin_animation.xml

```
<!-- Animation frames: sample1.png -> sample3.png in
                                     res/drawable -->
<animation-list
    xmlns:android="http://schemas.android.com/apk/res/android"
    android:id="@+id/selected" android:oneshot="false">
  <item android:drawable="@drawable/sample1"
                              android:duration="150" />
  <item android:drawable="@drawable/sample2"
                              android:duration="150" />
  <item android:drawable="@drawable/sample3"
                              android:duration="150" />
  <item android:drawable="@drawable/sample2"
                              android:duration="150" />
  <item android:drawable="@drawable/sample3"
                              android:duration="150" />
  <item android:drawable="@drawable/sample1"
                              android:duration="150" />
</animation-list>
```

Listing 5.6 specifies three PNG files called `sample1.png`, `sample2.png`, and `sample3.png`. The animation effect is for 200 milliseconds (which is the value of `android:duration`) and is performed once (because `android.oneshot` is set to true).

Note that you need to add the three PNG images `sample1.png`, `sample2.png`, and `sample3.png` to the `drawable` subdirectories. Finally, you need to add this code snippet to `activity_main.xml`:

```
<ImageView
    android:id="@+id/sample1"
    android:layout_width="fill_parent"
    android:layout_height="fill_parent"
    android:scaleType="centerCrop"
    android:src="@drawable/sample1"
/>
```

You need to include the preceding XML `<ImageView>` element for each of the three PNG files.

Working with Sprites in Android

Sprites are static images that are shown in rapid succession in order to create animation effects. Sprites are useful for creating various effects (such as movement or interaction between character figures) in games. A set of sprites can be placed in a so-called "sprite sheet," and an individual sprite can be rendered by specifying the coordinates of the upper-left corner of the sprite in a sprite sheet, as well as the width and height of the sprite. Consequently, a sprite sheet can contain sprites of different dimensions. A sprite sheet can be downloaded via a single HTTP request, which is more efficient than making multiple HTTP requests to download individual PNG files.

The following link displays an assortment of sprite sheets that show the variety of sprite sheets that other people have created: *https:// www.google.com/search?q=sample+sprite+sheet&hl=en&tbm= isch&tbo=u&source=univ&sa=X&ei=FT9XUdrSLu70igLR3YDw Bw&ved=0CC4QsAQ&biw=960&bih=567.*

Sprites are available in many programming languages, and you can even use sprites in CSS3. There are various open-source toolkits available for rendering and animating sprites in case you do not wish to write all the code yourself. In addition, you can also work with sprites using toolkits based on `OpenGL`.

In Chapter 4 you saw how to use the Android classes `BitmapFactory` and `Bitmap` to perform manipulations on images, so you already have some of the technical background to work with sprites in Android. Perform an Internet search for detailed code samples illustrating how to create mobile games with sprites that respond to touch-related events.

Summary

In this chapter you learned how to detect various touch-related events, including single tap and multi-tap events. Next you learned how to add touch-related functionality to a multi-line graph whose graphics code is based on material from Chapter 4.

Then you learned about the package with Java classes for handling various types of user gestures. In addition you learned about `Sprites` and why they can be useful in Android applications.

CHAPTER 6

SENSORS AND MULTIMEDIA

This chapter discusses various sensors that are accessible on Android mobile devices and also how to work with multimedia. Since support for sensors on Android devices does vary, you will learn how to obtain a list of sensors that are available on a given Android device. You will also see an example that combines graphics effects and gestures with the output from a sensor. In addition, you will learn some details about playing audio and video files on an Android device. As usual, the code samples in this section were deployed to Android phones (but simulators were not tested).

The first (and longest) part of this chapter contains code samples that illustrate how to list the sensors that are supported on an Android device, how to check for the availability of specific sensors on an Android device, and then how to report information about values related to those sensors. This section contains a "touch and shake" Android code sample that combines graphics and sensors. This code sample enables users to render circles by touching the screen, and then they can erase their "sketch" by shaking their mobile device.

The second part of this chapter contains Android code samples with media-related functionality, such as playing audio files and video files. One interesting point is that the code sample for playing an MP4 video file from YouTube works on a phone with Android 6.0.1 but not on a Pixel phone with Android 7.1. After reading these code samples, you will be in a better position to understand how to create Android applications that record audio files and video files. The latter functionality is beyond the scope of this chapter, but you can perform an Internet search to find articles that discuss how to record audio and video files.

The third part of this chapter (which is very short) discusses some ideas for Android applications that combine sensors and multimedia, along with some links that provide potentially useful code blocks.

The final part of this chapter delves into Android permissions. Starting from API level 23, Android permissions have become more user friendly (e.g., runtime permissions are available), and correspondingly more involved for developers.

As you will see, Android applications with multimedia—and examples from earlier chapters—require various permissions. In some cases, Android applications require multiple permissions.

Overview of Android Sensors

You are probably familiar with several types of sensors that are available on mobile devices. Before we discuss the features of specific sensors, let's look at the three categories of sensors that Android supports:

- Motion Sensors
- Environmental Sensors
- Position Sensors

Motion Sensors involve the measurement of acceleration and rotational forces in three dimensions, and they include accelerometers, gravity sensors, gyroscopes, and rotational vector sensors.

Environmental Sensors involve the measurement of environmental parameters, such as air temperature and pressure, illumination, and humidity. Examples of these sensors are barometers, photometers, and thermometers.

Position Sensors involve the measurement of the position of a device, and they include orientation sensors and magnetometers.

Many Android devices have built-in sensors that belong to the three categories described above. The Android sensor framework enables you to determine which sensors are available on a given Android device and to determine the capabilities of each sensor. In addition to obtaining raw sensor data, you can also specify the minimum rate at which you want to obtain sensor data. Furthermore, you can register (and also unregister) event listeners for sensors in order to monitor sensor changes.

If you prefer to use a sensor library, which is easier than reading raw data, the following link is helpful: *https://github.com/emotionsense/ SensorManager.*

A List of Some Android Sensors

The following list displays the sensors that Android 4 supports on mobile devices:

```
accelerometers
ambient temperature (added in Android 4.0)
gravity sensors
humidity sensor (added in Android 4.0)
gyroscopes
rotational vector
barometers
photometers
thermometers
orientation sensors
magnetometers
```

Each sensor typically has one or more constants associated with that sensor. The associated constants for the new sensors that were added in Android 4.0 are:

TYPE_AMBIENT_TEMPERATURE: A temperature sensor that provides the ambient (room) temperature in degrees Celsius.

TYPE_RELATIVE_HUMIDITY: A humidity sensor that provides the relative ambient (room) humidity as a percentage.

If TYPE_AMBIENT_TEMPERATURE and TYPE_RELATIVE_HUMIDITY sensors are both available on a device, you can use them to calculate the dew point and the absolute humidity.

Keep in mind that the temperature sensor TYPE_TEMPERATURE has been deprecated, so you should use the TYPE_AMBIENT_TEMPERATURE sensor instead.

In addition, Android's three synthetic sensors have been greatly improved, so they now have lower latency and smoother output. These sensors include:

- the gravity sensor (TYPE_GRAVITY)
- the rotation vector sensor (TYPE_ROTATION_VECTOR)
- the linear acceleration sensor (TYPE_LINEAR_ACCELERATION)

The improved sensors rely on the gyroscope sensor to improve their output, so the sensors appear only on devices that have a gyroscope.

There are two ways to obtain sensor data in an Android application: either deploy the application to an Android device, or use a simulator to test most of the supported sensors on Android devices.

Instantiating Sensor Managers in Android

Android code for sensors starts by instantiating a sensor manager, followed by some code that involves a particular sensor.

For example, the following code block instantiates a sensor manager and then checks for the presence of a gyroscope:

```
private SensorManager mSensorManager;
private Sensor mSensor;
// some details omitted

mSensorManager = (SensorManager)
getSystemService(Context.SENSOR_SERVICE);
mSensor = mSensorManager.getDefaultSensor(Sensor.
                                    TYPE_GYROSCOPE);
```

You can easily modify the preceding code block to check for different sensors. For example, if you are interested in getting gravity-related information, simply modify the final line of code in the preceding code block as follows (shown in bold):

```
mSensor = mSensorManager.getDefaultSensor(Sensor.TYPE_GRAVITY);
```

Always check whether or not a given sensor is available on a mobile device so that your Android application will not fail unexpectedly.

Listing the Available Sensors on a Mobile Device

The Android sensor framework is part of the `android.hardware` package, which includes the `SensorManager` that can check for available sensors.

Copy the directory `DeviceSensors` from the companion disc to a convenient location. Listing 6.1 displays the contents of `MainActivity.java`, which illustrates how to display the list of sensors on an Android device.

LISTING 6.1 MainActivity.java

```java
package com.example.oswaldcampesato2.devicesensors;

import android.content.Context;
import android.hardware.Sensor;
import android.hardware.SensorEventListener;
import android.hardware.SensorManager;
import android.os.Bundle;
import android.support.v7.app.AppCompatActivity;
import android.util.Log;
import android.widget.TextView;

import java.util.List;

public class DeviceSensors extends AppCompatActivity
        implements SensorEventListener
{
    private static final String TAG = "DeviceSensors";
    private SensorManager mSensorMgr;
    private TextView outView;
    private int sensor = SensorManager.SENSOR_ORIENTATION;

    @Override
    protected void onCreate(Bundle savedInstanceState)
    {
        super.onCreate(savedInstanceState);
        setContentView(R.layout.activity_device_sensors);

        mSensorMgr =
            (SensorManager) getSystemService(Context.
                                        SENSOR_SERVICE);
        List<Sensor> sensors = mSensorMgr.
                            getSensorList(Sensor.TYPE_ALL);

        // display list of sensors
        Log.i("sensor count: ", Integer.toString(sensors.
                                        size()));

        for(Sensor s : sensors) {
            Log.i(TAG, s.getName());
        }
    }

    @Override
    public void onAccuracyChanged(Sensor sensor, int accuracy)
    {
    }

    public void onSensorChanged(SensorEvent event) {}
}
```

Listing 6.1 contains boilerplate code, and the onCreate() method starts by instantiating a SensorManager object, after which you can obtain a list of sensors. Next, iterate over that list of available sensors on a device, as shown in this code block:

```
private mSensorManager sensorManager;
mSensorManager =
    (SensorManager) getSystemService(Context.SENSOR_SERVICE);
List<Sensor> sensors = mSensorMgr.getSensorList(Sensor.TYPE_ALL);

// display list of sensors
Log.i("sensor count: ", Integer.toString(sensors.size()));

for(Sensor s : sensors) {
    Log.i("sensor: ", s.getName());
}
```

The method onAccuracyChanged() is an abstract method in the interface SensorEventListener that is invoked when the accuracy of the registered sensor has changed. The other abstract method is onSensorChanged(), which is invoked when there is a new sensor event. In both cases, sensor-related information is displayed via the Log.d() method.

Listing 6.2 displays the list of seventeen sensors that are available on a Samsung Galaxy S5 with Android 6.0.1.

LISTING 6.2 Sensors on a Samsung Galaxy S5 with Android 6.0.1.

```
MPU6500 Acceleration Sensor
MPU6500 Gyroscope Sensor
MPU6500 Uncalibrated Gyroscope Sensor
AK09911C Magnetic field Sensor
AK09911C Magnetic Sensor UnCalibrated
Barometer Sensor
TMG399X Proximity Sensor
TMG399X RGB Sensor
MPL Rotation Vector
MPL Game Rotation Vector
SAMSUNG Step Detector Sensor
SAMSUNG Step Counter Sensor
SAMSUNG Significant Motion Sensor
Screen Orientation Sensor
Orientation Sensor
Gravity SensorLinear
Acceleration Sensor
```

Listing 6.3 displays the list of twenty-three sensors that are available on a Pixel phone with Android 7.1.

LISTING 6.3 Sensors on a Pixel phone with Android 7.1

```
BMI160 accelerometer
BMI160 gyroscope
AK09915 magnetometer
BMP285 pressure
BMP285 temperature
TMD4903 Proximity Sensor
TMD4903 Light Sensor
Orientation
BMI160 Step detector
Significant motion
Gravity
Linear Acceleration
Rotation Vector
Geomagnetic Rotation Vector
Game Rotation Vector
Tilt Detector
BMI160 Step counter
AK09915 magnetometer (uncalibrated)
BMI160 gyroscope (uncalibrated)
Sensors Sync
Double Twist
Double Tap
Device Orientation
```

The next section shows you how to check for the presence of specific sensors on an Android device.

Checking Sensor Availability on a Mobile Device

The number of sensors on Android smart phones varies from twelve to at least thirty-two, and possibly even more sensors in newer smart phones. Moreover, Google does not require hardware manufacturers to build any specific sensors into a device, which means that testing for sensors on Android devices is a necessity. For example, an application might require the gravity sensor that's of a particular version. The gravity sensor is actually a virtual sensor, but it still relies on a device having particular hardware sensors available for it to work.

You can check for a specific sensor by using one of the sensor-specific constants. For example, you can check for temperature, humidity, and pressure with the following constants:

```
TYPE_TEMPERATURE
TYPE_RELATIVE_HUMIDITY
TYPE_PRESSURE
```

After you have chosen the constant that is associated with a particular sensor, use the method getDefaultSensor() that accepts a sensor constant to determine whether or not a sensor is available on a device.

Note that if a device has more than one sensor of a given type, one of them is usually the default sensor. However, if no default sensor is available, then the method getDefaultSensor() returns null, which indicates that the sensor is not present.

As a simple example, you can check for a gyroscope sensor using the method getDefaultSensor(), as shown in the following code snippet:

```
if(mSensorMgr.getDefaultSensor(Sensor.TYPE_GYROSCOPE) != null)

{
    // determine the orientation of the gyroscope
}
else
{
    // the gyroscope is unavailable on this device
}
```

The following code first checks if the gravity sensor is present. If so, it then checks that the vendor is Google and that the sensor is version 3 (which you can replace with a different version number).

```
if(mSensorMgr.getDefaultSensor(Sensor.TYPE_GRAVITY) != null)
{
    List gravity = mSensorMgr.getSensorList(Sensor.
                                    TYPE_GRAVITY);
    for (int i = 0; i < gravity.size(); i++)
    {
        if (gravity.get(i).getVendor().contains("Google Inc.")
&&
            gravity.get(i).getVersion() == 3)
        {
            // I've got the version 3 Google gravity sensor I need.
            mGravity = gravity.get(i);
        }
    }
}
else
{
    // No Google gravity sensor version 3
}
```

If an application requires a specific sensor, it's also possible to use Google Play to target only devices that have that particular sensor. For example,

for devices that must have an accelerometer, add the following to the
`AndroidManifest.xml` file:

```
<uses-feature android:name="android.hardware.sensor.light" />
```

If users navigate to Google Play on a device that does not have a light
sensor and search for applications, Google Play will not show users any
applications that require a light sensor (which makes sense).

Another useful method is `getMinDelay()`, which determines the minimum time interval (measured in microseconds) that a sensor requires in
order to obtain sensor data. If `getMinDelay()` returns a non-zero value,
then the sensor is a streaming sensor.

Streaming sensors were introduced in Android 2.3, and they can sense
data at regular intervals. On the other hand, non-streaming sensors only
report data when the sensor's parameters change and will return zero
when `getMinDelay()` is invoked.

Device Orientation

This section shows you how to detect orientation changes (portrait mode
versus landscape mode) in a mobile device.

 Copy the directory DeviceOrientation from the companion disc to a
convenient location. Listing 6.2 displays the contents of `MainActivity.`
`java`, which illustrates how to detect and report orientation changes of an
Android mobile device.

LISTING 6.2 MainActivity.java

```
package com.example.oswaldcampesato2.deviceorientation;

import android.support.v7.app.AppCompatActivity;
import android.hardware.SensorEventListener;
import android.hardware.SensorManager;
import android.os.Bundle;
import android.util.Log;
import android.widget.TextView;

public class MainActivity extends AppCompatActivity
        implements SensorEventListener
{
    private static final String TAG = "SensorDemo";
    private SensorManager sensorManager;
    private TextView textView;
```

```
private int sensor = SensorManager.SENSOR_ORIENTATION;

@Override
public void onCreate(Bundle savedInstanceState)
{
    super.onCreate(savedInstanceState);
    setContentView(R.layout.activity_main);

    textView = (TextView) findViewById(R.id.textView);

    // Real sensor manager
    sensorManager = (SensorManager)
                getSystemService(SENSOR_SERVICE);
}

// Register for the updates when Activity is in foreground
@Override
protected void onResume()
{
    super.onResume();
    Log.d(TAG, "onResume");
    sensorManager.registerListener(this, sensor);
}

// Stop the updates when Activity is paused
@Override
protected void onPause()
{
    super.onPause();

    Log.d(TAG, "onPause");
    sensorManager.unregisterListener(this, sensor);
}

@Override
public void onAccuracyChanged(Sensor sensor, int accuracy)
{
    Log.d(TAG, String.format(
            "onAccuracyChanged  sensor: %d
            accuracy: %d", sensor, accuracy));
}

public void onSensorChanged(SensorEvent event)
{
    String apr = String.format(
        "Azimuth: %.2f\nPitch: %.2f\nRoll: %.2f",
        event.values[0], event.values[1], event.values[2]);

    Log.i(TAG, apr);
    textView.setText(apr);
}
}
```

The onCreate() method in Listing 6.2 obtains a reference to a TextView component that is defined in activity_main.xml and then initializes the variable sensorManager to the current sensor manager.

The method onAccuracyChanged() uses the Android Log class to print the current values of the parameters sensor and accuracy. Specifically, the output of the method Log.d() is displayed in the LogCat view.

The method onDeviceChanged() reports any changes in the sensor by printing the three values in the array values that is a parameter of the onDeviceChanged() method:

```
String apr = String.format(
    "Azimuth: %.2f\nPitch: %.2f\nRoll: %.2f",
    event.values[0], event.values[1], event.values[2]);

Log.d(TAG, apr);
outView.setText(apr);
```

The preceding code block displays the new values for the sensor in the LogCat view as well as the TextField component outView that was initialized in the onCreate() method.

Accessing the Compass

This section shows you how to create an Android mobile application that obtains compass information.

 Copy the directory SimpleCompass from the companion disc to a convenient location. Listing 6.3 displays the contents of MainActivity.java that illustrates how to read compass information in an Android application.

LISTING 6.3 MainActivity.java

```
package com.example.oswaldcampesato2.simplecompass;

import android.content.Context;
import android.graphics.Canvas;
import android.graphics.Paint;
import android.graphics.Paint.Style;
import android.hardware.Sensor;
import android.hardware.SensorEvent;
import android.hardware.SensorEventListener;
import android.hardware.SensorManager;
import android.os.Bundle;
import android.support.v7.app.AppCompatActivity;
```

```
import android.view.Menu;
import android.view.View;

public class MainActivity extends AppCompatActivity
        implements SensorEventListener
{
    // View to draw a compass
    Float azimuth;

    public class CustomDrawableView extends View
    {
        Paint paint = new Paint();

        public CustomDrawableView(Context context) {
            super(context);

            paint.setColor(0xff00ff00);
            paint.setStyle(Style.STROKE);
            paint.setStrokeWidth(2);
            paint.setAntiAlias(true);
        };

        protected void onDraw(Canvas canvas)
        {
            int width = getWidth();
            int height = getHeight();
            int centerx = width/2;
            int centery = height/2;

            canvas.drawLine(centerx, 0, centerx, height, paint);
            canvas.drawLine(0, centery, width, centery, paint);

            // Rotate the canvas with the azimuth
            if(azimuth != null) {
                canvas.rotate(-azimuth*360/(2*3.14159f),
                        centerx, centery);
            }

            paint.setColor(0xff0000ff);

            canvas.drawLine(centerx, -1000, centerx, +1000,
                                                        paint);
            canvas.drawLine(-1000, centery, 1000,
                                            centery, paint);
            canvas.drawText("N", centerx+5, centery-10, paint);
            canvas.drawText("S", centerx-10, centery+15, paint);

            paint.setColor(0xff00ff00);
        }
    }

    CustomDrawableView mCustomDrawableView;
```

```
private SensorManager mSensorManager;
Sensor accelerometer;
Sensor magnetometer;

protected void onCreate(Bundle savedInstanceState)
{
    super.onCreate(savedInstanceState);
    //setContentView(R.layout.activity_main);

    mCustomDrawableView = new CustomDrawableView(this);
    setContentView(mCustomDrawableView);

    // Register the sensor listeners
    mSensorManager = (SensorManager)
                        getSystemService(SENSOR_SERVICE);

    accelerometer  = mSensorManager.getDefaultSensor(
                            Sensor.TYPE_ACCELEROMETER);

    magnetometer   = mSensorManager.getDefaultSensor(
                            Sensor.TYPE_MAGNETIC_FIELD);
}

protected void onResume()
{
    super.onResume();
    mSensorManager.registerListener(this, accelerometer,
            SensorManager.SENSOR_DELAY_UI);

    mSensorManager.registerListener(this, magnetometer,
            SensorManager.SENSOR_DELAY_UI);
}

protected void onPause()
{
    super.onPause();
    mSensorManager.unregisterListener(this);
}

public void onAccuracyChanged(Sensor sensor, int
                                        accuracy) {}

float[] mGravity;
float[] mGeomagnetic;

public void onSensorChanged(SensorEvent event)
{
    if(event.sensor.getType() == Sensor.TYPE_ACCELEROMETER)
        mGravity = event.values.clone();

    if(event.sensor.getType() == Sensor.
                                TYPE_MAGNETIC_FIELD)
```

```
            mGeomagnetic = event.values.clone();

        if(mGravity != null && mGeomagnetic != null) {
            float R[] = new float[9];
            float I[] = new float[9];

            boolean success = SensorManager.getRotationMatrix(
                    R,I,mGravity,mGeomagnetic);

            if(success) {
                float orientation[] = new float[3];
                SensorManager.getOrientation(R, orientation);

                // orientation contains: azimuth, pitch and roll
                azimuth = orientation[0];
            }
        }

        mCustomDrawableView.invalidate();
    }

    @Override
    public boolean onCreateOptionsMenu(Menu menu) {
        return true;
    }
}
```

The onCreate() method in Listing 6.3 first instantiates mCustom-DrawableView that is an instance of the CustomDrawableView custom class. You saw an example of using this technique in Chapter 4 for rendering custom graphics in the onDraw() method. The next portion of the onCreate() method registers a sensor manager, an accelerometer, and a magnetometer.

The method onSensorChanged() uses conditional logic to determine which sensor has had its values modified, as shown here:

```
if(event.sensor.getType() == Sensor.TYPE_ACCELEROMETER)
    mGravity = event.values.clone();
if(event.sensor.getType() == Sensor.TYPE_MAGNETIC_FIELD)
    mGeomagnetic = event.values.clone();
```

The next portion of this method uses conditional logic before initializing a pair of arrays R and I, that are passed in to the getRotationMatrix() method of the SensorManager class, as shown here:

```
if(mGravity != null && mGeomagnetic != null) {
    float R[] = new float[9];
    float I[] = new float[9];
```

```
boolean success = SensorManager.getRotationMatrix(
                      R,I,mGravity,mGeomagnetic);

// additional code block shown below
}
```

If the value of the Boolean variable `success` is `true`, the final portion of code (which is nested inside the previous code block) passes the `R` array (initialized earlier in the code) and a second array to the `getOrientation()` method of the `SensorManager` class, as shown here:

```
if(success) {
    float orientation[] = new float[3];
    SensorManager.getOrientation(R, orientation);

    // orientation contains: azimuth, pitch and roll
    azimuth = orientation[0];
}
```

The most up-to-date value for the `azimuth` is assigned in the last line of code in the preceding code block.

Since the contents of the `Canvas` of this custom class has been modified, we need to explicitly trigger the `invalidate()` method of the `Canvas` class so that Android will refresh the contents of the `Canvas` with the latest updated value of the `azimuth`.

Vibration

This section provides an outline of the code that is required to detect vibrations in an Android mobile device. Copy the directory `Vibrate` from the companion disc to a convenient location.

Include this permission in the file `AndroidManifest.xml`:

```
<uses-permission android:name="android.permission.VIBRATE"/>
```

Listing 6.4 displays the contents of `MainActivity.java`, which illustrates how to generate a vibration in an Android phone.

LISTING 6.4 MainActivity.java

```
package com.example.oswaldcampesato2.vibrate;

import android.app.Notification;
import android.app.NotificationManager;
```

```
import android.app.Service;
import android.os.Bundle;
import android.os.Vibrator;
import android.support.v7.app.AppCompatActivity;
//import android.support.v7.app.NotificationCompat;
import android.support.v4.app.NotificationCompat;

import android.view.View;

public class MainActivity extends AppCompatActivity
{
    // The vibration times in mSec are pairs
    // of silent time and vibrate time values
    private static final long[] THREE_CYCLES =
      new long[] { 100, 1000, 1000, 1000, 1000, 1000 };

    @Override
    public void onCreate(Bundle savedInstanceState)
    {
        super.onCreate(savedInstanceState);
        setContentView(R.layout.activity_main);

        vibrateOnce();
        vibrateMulti(THREE_CYCLES);
    }

    public void shortVibrate(View v) {
        vibrateOnce();
    }

    public void longVibrate(View v) {
        vibrateMulti(THREE_CYCLES);
    }

    private void vibrateOnce() {
        Vibrator vibrator = (Vibrator)
                getApplication().getSystemService(
                        Service.VIBRATOR_SERVICE);

        vibrator.vibrate(1000);
    }

    private void vibrateMulti(long[] cycles) {
        NotificationManager notificationManager =
          (NotificationManager)
                        getSystemService(NOTIFICATION_SERVICE);

        NotificationCompat.Builder builder =
            new NotificationCompat.Builder(this)
                        .setSmallIcon(R.drawable.ic_launcher);

        builder.setVibrate(
```

```
        new long[] {2000, 500, 2000, 500, 2000, 500});

    notificationManager.notify(0, builder.build());
    }
}
```

Listing 6.4 contains some boilerplate code, followed by the onCreate() method that invokes vibrateOnce() and vibrateMulti(), which perform a single vibration and three vibrations, respectively.

The interesting code is the vibrateMulti() method, which contains an instance of the NotificationManager class and an instance of the Notification class. When you instantiate the variable builder, make sure that you invoke the setSmallIcon() method (otherwise the application will crash).

The method setVibrate() assigns an array of values that specify the vibration pattern. This sequence contains pairs of values, where the first number specifies the duration of the vibration and the second number specifies the duration of the "paused" vibration.

As an example, the following sequence specifies a vibration of 2 seconds followed by a pause of 500 milliseconds, and this pattern is specified three times:

```
builder.setVibrate(new long[] {2000,500,2000,500,2000,500});
```

This concludes the portion of the chapter regarding sensors. The remainder of this chapter provides an overview of multimedia, which includes playing audio files and video files.

Overview of Android Media

Android provides the following media-related packages containing interfaces and classes:

- android.media
- android.media.audiofx
- android.media.effect

In brief, the Android package android.media contains the MediaPlayer class that enables you to play audio files in an Android application. The Android package android.media.audiofx contains the AudioEffect base class for controlling audio effects, such as the bass (via the BaseBoost class). The Android package android.media.effect contains classes that enable you to apply visual effects to images and videos.

In addition, the `MediaPlayer` class allows you to control playback of audio/video files and streams. As you probably expect, the Android `AudioPlayer` class plays an audio resource, whereas the `VideoView` class (which is a subclass of the Android `View` class) specifies a video file to play. In your Java code, reference the `VideoView` control (specified in an XML file) and then instantiate a Java object to play a video file.

Android applications often use one of the following locations for audio clips:

- the `res/raw` subdirectory
- the `assets` subdirectory
- an application-local directory
- the SD card (`/sdcard`)

Note that Android Studio does not create the first two subdirectories, so you must create them manually.

If you store audio files as raw resources in the `res/raw` subdirectory, keep in mind that they cannot be replaced without upgrading the application. You can reference audio clips in the `assets` subdirectory using `file:///android_asset/` for URLs (which you can do in hybrid Android `HTML5` mobile applications). This technique works with APIs that expect `Uri` parameters instead of resource IDs, but you cannot modify the assets without upgrading the application. Audio clips that are stored in an application-local subdirectory can be replaced as needed, but you need to be mindful of the amount of available storage space.

The `SD` card typically provides more storage space, but remember that other Android applications can also access the `SD` card. Files saved to the external storage are world-readable and can be modified by users when they enable `USB` mass storage to transfer files on a computer: *https://developer.android.com/guide/topics/data/data-storage.html#filesExternal.*

Playing a Ringtone

The Android package `android.media` contains the `MediaPlayer` class that enables you to play ringtones in an Android application.

 Copy the directory `RingTone` from the companion disc to a convenient location. Listing 6.5 displays the contents of `MainActivity.java`, which illustrates how to generate a ringtone.

LISTING 6.5 RingToneActivity.java

```java
package com.example.oswaldcampesato2.ringtone;

import android.media.Ringtone;
import android.media.RingtoneManager;
import android.net.Uri;
import android.os.Bundle;
import android.support.v7.app.AppCompatActivity;
import android.view.View;
import android.view.View.OnClickListener;
import android.widget.Button;

public class RingToneActivity extends AppCompatActivity
{
    private Ringtone mCurrentRingtone;

    @Override
    protected void onCreate(Bundle savedInstanceState) {
        super.onCreate(savedInstanceState);
        setContentView(R.layout.activity_ring_tone);

        // Get the default Phone Ringer RingTone
        final Button ringtoneButton =
            (Button) findViewById(R.id.button1);

        ringtoneButton.setOnClickListener(new
                                    OnClickListener() {
          @Override
          public void onClick(View v) {
            Uri ringtoneUri = RingtoneManager
                 .getDefaultUri(RingtoneManager.
                                    TYPE_RINGTONE);

              playRingtone(RingtoneManager.getRingtone(
                        getApplicationContext(),
                                    ringtoneUri));
          }
        });
    }

    // Stop current Ringtone and play new one
    private void playRingtone(Ringtone newRingtone)
    {
        if(null != mCurrentRingtone && mCurrentRingtone.
                                        isPlaying())
            mCurrentRingtone.stop();

        mCurrentRingtone = newRingtone;

        if (null != newRingtone) {
            mCurrentRingtone.play();
```

```
        }
    }

    @Override
    protected void onPause() {
        playRingtone(null);
        super.onPause();
    }
}
```

The onCreate() method in Listing 6.5 initializes the variable ring-toneButton by referencing a Button control in activity_main.xml (displayed in Listing 6.6). The next portion of Listing 6.5 defines a click handler for this button via an anonymous inner class, which overrides the default onClick() method. As you can see, the onClick() method contains two lines of code. The first line of code initializes the variable ring-toneUri (of type Uri) that is a reference to the default ringtone on the given Android device.

The second line of code invokes the playRingTone() method, which takes an argument ringTone that is of type Ringtone. The play-RingTone() method stops any currently playing ringtone, and starts playing a new ringtone with the variable ringTone (provided that it is not null).

Listing 6.6 displays the contents of activity_main.xml, which contains a Button control that is referenced in Listing 6.5.

LISTING 6.6 activity_main.xml

```
<LinearLayout
    xmlns:android="http://schemas.android.com/apk/res/android"
    android:layout_width="match_parent"
    android:layout_height="match_parent"
    android:orientation="vertical" >

    <Button
        android:id="@+id/button1"
        android:layout_width="match_parent"
        android:layout_height="wrap_content"
        android:layout_marginTop="10dip"
        android:text="@string/ringtone_string" >
    </Button>
</LinearLayout>
```

Listing 6.6 contains a top-level <LinearLayout> element that in turn contains a <Button> element that (when pressed) will play a ringtone.

Playing an Audio File

In addition to playing ringtones, the `MediaPlayer` class in the Android package `android.media` also enables you to play audio files in an Android application.

 Copy the directory `SimpleAudio1` from the companion disc to a convenient location. Listing 6.7 displays the contents of `SimpleAudio1.java`, which illustrates how to play an `m4a` audio file in an Android application.

LISTING 6.7 SimpleAudio1.java

```
package com.example.oswaldcampesato2.simpleaudio1;

import android.media.MediaPlayer;
import android.media.MediaPlayer.OnCompletionListener;

import android.os.Bundle;
import android.support.v7.app.AppCompatActivity;
import android.util.Log;
import android.view.View;
import android.widget.Button;

public class SimpleAudio1 extends AppCompatActivity
{
    private String TAG = "SimpleAudio1";
    MediaPlayer mp;

    @Override
    protected void onCreate(Bundle savedInstanceState)
    {
        super.onCreate(savedInstanceState);
        setContentView(R.layout.activity_simple_audio1);

        // adjust the volume with these 2 lines:
        //AudioManager audioManager = (AudioManager)
        //                      getSystemService(Context.
                                        AUDIO_SERVICE);
        //audioManager.setStreamVolume(AudioManager.
                                STREAM_MUSIC,20,0);

        Button myButton = (Button) findViewById(R.id.playsong);

        myButton.setOnClickListener(new Button.OnClickListener()
{
        public void onClick(View v) {
            Log.i(TAG, "Playing audio file");

            // create also invokes the prepare() method
```

```
        mp = MediaPlayer.create(SimpleAudio1.this,
                                R.raw.japanese1);
        mp.start();

        mp.setOnCompletionListener(new
                            OnCompletionListener() {
            public void onCompletion(MediaPlayer arg0) {
                Log.i(TAG, "Inside onCompletion");
            }
          }
        );
      }
    }
  );
}

public void onDestroy() {
    super.onDestroy();

    if (mp != null) {
        mp.stop();
        mp.release();
        mp = null;
    }
  }
}
```

The onCreate() method in Listing 6.7 initializes the variable myButton by obtaining a reference to a Button component that is defined in the XML document activity_main.xml. The next portion of onCreate() defines a listener for this button, which contains the onClick() method that plays the audio file whenever users click on the button. The code for playing the audio file is reproduced here:

```
// create also invokes the prepare() method
mp = MediaPlayer.create(SimpleAudio1.this,
                        R.raw.japanese1);
mp.start();
```

The preceding code block initializes the variable mp (an instance of the MediaPlayer class) by passing a reference to the current Java class SimpleAudio1 as well as the audio file japanese1.m4a located in the res/raw subdirectory. After the initialization step, the code invokes the start() method order to play the audio clip.

The final portion of onCreate() defines a listener that invokes the method onComplete() when the audio file has finished playing (and you can put additional custom code in this method).

The `onDestroy()` method is included in order to deallocate resources, which in this case is just the variable `mp` that is an instance of the `MediaPlayer` class.

Another option for playing audio files is to use `SoundPool` class that is documented here: *https://developer.android.com/reference/android/media/SoundPool.html.*

Playing a YouTube Video

In addition to playing audio files, you can also play video files in an Android application.

One way to do so is to use the YouTube Android API, as described here (which also provides downloadable sample applications): *https://developers.google.com/youtube/android/player/.*

The YouTube Android API involves multiple configuration steps, such as a `JAR` file, a developer key, an update to `build.gradle`, and so forth. A detailed tutorial that provides step-by-step instructions for the YouTube Android API is here: *http://stacktips.com/tutorials/android/youtube-android-player-api-example.*

As an alternative, the code sample in this section uses an approach that is simpler than the samples that are downloadable from the preceding link. Compare the two approaches and decide which one is better for your needs.

NOTE *The video code sample in this section plays on a Samsung Galaxy S5 with Android 6.0.1, but not on a Pixel phone with Android 7.1.*

Copy the directory `YouTubeVideo` from the companion disc to a convenient location. Listing 6.8 displays the contents of `activity_you_tube.xml`, which contains a `VideoView` component where the YouTube video will be played.

LISTING 6.8 activity_you_tube.xml

```
<?xml version="1.0" encoding="utf-8"?>
<android.support.constraint.ConstraintLayout
    xmlns:android="http://schemas.android.com/apk/res/android"
    xmlns:tools="http://schemas.android.com/tools"
    android:id="@+id/activity_you_tube"
    android:layout_width="match_parent"
    android:layout_height="match_parent"
```

```
tools:context="com.example.oswaldcampesato2.
                        youtubevideo.YouTubeActivity">

<VideoView
    android:id="@+id/myvideoview"
    android:layout_width="fill_parent"
    android:layout_height="wrap_content" />
</android.support.constraint.ConstraintLayout>
```

Listing 6.9 displays the contents of YouTubeActivity.java, which illustrates how to play a YouTube video clip in an Android application.

LISTING 6.9 YouTubeActivity.java

```
package com.example.youtubevideo;

import android.app.Activity;
import android.content.Intent;
import android.net.Uri;
import android.os.Bundle;
import android.view.Menu;

public class YouTubeActivity extends Activity
{
    @Override
    protected void onCreate(Bundle savedInstanceState)
    {
        super.onCreate(savedInstanceState);
        setContentView(R.layout.activity_you_tube);

        String youTubeLink = "https://youtu.be/ESXgJ9-H-2U";

        // see the next section for generating a 3gp link

        Uri uri = Uri.parse("rtsp://r3---sn-a5mekned.
googlevideo.com/CjOLENy73wIaNAll-4ffJ-AlERMYDSANFCO
zUl5YMOCoAUIASARgt__7jfLH3vdWigELZTZEV0NOTmNRck0M/
AFB58984FDF12A453C9C17F5D5DF848838D214A4.6228BEB2775
CD11CEB648058FA09D1A0AB12B72C/yt6/1/video.3gp");

        VideoView myVideoView =
            (VideoView)findViewById(R.id.myvideoview);

        MediaController mediaController = new
                            MediaController(this);
        mediaController.setAnchorView(myVideoView);

        myVideoView.setMediaController(mediaController);
```

```
        myVideoView.setVideoPath(youTubeLink);
        myVideoView.setVideoURI(uri);

        myVideoView.requestFocus();
        myVideoView.start();
    }

    @Override
    public boolean onCreateOptionsMenu(Menu menu) {
        //getMenuInflater().inflate(R.menu.main, menu);
        return true;
    }
}
```

The `onCreate()` method in Listing 6.9 first initializes the variable `YouTubeLink` to a URL that is the location of a video clip. Next, the `uri` variable is constructed from an `rtsp` string (see the next section for instructions) that is based on the specified YouTube video link.

Next, the `myVideoView` variable is initialized as a reference to the `VideoView` component in `activity_you_tube.xml` and supplied as a parameter to an instance of the `MediaController` class. The next three lines of code set the values of the media controller, the video path, and the video URI.

The last two lines of code in the `onCreate()` method set the focus to the `VideoView` component and then start playing the video.

Make sure that you include the following snippet in `AndroidManifest.xml` before you deploy the application to an Android device:

```
<uses-permission android:name="android.permission.INTERNET" />
```

_____

OTE *The Android project `YouTubeVideo` works on a Samsung Galaxy S5 phone with Android 6.0.1, but does not work on a Pixel phone with Android 7.1.*

Generating a 3gp Link

Let's start with the YouTube link that is used in the preceding section: *www.youtube.com/watch?v=ESXgJ9-H-2U.*

Step 1: open a tab in your browser and navigate to the following URL:

```
m.youtube.com/watch?v=ESXgJ9-H-2U&app=m
```

Step 2: right click on the desired video, select `Copy Link Location`, and paste the result in another browser session, which will display something like this:

```
rtsp://r3---sn-a5mekned.googlevideo.com/CjOLENy73wIaNAll-4ffJ-
A1ERMYDSANFC0zU15YMOCoAUIASARgt__7jfLH3vdWigELZTZEVONOTmNRc
kOM/AFB58984FDF12A453C9C17F5D5DF848838D214A4.
6228BEB2775CD11CEB648058FA09D1A0AB12B72C/yt6/1/video.3gp
```

Step 3: use the string in Step 2 as a parameter for in `Uri.parse()` in Listing 6.9.

NOTE *3gp only works for mobile applications.*

Other Scenarios for Playing Videos

In addition to playing a YouTube video, you can play a video from the SD card or a video located in the `res/raw` subdirectory. However, keep in mind that placing a video file in the `res/raw` subdirectory increases the size of an Android application, whereas playing a video stream from an external site does not increase the application size. Moreover, you have more flexibility with external sites because you can provide a drop-down list of videos (from multiple sites) that users can play on their Android device, and even enable users to enter a link to a video in an input field, none of which increases the size of your Android application.

If you intend to use `VideoView` to read `MP4` files from the `SD` card of an Android phone, see the following post regarding a workaround for a bug in `VideoView` for Android API 16: *http://stackoverflow. com/questions/25696237/videoview-and-mediaplayer-error1- 2147483648.*

In addition, errors can arise due to incorrect or unsupported encoding. The following link contains the list of supported media formats for Android: *https://developer.android.com/guide/topics/media/media-for-mats.html.*

The following free Android application detects which codecs (encoders and decoders) are available on an Android device: *https://play.google. com/store/apps/details?id=net.tyniw.mediacodecinfo.application&hl=en.*

If you want to play video files that are included as part of an Android application, you must manually create the subdirectory `res/raw` and place MP4 files in that location. Next, use the following type of code snippet to access an MP4 file:

```
Uri video = Uri.parse(
  "android.resource://com.usecontentprovider/raw/
                                    MyVideo.mp4");
```

Recording audio and video files via Android applications is more complex than playing audio and video files, and they are beyond the scope of this book. However, you can find code samples in the Android SDK, in online tutorials, or from the following links:

https://github.com/steelkiwi/AndroidRecording

https://developer.android.com/guide/topics/media/audio-capture.html

A Runtime Check for Implicit Intents

When you develop multimedia applications, you sometimes need to use Implicit Intents. However, if the device cannot find an Activity to handle the Implicit Intent, then an ActivityNotFoundException will occur.

Fortunately, you can prevent such an error by checking whether or not an Activity is available to handle an Implicit Intent, as shown in the following code block:

```
public void dispatchTakePictureIntent(Fragment fragment) {
  Intent pIntent = new Intent(MediaStore.
                ACTION_IMAGE_CAPTURE);

  // is an Activity component available to handle this
     intent?
  if(pIntent.resolveActivity(mContext.
     getPackageManager())!=null){
     pIntent.putExtra(MediaStore.EXTRA_OUTPUT,
                getOutputPhotoFileUri());

     fragment.startActivityForResult(pIntent,
                          TAKE_PHOTO_RC);
  } else {
     String toastText = (String) mContext.
           getResources()
           .getText(R.string.toast_need_camera_app);
```

```
        Toast.makeText(mContext,toastText,Toast.LENGTH_
                                         SHORT).show();
    }
}
```

The preceding method contains conditional logic to detect the presence of an `Activity` to handle (in this case) the task of taking a picture. If so, a new `Activity` is started; if not, a `Toast` is displayed with the appropriate message.

ExoPlayer

As you have seen in this chapter, Android provides `MediaPlayer` for playing media with minimal code, and the `MediaCodec` and `MediaExtractor` classes are provided for building custom media players.

As an alternative, `ExoPlayer` is an open source project that supports features that are not currently provided by `MediaPlayer`, such as Dynamic adaptive streaming over HTTP (DASH), SmoothStreaming, and Common Encryption.

The `ExoPlayer` home page is here: *http://google.github.io/ExoPlayer*.

`ExoPlayer` can be customized and extended, allowing many components to be replaced with custom implementations. You can include the `ExoPlayer` library in Android applications. Keep in mind that `ExoPlayer` is not part of the Android framework and is distributed separately from the Android SDK. The `ExoPlayer` Github repository is here: *https://github.com/google/ExoPlayer*.

The next section regarding Android permissions is quite lengthy, so you might need to return to parts of this section as you encounter Android applications that involve various types of Android permissions.

Android Permissions

Although the code samples in this chapter do not contain Android permissions, you will discover that they are used in practically every non-trivial Android application. Android supports many types of permissions, and forgetting to include them in `AndroidManifest.xml` is a common error.

Android Permission Types

Android classifies permissions into three types: normal, dangerous, and system permissions.

Normal permissions are those that do not access the file system or built-in sensors, such as those that request access to network state, wifi state, and Bluetooth. Normal permissions are discussed in detail here: *https://developer.android.com/guide/topics/security/normal-permissions.html*.

So-called "dangerous" permissions are permissions that enable applications to access sensors or to access the file system of a device. A partial list of dangerous permissions includes: Calendar, Camera, Contacts, Location, Microphone, Phone, Sensors, SMS, and storage.

System permissions include SYSTEM_ALERT_WINDOW and WRITE_ SETTINGS. Applications that require these permissions must declare them in the manifest, and also send an intent requesting authorization from users. The system responds to the intent by showing a detailed management screen to the user. More detailed information regarding Android system permissions (including best practices) is here: *https://developer.android.com/training/permissions/index.html*.

One thing to keep in mind is that every Android application has a separate "sandbox," which shields the application from every other Android application. Android Application A can access resources in Android Application B if users grant permission (during installation time) for such access.

Permissions in Android 5.1 or Lower

Handling permissions in Android 5.1 or lower is summarized here:

1) If the device is running Android 5.1 or lower, or the targetSdkVersion of an application is 22 or lower, the system asks users to grant the permissions when users install the application.
2) If you add a new permission to an updated version of the application, the system asks users to grant that permission when users update the application.
3) After users install the application, the only way they can revoke the permission is by uninstalling the application.

Permissions in Android 6 or Higher

In Android permissions can be added dynamically and permissions can be revoked on the device. When revoking permissions from older applications, you'll see this message:

> This app was designed for an older version of Android. Denying permission may cause it to no longer function as intended.

If the device is running Android 6.0 or higher, and the `targetSdkVersion` is 23 or higher, the application will request permissions from the user at runtime. However, since users can revoke the permissions at any time, the application needs to check whether it has the necessary permissions *every time* it runs.

Android Permission Groups

Any permission can belong to a permission group, including normal permissions and permissions defined by your app. A permission's group only affects the user experience if the permission is dangerous, which means that you can ignore the permission group for normal permissions.

All dangerous Android system permissions belong to permission groups. If an application requests a dangerous permission that is listed in its manifest, and the application does not currently have any permissions in the permission group, the system displays a dialog box to the user describing the permission group that the application wants to access. The dialog box does not describe the specific permission within that group.

NOTE *All dangerous Android system permissions belong to permission groups.*

For example, if an application requests the `READ_CONTACTS` permission, the system dialog box simply indicates that the application needs access to the device's contacts. If the user grants approval, the system gives the application only the permission it requested.

How to Specify Permissions in Android

You can specify various permissions in `AndroidManifest.xml` using the XML `<uses-permission>` element. Examples of permissions for camera and Internet access are here:

```
<uses-permission android:name="android.permission.CAMERA" />
<uses-permission android:name="android.permission.INTERNET" />
```

Listing 6.10 illustrates how to include an Android permission in the XML document `AndroidManifest.xml`.

LISTING 6.10 Specifying Permissions in AndroidManifest.xml

```
<uses-permission android:name="android.permission.CAMERA"/>
<?xml version="1.0" encoding="utf-8"?>
<manifest xmlns:android="http://schemas.android.com/
                                              apk/res/android"
   package="com.sample.graphics "
   android:versionCode="1"
   android:versionName="1.0">

<uses-sdk android:minSdkVersion="14"/>
<uses-permission android:name="android.permission.CAMERA"/>

<application
// details omitted
</application>
</manifest>
```

In Listing 6.10 the Android permission (shown in bold) appears outside of the XML `<application>` element, which means that the permission is granted to the entire Android application. If you specify an Android permission inside the XML `<application>` element, but outside of an XML `<activity>` element (there can be more than one such element), then the permission applies to the `Activity` and not to the entire Android application (remember this difference).

Consult the online documentation for more detailed information regarding Android permissions: *http://developer.android.com/guide/topics/security/permissions.html*.

The entire list of Android permissions (there are many) is here: *https://gist.github.com/Arinerron/1bcaadc7b1cbeae77de0263f4e15156f.*

Android M and Runtime Permissions

Prior to Android M, Android applications gave users an "all-or-nothing" list of requested access during application installation, and users had to make decisions about permissions that they might not have fully understood. Android M supports a new permissions model: applications will ask for permission to use resources (the camera, microphone, and so forth) when first needed.

Android applications that target Android M can request permissions at any time, whereas "legacy" applications still require all permissions when the applications are installed on a device. Users can deny any permissions upon request, or deny any permissions later (even for legacy applications).

Although Android M users can revoke those privileges after they have been granted, it's unclear whether they can grant and revoke individual access permissions per application. The following link contains screenshots that illustrate how to manage permissions on Android 6:

http://www.howtogeek.com/230683/
how-to-manage-app-permissions-on-android-6.0.

Dealing with permission denial in Android M:

https://plus.google.com/+AndroidDevelopers/posts/8aaudh5n1zM.

An example of runtime permissions for Android Marshmallow:

https://github.com/googlesamples/android-RuntimePermissions.

Android Marshmallow has removed almost thirty permissions that are listed here:

https://commonsware.com/blog/2015/08/17/random-musings-android-6p0-sdk.html.

The preceding link discusses combinations of permissions that are possible (or required) when working with Android Marshmallow and older versions of Android.

Summary

This chapter showed you how to create Android mobile applications to detect the presence of various sensors on an Android device (which can vary between devices). You saw how to use the accelerometer, the gyroscope, and also how to detect the battery level of an Android device.

Then you learned about multimedia for playing ringtones, audio files, and video files. In particular, you learned how to play a YouTube video on an Android device. Next, you learned how to determine whether or not an `Activity` is available to handle an `Implicit Intent`, thereby avoiding a runtime error. In addition, you learned about the open source project `ExoPlayer` that supports features that are not currently provided by `MediaPlayer`, such as SmoothStreaming and Common Encryption.

Finally, you learned about various types of permissions for Android applications, how to request them, and how they differ based on the Android API level.

DATA STORAGE AND FILE I/O

This chapter discusses context-related Android classes that enable you to store data in a global context, followed by a discussion of the storage feature of a mobile device to maintain user-related information. You will learn about various storage-related options, managing text files, working with a database, and invoking system commands. As usual, the code samples in this section were deployed to Android phones (but simulators were not tested).

This chapter also addresses `Content Providers` vis-à-vis Android API level 23 and permissions. As you might have already discovered, code samples that work correctly with lower API levels sometimes no longer work when they are recompiled with Android Marshmallow or higher. Some code modifications are required, as illustrated in the contacts-related code section, which contains an example of conditional logic that compares the SDK version of an Android application against Android Marshmallow and then executes the appropriate code.

The first part of this chapter shows you how to work with content providers so that you can update and access data on a mobile device. This section also discusses various types of loaders for Android applications.

The second part of this chapter shows you how to create an Android application that uses a `SQLite` database to persist data on a mobile device. Next, you will learn about Realm, which is a good alternative to SQLite. Note that Firebase is a cloud-based database, whereas you would install Realm on your Android device.

The third part of this chapter involves managing text files and also how to store binary files on an Android device. The final section of this chapter contains an Android application that invokes the ps command (which displays a list of processes) in order to display the list of processes that are running on an Android device. Note that this code sample assumes that you are familiar with Java classes such as BufferedReader and InputStreamReader.

Before delving into Content Providers, let's take a look at how to use some Context-related classes in Android applications.

The Android Context Classes

The Android package android.app contains the abstract class Context that has numerous concrete subclasses, such as Activity, ApplicationContext, and Intent. An Android Context provides information about an Activity or Application to newly created components. The "relevant" Context (described shortly) should be provided to newly created components (whether application context or Activity context). There are two context-related methods available in Android that are summarized below:

View.getContext(): returns the context the view is currently running in (usually the currently active Activity)

Activity.getApplicationContext(): returns the context for the entire application (the process that contains all the active Activitys). Use this method instead of the current Activity context if you need a context tied to the lifecycle of the entire application, not just the current Activity. Note that Activity is an indirect subclass of Context, so you can use this to get the context of that activity.

The Android ApplicationContext Class

The application context enables you to access resources that are shared between Activity instances. The getApplicationContext() method makes it easy to get the application context using the following code snippet:

```
Context context = getApplicationContext();
```

You can also use this object when writing code in your Activity class (because the Activity class is derived from the Context class). After getting this valid application context, you can access features and services at a system level.

Listing 7.1 displays the contents of MyCustomApp.java, which illustrates how to keep track of variables in a global context in an Android application.

LISTING 7.1 MyCustomApp.java

```
public class MyCustomApp extends Application
{
    private static Context context;
    private String state = "someState";
    private String url = null;

    public void onCreate()
    {
        super.onCreate();
        context = getApplicationContext();
    }

    public static Context getApplicationContext(){
        return context;
    }

    public String getState(){
        return this.state;
    }

    public void setUrl(url){
        this.url = url;
    }

    public String getUrl(){
        return this.url;
    }
}
```

Listing 7.1 is essentially a "value object" (VO) class, with "getters" and "setters" for the private variables state and url. Listing 7.1 also contains the onCreate() method that invokes the onCreate() method of its parent class and then initializes the variable content, as shown here:

```
public void onCreate()
{
    super.onCreate();
    context = getApplicationContext();
}
```

Notice that Listing 7.1 contains the static method getApplicationContent() that simply returns the variable context. Another detail to keep in mind is that you can access variables in the global context class with this code snippet:

```
String state = MyCustomApp.getApplicationContext().getState();
```

The Android Lifecycle and Application Context

The application context enables you to access resources that are shared between `Activity` classes. However, before you rely on the preceding class to pass variables between two `Activity`s, consider the scenario in which a `url` in `Activity` A is used in a `WebView` component in `Activity` B, and the following occurs:

1) set the `url` in the global context
2) start `Activity` B
3) retrieve the `url` in the global context
4) the application is placed in the background
5) the application is killed in the background
6) retrieve the `url` in the `onResume()` method

After step 5) you have no guarantee that the global context is still valid, so it's possible that the value retrieved for the variable `url` is `null`. A better approach is either to use the `onSaveInstanceState()` method to store values of variables in a bundle, or to save the values of variables in `SharedPreferences`.

In addition, you could also first check for a variable in the application context, and if its value is `null`, then you can obtain its value from `SharedPreferences`.

Content Providers and User Contacts

A `Content Provider` in Android allows unrelated applications to share data based solely on the names of the tables and fields in the data. Android also offers a more general Remote Procedure mechanism that is based on `IDL` (interface definition language). However, this mechanism (which is not directly related to Content Providers) is beyond the scope of this book.

The Android `Contacts` data is a `Content Provider`, which is very straightforward to use in an Android application.

 Copy the directory `MyContactList` from the companion disc to a convenient location. Listing 7.2 displays the contents of `MainActivity.java`, which illustrates how to display your list of contacts in an Android application.

LISTING 7.2 MainActivity.java

```java
package com.example.oswaldcampesato2.mycontactlist;

import android.Manifest;
import android.app.ListActivity;
import android.content.ContentResolver;
import android.content.pm.PackageManager;
import android.database.Cursor;
import android.os.Build;
import android.os.Bundle;
import android.provider.ContactsContract;
import android.util.Log;
import android.widget.ArrayAdapter;
import android.widget.ListView;

import java.util.ArrayList;
import java.util.List;

import static com.example.oswaldcampesato2.mycontactlist.R.*;

public class MainActivity extends ListActivity
{
    private String TAG = "CONTACTS";

    // Request code for READ_CONTACTS (must be > 0)
    private static final int PERMISSIONS_REQUEST_READ_
                                        CONTACTS = 123;

    private ListView listNames;

    @Override
    protected void onCreate(Bundle savedInstanceState)
    {
        super.onCreate(savedInstanceState);
        setContentView(layout.activity_main);

        //-----------------------------------------------
        // ListView id MUST be '@android:id/list' else:
        // Caused by: java.lang.RuntimeException:
        // Your content must have a ListView whose id
        // attribute is 'android.R.id.list'
        //-----------------------------------------------

        this.listNames =
            (ListView) findViewById(android.R.id.list);

        showContacts();
    }

    private void showContacts()
    {
```

```
            // Check the SDK version and also if
            // the permission is already granted

            if(Build.VERSION.SDK_INT >= Build.VERSION_CODES.M &&
                checkSelfPermission(Manifest.permission.
                                                READ_CONTACTS) !=
                                PackageManager.
                                        PERMISSION_GRANTED)
            {
                requestPermissions(
                    new String[]{Manifest.permission.READ_CONTACTS},
                    PERMISSIONS_REQUEST_READ_CONTACTS);

            // Wait for callback in the overridden method
            // onRequestPermissionsResult(int,String[],int[])
             }
             else
             {
                 // Android version is lesser than 6.0
                 // or the permission is already granted
                 List<String> contacts = getContactNames();

                 ArrayAdapter<String> adapter =
                         new ArrayAdapter<String>(this,
                         android.R.layout.simple_list_item_1, contacts);

                 listNames.setAdapter(adapter);
             }
        }

    private List<String> getContactNames()
    {
        int userCount = 0;
        List<String> contacts = new ArrayList<>();

        // Get the ContentResolver
        ContentResolver cr = getContentResolver();

        // Get the Cursor of all the contacts
        Cursor cursor = cr.query(
                ContactsContract.Contacts.CONTENT_URI,
                            null, null, null, null);

        // Move the cursor to first and
        // check if the cursor is empty

        if (cursor.moveToFirst()) {
            // Iterate through the cursor
            do {
                // Get the contacts name
                String name = cursor.getString(
```

```
                    cursor.getColumnIndex(
            ContactsContract.Contacts.DISPLAY_NAME));

            contacts.add(name);
            ++userCount;
        } while (cursor.moveToNext());
    }
    cursor.close();

    Log.i(TAG, "Contact count: "+userCount);
    return contacts;
    }
}
```

Listing 7.2 contains boilerplate code and then defines the MainActivity class that extends the Android ListActivity class instead of the AppCompatActivity class that you have seen in almost all the other code samples.

The onCreate() method initializes the variable listNames as a reference to the ListView component in activity_main.xml. The last line of code in onCreate() invokes the showContacts() method that contains conditional logic to determine the SDK version and the build version.

If the API level of the Android application is at least Android Marshmallow and permission has been already granted, then the readPermissions() method is invoked with the READ_CONTACTS permission that has been added to AndroidManifest.xml.

Otherwise, the API level is lower than Marshmallow (or permission has been granted), in which case the contacts variable (which is a list of strings) is initialized as the return value of the getContactNames() method (discussed later). Then the adapter variable is initialized as an instance of the ArrayAdapter class, and then initialized as the adapter for the listNames variable.

The getContactNames() method initializes the cursor variable (an instance of the Cursor class) as a "pointer" to the contacts that are available on your Android device. If cursor is non-null, the do-while loop advances the cursor and simultaneously adds each user to the contacts variable (which is a list of strings). When the do-while loop completes, the cursor is closed and the contacts variable is returned.

The preceding description of the getContactNames() method is admittedly light, but you can read the online documentation for more information regarding cursors and the other classes that are referenced in this method.

Listing 7.3 displays the contents of `activity_main.xml`, which contains a `ListView` component in order to display a list of user contacts.

LISTING 7.3 activity_main.xml

```
<?xml version="1.0" encoding="utf-8"?>
<RelativeLayout
    xmlns:android="http://schemas.android.com/apk/res/android"
    xmlns:tools="http://schemas.android.com/tools"
    android:id="@+id/activity_main"
    android:layout_width="match_parent"
    android:layout_height="match_parent"
    android:paddingBottom="@dimen/activity_vertical_margin"
    android:paddingLeft="@dimen/activity_horizontal_margin"
    android:paddingRight="@dimen/activity_horizontal_margin"
    android:paddingTop="@dimen/activity_vertical_margin"
    tools:context="com.example.oswaldcampesato2.
                            mycontactlist.MainActivity">

    <ListView
        android:id="@android:id/list"
        android:layout_width="match_parent"
        android:layout_height="match_parent" />
</RelativeLayout>
```

The following link contains good information about how to prompt users for permissions (and other relevant aspects of permissions): *https://material.io/guidelines/patterns/permissions.html#*.

Note that this code sample was deployed to a Pixel phone with Android 7.1, but has not been tested on other devices or on a simulator.

Custom Content Provider Implementation

This section provides you with an overview of the main aspects of creating custom content providers.

An Android `ContentProvider` (part of the `android.content` package) shares content among applications. Android built-in `ContentProviders` include `Contacts` and the `MediaStore`, both of which are in the `android.provider` package.

The first point to understand is that custom content providers are subclasses of the class `android.content.ContentProvider` that is provided by Android. Custom content providers implement the following methods:

- `onCreate()`
- `delete()`
- `getType()`
- `insert()`
- `update()`

The `getType()` method returns the `MIME` type of the data that is stored by the content provider, and the other methods in the preceding list provide functionality that you would expect (based on their names).

The second point is that the Android system provides a `Content URI` in order to identify different content providers that are available on an Android device. The Android system stores references to content providers according to an authority string that is part of the provider's content URI. The Android system looks up the authority in its list of known providers and their authorities. The `Authority` section of the content URI identifies the content provider, and it's usually expressed as the package name of the content provider, an example of which is here:

```
com.iquarkt.myapp.myprovider
```

You can access the table `employee` in a content provider by appending the table name to the authority, as shown here:

```
com.iquarkt.myapp.myprovider/employee
```

You can access a specific row in the table `employee` by appending its `rowID` to the table name, as shown here:

```
com.iquarkt.myapp.myprovider/employee/50
```

Additional information regarding Android `Authority` is here: *https://developer.android.com/guide/topics/manifest/provider-element.html*.

The third point is that the `CRUD`-related methods listed at the beginning of this section must determine whether a given `URI` involves a single row or multiple rows in a table, which can create complexity in the implementation details of these methods. Fortunately, the Android `UriMatcher` class can help you reduce this complexity. The `UriMatcher` class is a convenience class that supports a many-to-one mapping via pattern matching, which simplifies the design communication in a list-style representation. The numeric assignment allows you to insert, remove, and rearrange patterns without affecting the match. This feature is useful when the match is part of a "case" value in a switch statement. More details regarding the `UriMatcher` class are here: *https://developer.android.com/reference/android/content/UriMatcher.html.*

In summary, if you want to define custom content providers, you must do the following:

- subclass the Android class `android.content.ContentProvider`
- implement CRUD operations
- make them accessible via a `Content URI`

If you want to learn more about how to create a custom content provider, the following link contains useful information: *https://developer.android.com/guide/topics/providers/content-provider-creating.html.*

Data Storage

You can store data on a mobile device in several ways (for different purposes), some of which are listed here:

- Shared Preferences
- Internal Storage
- External Storage
- SQLite Databases
- Network Connection

Shared Preferences is useful for storing private primitive data in key-value pairs.

Internal Storage can be used for storing private data on the device memory.

External Storage is handy for storing public data on shared external storage.

SQLite Databases are convenient for storing structured data in a private database.

Network Connection is good for storing data on the Web with your own network server.

The method that you select for persisting application data depends on factors such as:

- the volume of data
- private versus public data
- accessibility to other Android apps

You can use an Android `ContentProvider` to share data among multiple Android applications. The following sections discuss these storage techniques in more detail, along with some code samples that you can use in Android applications.

User Preferences

The Android package `android.app` contains the `PreferenceActivity` (a subclass of `android.app.ListActivity`) that is the base class for preference-related Android classes. According to the Android documentation:

> Prior to HONEYCOMB this class only allowed the display of a single set of preference; this functionality should now be found in the new PreferenceFragment class. If you are using PreferenceActivity in its old mode, the documentation there applies to the deprecated APIs here.

> This activity shows one or more headers of preferences, each of which is associated with a PreferenceFragment to display the preferences of that header.

The Android `SharedPreferences` class provides APIs for saving a relatively small collection of key-value pairs. A `SharedPreferences` object points to a file containing key-value pairs and provides simple methods to read and write them. Each `SharedPreferences` file is managed by the framework and can be private or shared. The `SharedPreferences` APIs enable you to store and retrieve simple values.

Keep in mind that the `SharedPreferences` APIs are only for reading and writing key-value pairs. By contrast, the `Preference` APIs are useful for creating a user interface for application settings.

Create a shared preference file or access an existing one by invoking one of two methods:

1) `getSharedPreferences()` is for multiple shared preference files
2) `getPreferences()` is invoked from an Activity when a single shared preference file is needed in the activity

More detailed information about shared preferences is here: *https://developer.android.com/training/basics/data-storage/shared-preferences.html*.

Loaders

This section provides a brief overview of Android Loaders, which include the main classes that Loaders use in order to provide data access to Android applications.

Starting with Android 3.0, loaders became the preferred way to access data of databases or content providers.

Loaders load data asynchronously and notify listeners when the results are ready. Loaders involve the following Android classes:

- LoaderManager
- LoaderManager.LoaderCallbacks (interface)
- Loader
- AsyncTaskLoader
- CursorLoader

The `LoaderManager` class manages loaders and it's also responsible for dealing with the `Activity` or `Fragment` lifecycle. The `LoaderManager.LoaderCallbacks` interface contains methods that you must implement. The `Loader` class is the base class for all Loaders. The `AsyncTaskLoader` class is an implementation that uses an `AsyncTask` to do its work. Finally, the `CursorLoader` class is a subclass of `AsyncTaskLoader` for accessing `ContentProvider` data.

In addition, the older technique for handling a `Cursor` is deprecated, which means that you need to avoid the use of the two methods `startManagingCursor()` and `managedQuery()` in Android projects.

Managed cursor queries are executed on the UI thread, so it's possible that your application will appear sluggish. On the other hand, loaders do not use the UI thread, so your Android applications will be responsive.

AsyncTask versus Observables (RxJava)

Many Android applications use `AsyncTask` for handling long-running tasks. However, as you learned in Chapter 2, an Android `Activity` is destroyed whenever users rotate their Android device from portrait to landscape (or vice versa). If you intend to update the UI with the result of the long-running task, you will encounter a `NullPointerException` if you attempt to access the original `Activity`. The solution involves writing custom code because `AsyncTask` does not provide a mechanism to handle this scenario.

As you will see in Chapter 10, `RxJava` provides a better solution. If you have Android applications that use `AsyncTask` and `AsyncTaskLoader`, consider replacing them with `rx.Observable` and `RxJava`, as discussed in Chapter 10.

SQLite Versus ContentProvider on Android

A SQLite database is convenient when you need to store a larger amount of data (involving thousands of records) in persistent storage. Moreover, you can also query (retrieve, update, insert, delete) the data in SQLite database and the data retrieval is much more robust. However, there are two important points to keep in mind:

- SQLite is not multi-threaded
- SQLite data is only accessible to the app that created the instance

On the other hand, if you need to share data between Android applications, the recommended model for Android is the content provider model. This following article contains useful information about content providers and also how to implement one: *http://www.devx.com/wireless/ Artiolo/11133.*

A `ContentProvider` is essentially a facade that provides an API that you can implement in order to expose databases to other processes. If you need to expose data to multiple Android applications, consider using a `ContentProvider`. Incidentally, it's possible to implement a `ContentProvider` in various ways; in fact, you can even store the data in a `SQLite` database.

A SQLite Example

The Android package `android.database.sql` contains classes for creating and opening a `SQLite` database on an Android mobile device. In addition, the Android package `android.view` contains the `Cursor` class that enables you to iterate through the result set that returned from a database query.

 Copy the directory `SaveDataToSQLite` from the companion disc to a convenient location. Listing 7.4 displays the contents of `MainActivity. java`, which illustrates how to store and retrieve a set of names in a `SQLite` database in an Android application.

LISTING 7.4 MainActivity.java

```java
package com.iquarkt.savedatatosqlite;

import android.os.Bundle;
import android.support.v7.app.AppCompatActivity;
import android.widget.TextView;

public class MainActivity extends AppCompatActivity
{
    @Override
    public void onCreate(Bundle savedInstanceState)
    {
        super.onCreate(savedInstanceState);
        setContentView(R.layout.activity_main);

        saveData();
        TextView tv = (TextView)findViewById(R.id.text1);
        tv.setText("Data saved on SQLite database!");

        loadData();
    }

    private void saveData() {
        MySQLiteHelper db = new MySQLiteHelper(this);

        db.addUser(new User("John",   1829));
        db.addUser(new User("Zoe",    2060));
        db.addUser(new User("David", 2377));
        db.addUser(new User("Sandy", 1934));
    }

    private void loadData() {
        MySQLiteHelper db = new MySQLiteHelper(this);
        User user = db.getUser(2);

        TextView tv = (TextView)findViewById(R.id.text1);
        //tv.setText(user.toString());
        tv.setText("Name: "+user.name+" Rating: "+user.
                                                        rating);
    }

    @Override
    protected void onPause() {
        super.onPause();
        saveData();
    }

    @Override
    protected void onResume() {
```

```
        super.onResume();
        loadData();
    }
}
```

The `onCreate()` method in Listing 7.4 contains six steps (as you can see from the comments in the code) that start with obtaining a reference to the `DAODelegate` class (displayed in Listing 7.5). Next, the code deletes the current list of friends, populates a new list of friends, and displays that new list in a `TextView` component.

LISTING 7.5 MySQLiteHelper.java

```java
package com.iquarkt.savedatatosqlite;

import android.content.ContentValues;
import android.content.Context;
import android.database.Cursor;
import android.database.sqlite.SQLiteDatabase;
import android.database.sqlite.SQLiteOpenHelper;

public class MySQLiteHelper extends SQLiteOpenHelper
{
    private static final int DATABASE_VERSION = 1;
    private static final String DATABASE_NAME = "UsersDB";
    private static final String TABLE_USERS   = "users";

    public MySQLiteHelper(Context context) {
        super(context, DATABASE_NAME, null, DATABASE_VERSION);
    }

    @Override
    public void onCreate(SQLiteDatabase db) {
        String CREATE_USERS_TABLE = "CREATE TABLE "
                + TABLE_USERS + " ( " +
                "id INTEGER PRIMARY KEY AUTOINCREMENT, " +
                "name TEXT, " +
                "rating INTEGER )";

        db.execSQL(CREATE_USERS_TABLE);
    }

    @Override
    public void onUpgrade(SQLiteDatabase db,
                    int oldVersion, int newVersion) {
        db.execSQL("DROP TABLE IF EXISTS " + TABLE_USERS);
        this.onCreate(db);
    }
```

```
public void addUser(User user)
{
    SQLiteDatabase db = this.getWritableDatabase();

    ContentValues values = new ContentValues();
    values.put("name", user.name);
    values.put("rating", user.rating);

    db.insert(TABLE_USERS, null, values);
    db.close();
}

public User getUser(int id)
{
    SQLiteDatabase db = this.getReadableDatabase();

    Cursor cursor = db.query(TABLE_USERS,
            new String[]{"id", "name", "rating"},
            " id = ?", new String[]{ String.valueOf(id) },
            null, null, null, null);

    if (cursor == null) return null;

    cursor.moveToFirst();

    User user = new User();
    user.id = Integer.parseInt(cursor.getString(0));
    user.name = cursor.getString(1);
    user.rating = Integer.parseInt(cursor.getString(2));

    return user;
}
}
```

Listing 7.5 starts with some boilerplate code and some database-related initialization, such as defining the INSERT variable, which is a SQL statement for inserting new rows into the database.

The constructor in Listing 7.5 is passed a reference to the MainActivity class that is used for obtaining a reference to the current database.

Listing 7.5 also contains an assortment of "helper" methods with straight-forward code for inserting and deleting rows from the friends table in the database called database1. As you can see in Listing 7.5, these helper methods are invoked from an instance of the SaveDataToSQLite class.

Listing 7.6 displays the contents of User.java, which is a convenience class for keeping track of user-related information.

LISTING 7.6 User.java

```java
package com.iquarkt.savedatatosqlite;

public class User
{
    public int id;
    public String name;
    public int rating;

    public User() {}

    public User(String name, int rating)
    {
        this.name = name;
        this.rating = rating;
    }
}
```

As you may recall from other examples, the preceding class is a "VO" (value object) that contains field-level data, and also setters and getters. In this case such methods are not required because the user-related fields have `public` scope.

Figure 7.1 displays the result of launching `SaveDataToSQLite` on a Pixel phone with Android 7.1.

At this point you understand how to create `SQLite` databases, create tables, and also how to store and read both text data and binary data. In the case of binary data, you can use the concepts that you have learned in order to write a complete Android mobile application for reading and writing binary data.

FIGURE 7.1 A `SQLite` table in an Android application.

Working with Other Databases

There are various alternatives to SQLite (with varying levels of feature support), some of which are NoSQL databases. This section touches on two of the available alternatives to SQLite.

The Debug Database

The Android `Debug Database` allows you to view databases and shared preferences directly in your browser, and its home page is here:

https://github.com/amitshekhariitbhu/Android-Debug-Database.

Features of the `Debug Database` include:

- view all databases
- view all data in shared preferences in your application
- run any sql query on a database to update/delete data
- directly edit database values
- perform data searches
- perform data sorting

Create an Android application in Android Studio and add the following code snippet in `build.gradle`:

```
debugCompile 'com.amitshekhar.android:debug-db:0.3.0'
```

Use `debugCompile` so that it will only compile in your debug build and not in your release `apk`.

Now start the application, and `logcat` will contain the following type of entry:

```
D/DebugDB: Open http://XXX.XXX.X.XXX:8080 in your browser
```

You can also always get the debug address URL from your code by invoking the following method:

```
DebugDB.getAddressLog();
```

Now open the provided link in your browser.

NOTE *Your Android phone and laptop should be connected to the same Network (Wifi or LAN).*

If you want use a different port other than `8080`, make the following change in the `build.gradle` file under `buildTypes`:

```
debug {
    resValue("string", "PORT_NUMBER", "8081")
}
```

The Realm Database

One of the most popular database alternatives to SQLite is `Realm`, which is available on multiple platforms. Realm is a mobile database that is a replacement for SQLite and ORMs, and runs directly inside phones, tablets or wearables: *https://github.com/realm/realm-java*.

As you have already seen, SQLite enables you to store data in a relational database. Although the code sample uses SQL statements, it's also possible to use an Object-Relational Mapper (ORM) as an abstraction layer.

However, Realm is an alternative to SQLite that is not an ORM: instead of a relational model, Realm is based on an object store. In addition, Realm "lazy loads" data as it's required, which provides a performance advantage over ORMs that usually perform an initial load of all the data from SQL rows.

Realm provides support for Android, iOS (Objective-C as well as Swift), Xamarin, and React Native. All components from the Realm Mobile Database are available here: *https://github.com/realm*.

In addition to Realm, there are many other alternatives to SQLite, which includes relational databases as well as NoSQL databases. A quick Internet search will yield many links that will help you explore those alternatives.

File I/O and Supported Image Formats in Android

Android supports multiple binary file formats, including PNG, JPG, and GIF. If you consider using the transparency feature for the image, the PNG format would be a better choice.

If you need to read an image file that is part of your application, place that file under the `res/drawable` folder relative to the top-level directory of the Android project. After importing the image into this folder, a resource ID will be generated automatically when you recompile the package. For example, if you import the image file called `sample1.jpg`, the corresponding entry in the Java class `R.java` is `R.drawable.sample1` (without the file extension).

The following code snippet shows you how to reference an image by its resource ID:

```
Bitmap mBitmap = BitmapFactory.
            decodeResource(getResources(), R.drawable.pic1);
int mPhotoWidth = mBitmap.getWidth();
int mPhotoHeight = mBitmap.getHeight();
```

Each Android application starts with its own user and group ID, so some file folders are accessible through a given Android application only if they are specifically given the following access permission in AndroidManifest.xml:

```
<uses-permission
    android:name="android.permission.WRITE_EXTERNAL_STORAGE"/>
```

The following code block ensures that the subdirectory sampleimages exists:

```
String dirname = Environment.getExternalStorageDirectory() +
                "/sampleimages/";

File sddir = new File(dirname);

if (!sddir.mkdirs()) {
    if (sddir.exists()) {
    }
    else {
        Toast.makeText(TutorialOnImages.this,
                    "Folder error", Toast.LENGTH_SHORT)
            .show();
        return;
    }
}
```

The following code block saves the resulting image onto the SD card under our folder:

```
try {
    FileOutputStream fos = new FileOutputStream(
                        dirname + "sample1.png");
    mBitmap.compress(CompressFormat.JPEG, 75, fos);

    fos.flush();
    fos.close();
} catch (Exception e) {
    Log.e("MyLog", e.toString());
}
```

The fos variable is an instance of the FileOutStream class, and the mBitmap variable is an instance of the Bitmap class. Notice how the compression rate is set to 75%. Next, the compressed image is "flushed" to the file system, and the stream is explicitly closed. Any error that occurs in this code block is displayed as an error in the LogCat view.

Overview of Accessing Files in Android

Earlier in this chapter you saw code samples with file-related code without delving into the details of file I/O, whereas this section contains an overview of file-related operations in Android.

Android provides a `File` class that represents a file system entity that is identified by a pathname. According to the Android documentation for the `File` class:

> [The File class is] An "abstract" representation of a file system entity identified by a pathname. The pathname may be absolute (relative to the root directory of the file system) or relative to the current directory in which the program is running.
>
> The actual file referenced by a File may or may not exist. It may also, despite the name File, be a directory or other non-regular file.
>
> This class provides limited functionality for getting/setting file permissions, file type, and last modified time.

NOTE *A `File` object can reference a file, a directory, or a non-regular file.*

The `java.io.File` class contains the methods `list()` and `list-Files()` that you can use to list the contents of a directory. As a simple example, the following code snippet returns the list of filenames in the current directory:

```
String list = new File(".").list();
```

The following code snippet returns an array of `File` objects (where each object is associated with one filename) in the current directory:

```
File arrayOfFiles = new File(".").listFiles();
```

In Android you can easily retrieve the list of files in a directory on the SD card, as shown here:

```
File mFile = new File(Environment.getExternalStorageDirectory()
                 + "yourDirectory");
File myList = Arrays.asList(mFile.list());
```

Another technique for retrieving the list of files in a directory is to use the `FileFilter` class, as shown here:

```
File dir = new File("directoryPath");
FileFilter fileFilter = new FileFilter() {
    public boolean accept(File file) {
        return file.isDirectory();
    }
}
File[] files = dir.listFiles(fileFilter);
```

The next several sections contain code samples that illustrate how to write data to files and how to write data to the /sdcard directory of Android devices.

Writing to Files

Listing 7.7 displays the contents of `MainActivity.java`, which illustrates how to write to a file in an Android application.

LISTING 7.7 MainActivity.java

```
package com.example.oswaldcampesato2.writetofile;

import android.content.Context;
import android.os.Bundle;
import android.support.v7.app.AppCompatActivity;
import android.util.Log;

import java.io.IOException;
import java.io.OutputStreamWriter;

import static android.provider.Telephony.Mms.Part.FILENAME;

public class MainActivity extends AppCompatActivity
{
    private String TAG = "WRITEFILE";

    @Override
    public void onCreate(Bundle savedInstanceState)
    {
        super.onCreate(savedInstanceState);
        setContentView(R.layout.activity_main);

        String text1 = "Text for a File";

        try {
```

```
            OutputStreamWriter oStreamWriter =
                   new OutputStreamWriter(
                          openFileOutput(FILENAME,
                          Context.MODE_PRIVATE));

            oStreamWriter.write(text1);
            oStreamWriter.close();

            Log.i(TAG, "File write successful");
        }
        catch (IOException e) {
            Log.e(TAG, "File write failed: " + e.toString());
        }
    }
}
```

The onCreate() method in Listing 7.7 is straightforward: a try/catch block contains stream-related code to open a file for output and then write a text string to that file. If an error occurs, the error message is displayed via the Log.e() method.

Working with the SD Card

The SD Card is a storage area on an Android mobile device. All Android applications can read or write data to the SD Card, provided that they have the following permission in their AndroidManifest.xml file:

```
<uses-permission
   android:name="android.permission.WRITE_EXTERNAL_STORAGE"/>
```

Earlier in this chapter you learned how to work with files and directories on an Android mobile device. You can also process the contents of a directory on the SD Card, as shown here:

```
File file[] = Environment.getExternalStorageDirectory().
                                            listFiles();
for (File f : file)
{
    if (f.isDirectory()) {
        // append to the list of directories
    }
    else {
        // do something with a non-directory file
    }
}
```

You can determine the total and available space on the SD Card by using the StatFs and Environment classes from the android.os package, as shown here:

```
StatFs statFs = new StatFs(Environment
                    .getExternalStorageDirectory()
                    .getPath());

double totalBytes = (long) statFs.getBlockSize()*
                    (long) statFs.getBlockCount();

double totalMB = totalBytes/1048576;
```

You can display the value with two decimal places via a DecimalFormat object in java.text, as shown here:

```
DecimalFormat twoDecimalForm = new DecimalFormat("#.##");
```

If you need to create, read, or write files on the SD Card, consult the Android documentation for sample code.

Writing PNG Files to the SD Card

This section shows you how to programmatically save a JPG file to the sdcard on an Android device. One of the Appendices describes how to perform various file-related tasks from the command line using the Android adb utility (as discussed in Chapter 1). Listing 7.8 displays the contents of the method saveImageToSDCard(), which saves JPG files to the /sdcard directory on an Android mobile device.

LISTING 7.8 SaveImages.java

```
public void saveImageToSDCard(byte[] data, String targetName)
{
    FileOutputStream outStream = null;
    String location = "/sdcard/" +targetName;
    String TAG = "saveImageToSDCard";

    try {
        // write to sdcard
        outStream = new FileOutputStream(location);
        outStream.write(data);
        outStream.close();

        Log.d(TAG, "Saved image to filename: " + targetName);
        Log.d(TAG, "Number of bytes written: " + data.length);
    }
```

```
catch (IOException e) {
   e.printStackTrace();
}
finally {}

Log.d(TAG, "saveImageToSDCard completed");
}
```

Listing 7.8 displays the contents of the method `saveImageToSDCard()` that can be invoked (in an Android application) to save an image, and you need to pass two parameters. The first parameter is a byte array `data` with the contents of a JPG file, and the second parameter is a filename `targetName` which will contain the contents of the byte array and is saved under the `/sdcard` directory. Next, this method defines a location variable that appends the target filename to the directory `/sdcard`, as well as two other variables that are used in the code.

The next portion of code consists of a standard `try/catch` block that creates the output file.

You can enhance Listing 7.8 in at least two ways. First, you can generalize this method by including a third parameter that specifies the directory location to save a file. Note that you must check if the directory exists and if the application has the permissions to create files in the directory. Second, notify users when the target file already exists and give users the option of canceling the file creation and the option to overwrite the existing file.

The following code block illustrates how to create a directory and check whether or not it was successfully created:

```
String dirname =
    Environment.getExternalStorageDirectory() + "/
                                       newdirectory/";

File sddir = new File(dirname);

if (!sddir.mkdirs())
{
   if (sddir.exists())
   {
      // save the file here
   }
   else
   {        Toast.makeText(MainActivity.this,
            "Folder creation error", Toast.LENGTH_
                                     SHORT).show();

   }
}
```

The following projects on the companion disc contain some relevant file-related functionality:

```
ReadTextFile1
SaveDataToFile
SaveTextFile
```

In Chapter 3 you saw an example of an `AlertDialog` to prompt users for a response, which you can use in one of the aforementioned enhancements.

Making System Calls in Android

The Android application in this section executes the system command `ps` that displays the list of processes (and status-related information) that are running on an Android mobile device. Although you can obtain information about running processes via third-party applications that you can install on an Android device, this is a "fun" code sample that illustrates how you can obtain the result programmatically.

In addition, you can use this code as a starting point for code that involves other commands. For example, the following command displays the binary executables on an Android device:

```
adb shell ls /system/bin
```

A very short partial list of the binary executables on a Samsung Galaxy S5 includes: `cat, chmod, cmp, cut, dd, df, grep, uniq,` and `xargs`.

After you have read the code in this section, experiment with the code by replacing the `ps` command with one of the preceding commands (or some other combination). Some of the available binary executables access the file system, which is the rationale for the inclusion of this code sample in this chapter.

The code sample in this section uses a `LinearLayout` as the main layout, and the list of processes is displayed in a `ListView` component. In addition, each process has its status information displayed in a `TextView` component that is defined in the `onerow.xml` configuration file. Although the details about streams and buffered readers are omitted, you can still understand the overall logic and the other code details. If necessary, you can perform an Internet search to find documentation regarding streams and buffered readers in Java.

NOTE *This code sample displays a different output on a Samsung Galaxy S5 phone with Android 6.0.1 than on a Pixel phone with Android 7.1 (root-owned processes are not displayed in the latter).*

Copy the directory `ExecCommand` from the companion disc to a convenient location. Listing 7.9 displays the contents of `MainActivity.java`, which illustrates how to obtain information about processes that are running on an Android mobile device.

LISTING 7.9 MainActivity.java

```java
package com.iquarkt.execcommand;

import android.os.Bundle;
import android.support.v7.app.AppCompatActivity;
import android.widget.ArrayAdapter;
import android.widget.ListView;

import java.io.BufferedReader;
import java.io.IOException;
import java.io.InputStreamReader;
import java.util.ArrayList;

public class ExecCommandActivity extends AppCompatActivity
{
    private String TAG = "ExecCommand";
    private ListView mainListView;
    private ArrayAdapter<String> listAdapter;
    Process process = null;
    String line;
    BufferedReader in = null;

    @Override
    public void onCreate(Bundle savedInstanceState) {
        super.onCreate(savedInstanceState);
        setContentView(R.layout.activity_main);

        mainListView = (ListView) findViewById(R.
                                        id.mainListView);

        listAdapter = new ArrayAdapter<String>
                (this, R.layout.onerow, new ArrayList());

        runCommand();
    }

    private void runCommand()
    {
        try {
```

```
        process = Runtime.getRuntime().exec("ps");

        in = new BufferedReader(new InputStreamReader(
                process.getInputStream()));

        while((line = in.readLine()) != null) {
            if(line.length() != 0) {
                listAdapter.add(line);
            }
        }
    }
    catch (IOException ioex) {
        ioex.printStackTrace();
    }

    // Set the ArrayAdapter as the adapter for ListView
    mainListView.setAdapter( listAdapter );
    }
}
```

Listing 7.9 starts with boilerplate code, followed by the onCreate() method with the usual functionality. This method also instantiates the variables mainListView and listAdapter that are instances of the ListView component and the ArrayAdapter class, respectively.

The private method runCommand() starts by executing the ps command to obtain a list of current processes on an Android device with the following code snippet:

```
process = Runtime.getRuntime().exec("ps");
```

The next step obtains a buffered input stream with all the details of the running processes on the Android device:

```
in = new BufferedReader(new InputStreamReader(
                    process.getInputStream()));
```

The next portion of code contains a loop that reads one "line" at a time from the input stream, where each "line" contains the information about a single process. Each line of data is then added to listAdapter, as shown here:

```
while((line = in.readLine()) != null) {
    if(line.length() != 0) {
        listAdapter.add(line);
    }
}
```

Note that the code in `runCommand()` is inside a `try/catch` block in order to handle a possible `IOException` error (which is ignored in this code sample).

Listing 7.10 displays the contents of `activity_main.xml`, which contains a `ListView` inside a `LinearLayout` manager.

LISTING 7.10 activity_main.xml

```xml
<?xml version="1.0" encoding="utf-8"?>
<LinearLayout
    xmlns:android="http://schemas.android.com/apk/res/android"
            android:orientation="vertical"
            android:layout_width="fill_parent"
            android:layout_height="fill_parent">

    <ListView android:layout_width="fill_parent"
      android:layout_height="fill_parent"
      android:id="@+id/mainListView">
    </ListView>
</LinearLayout>
```

The `XML` `<ListView>` element in Listing 7.10 specifies that the data returned from the `ps` command will be displayed as a list of items. However, the format for each row in the list of items needs to be specified as well. This format is defined in Listing 7.11: it displays the contents of `onerow.xml`, which contains a single `TextView` component.

LISTING 7.11 onerow.xml

```xml
<TextView xmlns:android="http://schemas.android.com/
                                        apk/res/android"
            android:id="@+id/rowTextView"
            android:layout_width="fill_parent"
            android:layout_height="wrap_content"
            android:padding="10dp"
            android:textSize="16sp" >
</TextView>
```

Listing 7.11 defines a `TextView` component that specifies the format for rendering a single row of data, where each row corresponds to a "line" of output from the `ps` command.

Figure 7.2 displays the result of launching the `ExecCommand` project on a Pixel phone with Android 7.1.

Figure 7.3 displays the result of launching the `ExecCommand` project on a Samsung Galaxy S5 phone with Android 6.0.1.

USER	PID	PPID	VSIZE	RSS	WCHAN	PC	NAME
u0_a135	2101	609	1704516	46964	pipe_wait	6fff4d2d90 S	com.iquarkt.execcommand
u0_a135	2222	2101	9104	1624		0 78103a7d90 R	ps

FIGURE 7.2 A List of processes on a Pixel phone with Android 7.1.

As another example, you can display the output from the `LogCat` command with the following `onCreate()` method:

USER	PID	PPID	VSIZE	RSS	WCHAN	PC	NAME
root	1	0	3140	828	sys_epoll_	00000000 S	/init
root	2	0	0		kthreadd	00000000 S	kthreadd
root	3	2	0	0	run_ksofti	00000000 S	ksoftirqd/0
root	6	2	0	0	msm_mpm_wo	00000000 D	kworker/u:0
root	7	2	0	0	msm_rpm_sm	00000000 D	kworker/u:0H
root	8	2	0	0	cpu_stoppe	00000000 S	migration/0

FIGURE 7.3 A List of processes on a Samsung Galaxy phone with Android 6.0.1.

```
@Override
protected void onCreate(Bundle savedInstanceState)
{
    super.onCreate(savedInstanceState);
    setContentView(R.layout.activity_my_log_cat);

    try {
        Process process = Runtime.getRuntime().exec("logcat -d");

        BufferedReader bufferedReader = new  BufferedReader(
```

```
    new InputStreamReader(process.getInputStream()));

    StringBuilder log=new StringBuilder();
    String line = "";

    while ((line = bufferedReader.readLine()) != null) {
        log.append(line+"\n");
    }

    TextView tv = (TextView)findViewById(R.id.textView1);
    tv.setText(log.toString());
    }
    catch (IOException e) {}
}
```

The preceding code block contains one code snippet that differs from Listing 7.9:

```
Process process = Runtime.getRuntime().exec("logcat -d");
```

Keep in mind that you need to provide additional code in order to improve the alignment of the data that is displayed on an Android device.

Summary

Tho first part of this chapter described how to work with content providers and loaders for Android applications. Then you saw how to create an Android application that uses a SQLite database to persist data on a mobile device, and also how to work with the Realm database.

Next you learned how to manage text files in Android, and also how to store binary files on an Android device. Finally, you saw an Android application that invokes the ps command in order to display the list of processes that are running on an Android device.

CHAPTER 8

SERVICES AND BROADCAST RECEIVERS

This chapter discusses Android services and Android broadcast receivers, both of which provide useful functionality in Android applications. One use case for an Android Service involves downloading music in the background. A use case for an Android Broadcast Receiver involves detecting a change in the battery level of a mobile device; another use case involves receiving a notification when your Android device has rebooted.

The first part of this chapter delves into Android Services, which are suitable for various tasks. A Service runs in the main UI thread, and you can launch a separate Thread in a Service in order to perform long-running tasks. This section discusses several types of services and also contains code samples. If you are unfamiliar with threads, read the appropriate Appendix that discusses threads and networking, which also contains an example of a custom Service that uses a custom thread.

The second part of this chapter discusses Broadcast Receivers, which can respond to system-wide broadcasts as well as broadcast messages from other Android applications on the same device. The system delivers broadcasts for system events, and you can use a Broadcast Receiver to receive a notification about those events. This section also contains an example of an Android Alarm that performs a simple background task.

Android Intents, Services, and Broadcast Receivers

As you read the material in this chapter, keep in mind the following condensed set of use cases, because they can help you understand the differences among various features of Android.

Intent listeners are good for showing notifications. AsyncTasks provide a reasonable solution for non-critical background tasks (on behalf of the UI) that are completed in under one or two seconds. Services are useful for tasks that require more than a few seconds to complete, or need to run continuously in the background. Broadcast receivers are good for system-related events (e.g., a device has rebooted) or sensor-related events (e.g., the battery level has changed). In addition, if you need to execute jobs in the background, consider the following Android library: *https://github.com/evernote/android-job*.

`ReactiveNetwork` is an Android library that uses `RxObservables` (discussed in Chapter 10) to listen for network connection state and Internet connectivity: *https://github.com/pwittchen/ReactiveNetwork*.

One additional point: the component types `Service`, `BroadcastReceiver`, and `ContentProvider` have their own lifecycle (simpler than the `Activity` lifecycle). A lifecycle is useful for memory management of various components. Chapter 2 discusses the `Activity` lifecycle, but this chapter does not delve into the details about the other lifecycles. More information is available in the Android documentation, and some relevant links are here:

> *https://developer.android.com/guide/components/services.html#Lifecycle*

> *https://developer.android.com/reference/android/content/BroadcastReceiver.html#ReceiverLifecycle*

Android Services

Android supports Services via a `<service>` element. Every `Service` in an Android application must have its associated XML `<service>` element included in `AndroidManifest.xml`. These XML elements are placed as siblings of the `Activity` element(s).

An Android `Service` provides a mechanism to communicate with the Android system regarding a background task or operation. The associated method in this case is `Context.startService()`, which starts the execution of the task.

In addition, an Android `Service` provides a mechanism for exposing functionality to other Android applications. The associated method in this case is `Context.bindService()`, which makes available a long-lasting connection with the `Service`.

An Android `Service` is part of the `android.app` package, and a custom service is a subclass of the Android `Service` class. A custom Android `Service` must be a subclass of `android.app.Service` or one of its subclasses (such as the Android class `android.app.IntentService`).

Keep in mind that a `Service` is a component that performs operations without a user interface, along with other features that are discussed later. Another important point: although a `Service` performs in the foreground, a `Service` can also create and launch a custom `Thread` that performs a task in the background. You can start a `Service` to perform a one-time operation (such as downloading a file) by passing an `Intent` to `startService()`. The `Intent` describes the service to start and also provides any necessary data.

Since Android Services run in the main thread of the main process, Android Services typically start a new thread when they need to perform work without blocking the UI (which is handled in the main thread) of the Android application. Thus, an Android application can "bind" to a service through a set of APIs that are exposed by that service.

An Android `Service` is defined via an XML `<service>` element in the XML document `AndroidManifest.xml`, as shown here:

```
<service android:name=".subpackagename.SimpleService"/>
```

Features of Android Services

The following list contains characteristics of Android services, some of which have been discussed in previous sections:

- They are an application component
- They can perform long-running background tasks
- They do not have a user interface
- They cannot communicate directly with an activity
- They usually run in a separate thread

Android `Services` can run in the foreground and as well as the background. Note that Services can run in the background indefinitely, even if the component that started the service is destroyed. In general, a service performs a single operation and stops after completing its task. If a service involves any long running blocking operation, it's better to place that code in a separate Thread, thereby avoiding an Application Not Responding (ANR) event.

Now that you have an overview of Android Services, let's take a look at a simple example, after which we'll discuss the `Service` lifecycle methods.

A Minimalistic Android Service

This section shows you how to create a minimalistic Android application that contains a custom `Service`.

 Copy the directory `MySimpleService` from the companion disc to a convenient location. Listing 8.1 displays the contents of `MainActivity.java`, which illustrates how an `Activity` can communicate with a custom `Service`.

LISTING 8.1 MainActivity.java

```java
package com.iquarkt.mysimpleservice;

import android.content.Intent;
import android.os.Bundle;
import android.support.v7.app.ActionBarActivity;
import android.view.Menu;
import android.view.MenuItem;

public class MainActivity extends ActionBarActivity
{
    @Override
    protected void onCreate(Bundle savedInstanceState)
    {
        super.onCreate(savedInstanceState);
        setContentView(R.layout.activity_main);

        // use this to start and trigger a service
        Intent intent = new Intent(this, MyBasicService.class);

        // add data to the intent
        intent.putExtra("APP1", "A value for my service");
        this.startService(intent);
    }

    @Override
    public boolean onCreateOptionsMenu(Menu menu)
    {
      //getMenuInflater().inflate(R.menu.menu_main, menu);
        return true;
    }

    @Override
    public boolean onOptionsItemSelected(MenuItem item)
```

```
    {
        // Handle action bar item clicks here. The action
                                          bar will
        // automatically handle clicks on the Home/Up button,
                                          so long
        // as you specify a parent activity in
                              AndroidManifest.xml.
        int id = item.getItemId();

        //noinspection SimplifiableIfStatement
        if (id == R.id.action_settings) {
            return true;
        }

        return super.onOptionsItemSelected(item);
    }
}
```

Listing 8.1 contains familiar code. The new section of code is in the onCreate() method, which defines an Android Intent, places some extra information in the intent, and then involves the startService() method.

Now let's look at Listing 8.2, which displays the contents of the class MyBasicScrvice.java that illustrates how to define a custom Service class.

LISTING 8.2 MyBasicService.java

```java
package com.iquarkt.mysimpleservice;

import android.app.Service;
import android.content.Intent;
import android.os.IBinder;
import android.util.Log;

public class MyBasicService extends Service
{
    private String TAG = "MyBasicService";

    @Override
    public int onStartCommand(Intent intent, int flags,
                                          int startId)
    {
        String extra = intent.getStringExtra("APP1");
        Log.i(TAG, "onStartCommand APP1 = "+extra);
        return Service.START_NOT_STICKY;
    }

    @Override
```

```
    public IBinder onBind(Intent intent)
    {
        // for communication return IBinder implementation
        return null;
    }
}
```

Listing 8.2 contains two new methods: the `onStartCommand()` and the `onBind()` method, both of which are part of the `Service` lifecycle that is discussed in the next section. The only thing that this code does is to retrieve the "extra" information (specified on the `onCreate()` method in `MainActivity.java`) and then use the `Log.i()` method to display the value of the extra information.

Next, update `AndroidManifest.xml` by inserting the following code immediately after the closing tag for the `<activity>` element in order to register the custom service:

```
<service android:name="MyBasicService"
        android:icon="@drawable/sample1"
        android:label="@string/service_name">
</service>
```

Finally, insert this code snippet in the `strings.xml` file:

```
<string name="service_name">My Basic Service</string>
```

Note that if you want to display a custom icon for this application, change the `icon` attribute in the `<application>` element, which in this case equals sample1, and therefore refers to the `sample1.png` file.

Launch this application from Android Studio and deploy to an Android device, after which you will see the familiar "Hello, World" text string on the screen. If you list the applications on our device and search for the `MySimpleService` application, you will see your custom icon if you have made the preceding change; otherwise you will see the default Android icon.

As noted above, Listing 8.2 contains two methods that belong to the `Service` class lifecycle, which are briefly discussed in the next section.

Service Lifecycle Methods

Whenever you define a custom `Service`, one or more of the following superclass callback methods must be overridden, depending on the nature of the service being created:

- onStartCommand()
- onBind()
- onCreate()
- onDestroy()

The onStartCommand() method is invoked (via the startService() method) when the service is started by another component. This method does not need to be implemented for bound services.

The onCreate() method, which handles initialization tasks, is invoked before the method onStartCommand() or the initial invocation of the onBind() method (discussed later). As you probably expect, the onDestroy() method is invoked when the service is being destroyed.

The onBind() method is invoked when a component binds to the service via a call to the bindService() method. Keep in mind the following detail: when you implement a bound service, this method must return an IBinder object whose purpose is to communicate with the client. In the case of started services, make sure that this method returns a NULL value.

Listing 8.3 displays the contents of MyService.java, which illustrates how to override the methods that belong to the Service lifecycle.

LISTING 8.3 MyService.java

```java
public class MyService extends Service
{
    @Override
    public IBinder onBind(Intent intent) {
        return null;
    }

    @Override
    protected void onCreate() {
        super.onCreate();
        startservice(); // defined elsewhere
    }

    @Override
    protected void startService() {
        // insert your code here
    }

    @Override
    protected void onStart() {
        // insert your code here
    }
}
```

Listing 8.3 shows you a minimalistic example of overriding lifecycle methods that you can use as a template for custom code.

For example, if you need to execute something on a regular basis, you can include an instance of a `Timer` class that schedules and executes a `TimerTask` as often as required for your application needs. In addition, you need some code to start the `Timer` class as well.

Managing Android Services

You can perform various actions with an Android `Service`, some of which are described in the following sections.

How to Start and Stop an Android Service

Start a `Service` from an `Activity` (or some other component) by passing an `Intent` to the `startService()` method. The Android system then invokes the `onStartCommand()` method of the `Service` and also passes the `Intent` to the `Service`.

For example, suppose that `HelloService.java` is an Android `Service` class, and that the UI contains a `<button>` element for starting the `Service`. In the click handler for the `<button>` element, add the following code snippet:

```
Intent intent = new Intent(this, HelloService.class);
startService(intent);
```

When users click on the `<button>` element, the custom code in the `startService()` method of the `HelloService` class is executed.

On the other hand, a `Service` can be stopped in two ways. The first way is to invoke the `stopSelf()` method after the `Service` finishes its task. The second way is to invoke the method `stopService()`. In this case, the method `stopService()` invokes the `onDestroy()` method that is defined in the custom `Service`.

Restricting Access to Services

You can ensure that only your Android application can access your custom `Service` by including the `android:exported` attribute with a value of `false`, as shown here:

```
<service android:name=".HelloService"
    android:exported="false"/>
</application>
```

In fact, not even an explicit `Intent` can start the preceding service.

Set the `android:exported` attribute to `false` in order to restrict access to a custom `Service`.

Types of Services

Although Android Services have a simple foundation, there are various types of Services available, and they can become quite complex. Just to summarize, Android supports the following types of Services:

- bound and unbound services
- sticky and non-sticky services
- IntentService services

The preceding services differ in terms of their lifespan, whether or not their methods can be accessed directly from other components, and whether or not they are restarted. The following subsections provide more details about these Services.

Bound and Unbound Services

A *bound* `Service` is a `Service` that is bound to an Android component via the `bindservice()` method. There are two points to keep in mind. First, the duration of a bound service is the same as the Android component to which it is bound. Second, the bound `Service` destroys itself as soon as it is unbound from its Android component.

In addition, a bound `Service` involves a `ServiceConnection` instance whose methods can be invoked directly. The binding is performed via the `bindService()` method, which has the following signature:

```
bindService(Intent, ServiceConnection, int)
```

By contrast, an *unbound* `Service` is started by an application component and then runs in the background, which continues to execute even if the original component that initiated it is destroyed. An unbound `Service` is useful for playing music continuously in the background.

Non-Sticky and Sticky Services

Non-sticky Services are more short-lived than a bound Service: they always terminate after completing their task. By contrast, a bound Service terminates only after it is unbound. Non-sticky Services are terminated by the service itself via the stopSelf() method, which can take 0 or 1 arguments. If you invoke stopSelf(), the service is stopped unconditionally; if you invoke stopSelf(int), then the Service whose id matches the integer-valued argument is stopped.

On the other hand, a sticky service remains "alive" until an external component instructs the service to terminate itself. Thus, a sticky service is similar to an unbound service; however, the former can be stopped and restarted multiple times, whereas the latter runs continuously.

Restarting Non-Sticky and Sticky Services

The onStartCommand() callback method returns the following integer values in the event that Android destroys a service. There are three cases to consider, as discussed in the following:

Case #1: START_NOT_STICKY restarts a service only if there are pending intents awaiting delivery.

Case #2: START_STICKY restarts a service as soon as possible if it was destroyed after the onStartCommand() method returned. If there are no pending intents waiting to be delivered, the onStartCommand() callback method is called with a NULL intent value. The intent being processed at the time that the service was destroyed is discarded.

Case #3: START_REDELIVER_INTENT restarts a service that was destroyed after returning from the onStartCommand() callback method, using the current intent redelivered to the onStart-Command() method, followed by any pending intents.

JobScheduler

The Android JobScheduler class provides APIs for scheduling various types of jobs that will be executed in the same process as your application. For example, you can extend the JobScheduler class in order to batch network requests in order to improve the performance of your Android application. The JobScheduler class is an abstract class that is available from API level 21.

The JobScheduler API provides an interface for scheduling background tasks when certain tasks apply. The prerequisites for using the JobScheduler API are here:

- Android SDK 25
- Android Build Tools v25.0.2
- Android Support Repository

The JobInfo class is used for scheduling Job requests via the JobScheduler, and more information about this class is here: *https://developer.android.com/reference/android/app/job/JobInfo.html.*

Now download the code from this repository: *https://github.com/googlesamples/android-JobScheduler.*

Listing 8.4 displays the contents of AndroidManifest.xml with <permission> elements and a <service> element that are shown in bold.

LISTING 8.4 AndroidManifest.xml

```
<?xml version="1.0" encoding="UTF-8"?>
<!--
Copyright 2013 The Android Open Source Project
Licensed under the Apache License, Version 2.0 (the
                                    "License");
you may not use this file except in compliance with the
                                    License.
You may obtain a copy of the License at
     http://www.apache.org/licenses/LICENSE-2.0
Unless required by applicable law or agreed to in
                            writing, software
distributed under the License is distributed on an "AS
                                IS" BASIS,
WITHOUT WARRANTIES OR CONDITIONS OF ANY KIND, either
                            express or implied.
See the License for the specific language governing
                            permissions and
limitations under the License.
-->

<manifest xmlns:android="http://schemas.android.com/
                            apk/res/android"
    package="com.example.android.jobscheduler" >

    <!-- Min/target SDK versions (<uses-sdk>) managed
                            by build.gradle -->

    <uses-permission android:name="android.permission.
                            INTERNET" />
```

```
<uses-permission
    android:name="android.permission.RECEIVE_BOOT_
                                        COMPLETED" />

<application
    android:icon="@drawable/ic_launcher"
    android:label="@string/app_name"
    android:theme="@style/AppTheme" >
    <activity
        android:name=".MainActivity"
        android:label="@string/app_name"
        android:windowSoftInputMode="stateHidden" >
        <intent-filter>
            <action android:name="android.intent.
                                    action.MAIN" />
            <category
                android:name="android.intent.
                                category.LAUNCHER" />
        </intent-filter>
    </activity>

    <service
        android:name=".service.MyJobService"
        android:permission="android.permission.
                                BIND_JOB_SERVICE"
        android:exported="true"/>
</application>
</manifest>
```

Listing 8.4 contains boilerplate code and a `<service>` element that references the class `MyJobService`. As you can see, the `<service>` element specifies the permission `android.permission.BIND_JOB_SERVICE`, and the Android documentation states that: "If a job service is declared in the manifest but not protected with this permission, that service will be ignored by the OS."

Additional information about the `JobScheduler` class and the `JobService` class is here:

> *https://developer.android.com/reference/android/app/job/ JobScheduler.html*

> *https://developer.android.com/reference/android/app/job/JobService. html*

A good blog post that provides more detailed information about various options for a `JobScheduler` is here: *http://toastdroid.com/2015/02/21/ how-to-use-androids-job-scheduler/*.

This concludes the `Service`-related portion of this chapter. The remainder of this chapter discusses Broadcast Receivers, along with code samples that contain both Services and Broadcast Receivers.

Android Broadcast Receivers

A `Broadcast Receiver` (part of the `android.content` package) is a publish-and-subscribe system that is based on an `Intent`. In a sense, the purpose of an Android `BroadcastReceiver` is to "listen" to Android `Intents`.

A `Broadcast Intent` is a system-wide intent that is sent to all applications that have registered an interested `Broadcast Receiver`. When the Android system sends `Broadcast` intents to indicate changes on a device, Android applications that contain a corresponding `<receiver>` element can handle those `Broadcast` events.

For example, you can define an Android `Broadcast Receiver` that receives a notification when your Android device is rebooted or when the battery level has changed (shown later in this chapter). Note that a `Broadcast Receiver` is defined via a `<receiver>` element that must be included in `AndroidManifest.xml`.

You can also think of a broadcast as simply a message that any application can receive. The Android system delivers different broadcasts for different system events, which can be delivered to other applications by passing an `Intent` to `sendBroadcast()`, `sendOrderedBroadcast()`, or `sendStickyBroadcast()` methods.

With the preceding points in mind, let's take a look at a basic broadcast receiver, which is the topic of the next section.

A Simple Broadcast Receiver

The code samples in this section contain two Java classes: `MainActivity.java` (which is the main `Activity` class) and `MyBroadcastReceiver.java` (which is launched from the main `Activity` class).

Copy the directory `MySimpleBroadcastReceiver` from the companion disc to a convenient location. Listing 8.5 displays the contents of `MainActivity.java`, which prompts users for an input string, and when they click the "send" button, this class invokes a custom `Broadcast Receiver` that displays the transmitted text string as a "toast."

After creating these two Java classes, you will see how to register the custom Broadcast Receiver in AndroidManifest.xml and update activity_main.xml with an <EditText> element for user input and a <Button> element to submit the text string.

LISTING 8.5 MainActivity.java

```
package com.iquarkt.mysimplebroadcastreceiver;

import android.os.Bundle;
import android.app.Activity;
import android.content.Intent;
import android.view.Menu;
import android.view.View;
import android.widget.EditText;

public class MainActivity extends Activity
{
    @Override
    protected void onCreate(Bundle savedInstanceState)
    {
        super.onCreate(savedInstanceState);
        setContentView(R.layout.activity_main);
    }

    @Override
    public boolean onCreateOptionsMenu(Menu menu)
    {
        getMenuInflater().inflate(R.menu.menu_main, menu);
        return true;
    }

    public void broadcastCustomIntent(View view)
    {
        Intent intent = new Intent("MyCustomIntent");

        EditText editText =
                (EditText)findViewById(R.id.intent_data);

        // add data to the Intent
        intent.putExtra("message",
                (CharSequence)editText.getText().toString());

        intent.setAction(
          "com.iquarkt.mysimplebroadcastreceiver.
                                    A_CUSTOM_INTENT");

        // send the string...
        sendBroadcast(intent);
    }
}
```

Listing 8.5 contains familiar boilerplate code, and the relevant code is specified in the broadcastCustomIntent method. When users click the Button component, this method reads the text string supplied by users and populates the message property with that text string. This method also sets the "action" to a custom string via the setAction() method, and this custom string is required in Listing 8.5 in order to correctly match the launched Intent. The final portion of this method specifies the action property and then invokes the sendBroadcast() method with the populated Intent.

One more detail: Listing 8.5 does not contain click-related code because the XML file activity_main.xml (displayed in Listing 8.6) specifies that the method broadcastCustomIntent will be invoked when users click on the Button control, as shown here:

```
<Button android:id="@+id/startBroadcastButton"
        android:layout_width="fill_parent"
        android:layout_height="wrap_content"
        android:layout_alignParentLeft="true"
        android:layout_below="@+id/intentdatat"
        android:onClick="broadcastCustomIntent"
        android:text="@string/myBroadcastIntent" />
```

The Java class MyBroadcastReceiver.java in this Android application processes the Intent that is launched from MainActivity.java in Listing 8.5.

Listing 8.6 displays the contents of MyBroadcastReceiver.java, which provides some "skeleton" code for the definition of a custom Android BroadcastReceiver class.

LISTING 8.6 MyBroadcastReceiver.java

```
package com.iquarkt.mybroadcastreceiver;

import android.content.BroadcastReceiver;
import android.content.Context;
import android.content.Intent;
import android.widget.Toast;

public class MyBroadcastReceiver extends BroadcastReceiver
{
    @Override
    public void onReceive(Context context, Intent intent)
    {
        // Extract data included in the Intent
        CharSequence intentData =
```

```
                          intent.getCharSequenceExtra("message");

      Toast.makeText(context,
                     "Message from Intent: "+intentData,
                     Toast.LENGTH_LONG).show();
  }
}
```

Listing 8.6 contains the `onReceive()` method that has a `Context` argument and an `Intent` argument. The `Intent` argument contains the text string that users entered in the `EditText` control, and the `getChar-SequenceExtra()` method is used to extract that text string (as a `CharSequence` instead of a `String`). Next, the `onReceive()` method launches a `Toast` via the `makeText()` method in order to display the users' text string in the form of a `Toast`.

Listing 8.7 displays the contents of `AndroidManifest.xml`, which registers the custom `Broadcast Receiver`.

LISTING 8.7 AndroidManifest.xml

```
package com.iquarkt.mybroadcastreceiver;
<?xml version="1.0" encoding="utf-8"?>
<manifest xmlns:android="http://schemas.android.com/apk/res/
                                                       android"
    package="com.iquarkt.mysimplebroadcastreceiver" >

  <application
    android:allowBackup="true"
    android:icon="@mipmap/ic_launcher"
    android:label="@string/app_name"
    android:theme="@style/AppTheme" >
    <activity
        android:name=".MainActivity"
        android:label="@string/app_name" >
        <intent-filter>
          <action android:name="android.intent.action.MAIN" />
          <category android:name="android.intent.
                                      category.LAUNCHER" />
        </intent-filter>
    </activity>

    <receiver android:name="MyBroadcastReceiver">
      <intent-filter>
        <action
          android:name="com.iquarkt.
                     mysimplebroadcastreceiver.A_CUSTOM_INTENT">
        </action>
      </intent-filter>
```

```
    </receiver>
  </application>

</manifest>
```

Listing 8.7 contains a `<receiver>` element that specifies the custom `Broadcast Receiver` that is defined in `MyBroadcastReceiver.java`. The `<receiver>` element also contains an `<intent-filter>` child element that in turn contains an `<action>` child element. The `<action>` element contains a name property whose value is the same custom string that is specified in Listing 8.6.

Lastly, Listing 8.8 displays the contents of `activity_main.xml`, which contains an `EditText` control and a `Button` control.

LISTING 8.8 activity_main.xml

```
<receiver android:name="MySimpleBroadcastReceiver">
  <intent-filter>
    <action android:name="com.iquarkt.
                mysimplebroadcastreceiver.A_CUSTOM_INTENT">
    </action>
  </intent-filter>
</receiver>

<RelativeLayout
    xmlns:android="http://schemas.android.com/apk/res/android"
    xmlns:tools="http://schemas.android.com/tools"
    android:layout_width="match_parent"
    android:layout_height="match_parent"
    android:paddingLeft="@dimen/activity_horizontal_margin"
    android:paddingRight="@dimen/activity_horizontal_margin"
    android:paddingTop="@dimen/activity_vertical_margin"
    android:paddingBottom="@dimen/activity_vertical_margin"
    tools:context=".MainActivity">

    <EditText android:id="@+id/intent_data"
        android:layout_width="fill_parent"
        android:layout_height="wrap_content"
        android:hint="@string/send_message" />

    <Button
        android:id="@+id/startBroadcastButton"
        android:layout_width="fill_parent"
        android:layout_height="wrap_content"
        android:layout_alignParentLeft="true"
        android:layout_below="@+id/intentdata"
        android:onClick="broadcastCustomIntent"
        android:text="@string/myBroadcastIntent" />
</RelativeLayout>
```

Listing 8.8 contains basic layout details, as well as the `onClick` attribute for the `Button` control that specifies the method `broadcastCustom-Intent()` in Listing 8.5 as the method to be executed whenever users click on the `Button` control.

Alarms

The code sample in this section shows you how to create an Android `Alarm` that uses an Android `Toast` as well as an Android `Notification`.

Earlier you saw how to create an Android `Alert` in an Android application, which you can use for simple situations (somewhat analogous to an alert in JavaScript). On the other hand, an Android `Alarm` is something that you can schedule to execute at some point in the future (comparable to setting an alarm clock). Although an Android `Alarm` is conceptually simple (i.e., do something at a future point in time), the code is more complex than the code for an Android `Alert`.

The code in this Android application requires two Java classes. The Java class that schedules an alarm is `SimpleAlarm1.java`. The Java class `ReceiveAlarm1.java` contains code that executes the alarm-related code at the appropriate point in time. In this code sample, the code in `ReceiveAlarm1.java` displays a toast-based message on the screen.

 Copy the directory `MySimpleAlarm` from the companion disc to a convenient location. Listing 8.9 displays the contents of `SimpleAlarm1.java`, which illustrates how to define an `Alarm` in Android.

LISTING 8.9 SimpleAlarm1.java

```
package com.iquarkt.gui;

import android.app.Activity;
import android.app.AlarmManager;
import android.app.Notification;
import android.app.NotificationManager;
import android.app.PendingIntent;
import android.content.Context;
import android.content.Intent;
import android.os.Bundle;
import android.util.Log;
import android.view.View;
import android.view.View.OnClickListener;
import android.widget.Button;
```

```
import android.widget.Toast;

import java.util.Calendar;

public class SimpleAlarm1 extends Activity
{
    private int APP_NOTIFICATION_ID = 123;
    private int alarmDelay = 5;  // seconds
    private Toast mToast;
    private NotificationManager nm;

    @Override
    public void onCreate(Bundle savedInstanceState)
    {
        super.onCreate(savedInstanceState);
        setContentView(R.layout.activity_main);

        Button button = (Button) findViewById(R.
                                    id.set_alarm_button);
        button.setOnClickListener(this.onClickListener);
    }

    private void showNotification(int statusBarIconID,
                            int statusBarTextID,
                            int detailedTextID,
                            boolean showIconOnly)
    {
     Log.i("showNotification ", "showNotification");

        Intent contentIntent = new Intent(this,
                                    SimpleAlarm1.class);
        PendingIntent theappIntent = PendingIntent.getBroadcast(
                            SimpleAlarm1.this, 0,
                            contentIntent, 0);

        CharSequence from = "Alarm Manager";
        CharSequence message = "ZZZZZZZZZZZZZZZZZZ";

        String tickerText =
            showIconOnly ? null : this.
                            getString(statusBarTextID);

        Notification notif = new Notification(statusBarIconID,
                            tickerText,
                            System.
                            currentTimeMillis());

        notif.setLatestEventInfo(this, from, message,
                                    theappIntent);

        notif.setLatestEventInfo(this, from, message,
                                    theappIntent);
```

```
        this.nm.notify(this.APP_NOTIFICATION_ID, notif);
    }

    private OnClickListener onClickListener = new
                                        OnClickListener() {
        public void onClick(View v) {
            Intent intent =
                new Intent(SimpleAlarm1.this,
                                    ReceiveAlarm.class);

            PendingIntent appIntent = PendingIntent.getBroadcast(
                    SimpleAlarm1.this, 0, intent, 0);

            Calendar calendar = Calendar.getInstance();
            calendar.setTimeInMillis(System.
                                    currentTimeMillis());
            calendar.add(Calendar.SECOND, alarmDelay);

            AlarmManager am =
                (AlarmManager) getSystemService(Context.
                                        ALARM_SERVICE);

            am.set(AlarmManager.RTC_WAKEUP,
                    calendar.getTimeInMillis(),
                    appIntent);

            // first cancel any active Toast:
            if(SimpleAlarm1.this.mToast != null) {
                SimpleAlarm1.this.mToast.cancel();
            }

            // now create and launch a new Toast:
            SimpleAlarm1.this.mToast = Toast.makeText(SimpleAlarm1.this,
                                    R.string.alarm_message,
                                    Toast.LENGTH_LONG);
            SimpleAlarm1.this.mToast.show();
        }
    };
}
```

The first part of Listing 8.9 contains an extensive list of import statements, some of which are needed for alarm-related and notification-related functionality. The method onCreate() obtains a reference to a Button component and then sets a listener that is defined later in the code.

Next, the private method showNotification() handles the details of instantiating an Android Intent that sends the notification-related information to the Android device.

The private inner class `onClickListener` contains the method `onClick()` that is executed whenever users click on the lone Android `Button` component in this Android application. This method instantiates an `Intent` called `intent` that is used to create an Android `PendingIntent` called `appIntent`, as shown here:

```
PendingIntent appIntent = PendingIntent.getBroadcast(
                    SimpleAlarm1.this, 0, intent, 0);
```

The next portion of this method creates a `Calendar` instance called `calendar` and an `AlarmManager` instance called `am` in order to set the time at which the alarm will be invoked, as shown here:

```
am.set(AlarmManager.RTC_WAKEUP,
        calendar.getTimeInMillis(),
        appIntent);
```

The final portion of the `onClick()` method uses conditional logic to determine whether or not to display a toast-based message, as shown here:

```
SimpleAlarm1.this.mToast = Toast.makeText(SimpleAlarm1.this,
                    R.string.alarm_message,
                    Toast.LENGTH_LONG);
SimpleAlarm1.this.mToast.show();
```

Listing 8.10 displays the contents of `ReceiveAlarm1.java`, which illustrates how to define a Java class that receives an alarm from the `SimpleAlarm1` class in Listing 8.8.

LISTING 8.10 ReceiveAlarm1.java

```
package com.iquarkt.gui;

import android.content.BroadcastReceiver;
import android.content.Context;
import android.content.Intent;
import android.util.Log;
import android.widget.Toast;

public class ReceiveAlarm extends BroadcastReceiver
{
    @Override
    public void onReceive(Context context, Intent intent)
    {
        Log.i("onReceive: ", "received intent2");
```

```
Toast.makeText(context,
               "hello from
          received alarm",
               Toast.
          LENGTH_SHORT).show();
     }
}
```

As you can see, Listing 8.10 is much simpler than Listing 8.9. The first part of Listing 8.10 contains some boiler-plate code with various `import` statements. The next portion of Listing 8.10 involves the method `onReceive()` that is invoked when a broadcast event is received, which in this example displays a toast-based message.

Figure 8.1 displays the result of launching the `Alarm1` project on a Pixel phone with Android 7.1.

FIGURE 8.1 An Alarm in an Android Application.

Accessing the Battery

This section contains a code sample that reads the battery level of a mobile device via a `Broadcast Receiver`.

 Copy the directory `SimpleBattery1` from the companion disc to a convenient location. Listing 8.11 displays the contents of `SimpleBattery1.java`, which illustrates how to read the battery level of a mobile device from an Android application.

LISTING 8.11 SimpleBattery1.java

```
package com.example.simplebattery1;

import android.os.Bundle;
import android.app.Activity;
import android.content.BroadcastReceiver;
import android.content.Context;
import android.content.Intent;
import android.content.IntentFilter;
import android.view.Menu;
import android.widget.ProgressBar;
import android.widget.TextView;

public class MainActivity extends Activity
```

```
{
    @Override
    public void onCreate(Bundle savedInstanceState)
    {
        super.onCreate(savedInstanceState);

        //Set layout we created
        setContentView(R.layout.activity_main);

        //Register the receiver that triggers an
        //event when the battery charge is changed
        registerReceiver(mBatInfoReceiver, new IntentFilter(
                        Intent.ACTION_BATTERY_CHANGED));
    }

    //Create Broadcast Receiver Object and class definition
    private BroadcastReceiver mBatInfoReceiver =
        new BroadcastReceiver() {
        @Override
        //When Event is published, onReceive method is called
        public void onReceive(Context c, Intent i) {
            //Get Battery percentage
            int level = i.getIntExtra("level", 0);

            //Find the progressbar creating in main.xml
            ProgressBar pb =
                    (ProgressBar) findViewById(R.
                                    id.progressbar);

            //Set progress level with battery percentage value
            pb.setProgress(level);

            //Find textview control created in main.xml
            TextView tv = (TextView) findViewById(R.
                                    id.textfield);

            //Set TextView with text
            tv.setText("Battery Level: "+Integer.
                                    toString(level)+"%");
        }
    };

    @Override
    public boolean onCreateOptionsMenu(Menu menu) {
        getMenuInflater().inflate(R.menu.main, menu);
        return true;
    }
}
```

The onCreate() method in Listing 8.11 registers a broadcast receiver that responds to changes in the battery by specifying mBatInfoReceiver, which is an instance of the BroadcastReceiver class that is defined later in the code. The onCreate() method also specifies an IntentFilter with the ACTION_BATTERY_CHANGED event, as shown here:

```
registerReceiver(mBatInfoReceiver, new IntentFilter(
                Intent.ACTION_BATTERY_CHANGED));
```

The next portion of Listing 8.11 instantiates mBatInfoReceiver and overrides the method onReceive() in order to render the current value of the battery whenever it has changed. This method references the two UI components that are defined in Listing 8.12.

LISTING 8.12 activity_main.xml

```xml
<?xml version="1.0" encoding="utf-8"?>
<LinearLayout
    xmlns:android="http://schemas.android.com/apk/res/android"
    android:layout_width="fill_parent"
    android:layout_height="fill_parent"
    android:orientation="vertical" >

<TextView
    android:id="@+id/textfield"
    android:layout_marginTop="40dip"
    android:layout_width="wrap_content"
    android:layout_height="wrap_content"
    android:layout_gravity="center"/>

<ProgressBar
    android:id="@+id/progressbar"
    android:layout_width="wrap_content"
    android:layout_height="wrap_content"
    android:layout_marginTop="20dip"
    android:layout_gravity="center"
    android:minWidth="200dip"
    android:minHeight="100dip"
    android:max="100"
    style="?android:attr/progressBarStyleHorizontal"/>
</LinearLayout>
```

Listing 8.12 contains an XML <LinearLayout> root element that contains an XML <TextView> element and an XML <ProgressBar> child element that are used for displaying the battery level as a decimal value and as a percentage of the progress bar, respectively.

Application Shortcuts (Android 7)

The Android SDK (API 25) provides an example of "app" shortcuts, which you can also download from here: *https://github.com/googlesamples/android-AppShortcuts/*.

Download the code (or clone the repository) in a convenient location, after which you will see that the Java-related directory contains four Java classes:

- Main.java
- MyReceiver.java
- ShortcutHelper.java
- Utils.java

Listing 8.13 displays the contents of MyReceiver.java, which illustrates how to set up app shortcuts in an Android application.

LISTING 8.13 MyReceiver.java

```
*
* Copyright (C) 2016 The Android Open Source Project
*
* Licensed under the Apache License, Version 2.0 (the
                                            "License");
* you may not use this file except in compliance with
                                         the License.
* You may obtain a copy of the License at
*
*       http://www.apache.org/licenses/LICENSE-2.0
*
* Unless required by applicable law or agreed to in
                                    writing, software
* distributed under the License is distributed on an
                                    "AS IS" BASIS,
* WITHOUT WARRANTIES OR CONDITIONS OF ANY KIND, either
                                    express or implied.
* See the License for the specific language governing
                                    permissions and
* limitations under the License.
*/
package com.example.android.appshortcuts;

import android.content.BroadcastReceiver;
import android.content.Context;
```

```
import android.content.Intent;
import android.util.Log;

public class MyReceiver extends BroadcastReceiver
{
    private static final String TAG = Main.TAG;

    @Override
    public void onReceive(Context context, Intent intent)
    {
        Log.i(TAG, "onReceive: " + intent);

        if (Intent.ACTION_LOCALE_CHANGED.equals(intent.
                                        getAction()))
        {
            // Refresh all shortcut to update the labels
            // (Right now shortcut labels don't contain
            // localized strings though)
            new ShortcutHelper(context).
                        refreshShortcuts(/*force=*/ true);
        }
    }
}
```

Listing 8.13 extends the BroadcastReceiver class, and also overrides the method onReceive that displays a log message via the Log.i() method and uses conditional logic to determine when to create a new instance of the custom ShortcutHelper class (not shown here) to refresh the list of available shortcuts.

You can deploy this application to an Android device that supports version 7.x of Android.

Summary

This chapter discussed Android Services, their lifecycle, and also an example of creating a custom Service in an Android application. Next you learned about Android Broadcast Receivers, and a simple example of implementing a Broadcast Receiver. You also saw how to use a Broadcast Receiver to receive a notification whenever the battery levels change on an Android device.

CHAPTER 9

ANDROID VR, TV, AUTO, AND THINGS

T his chapter contains an introduction to an assortment of Android topics, including Android VR (Virtual Reality), Android TV, Android Auto, and Android Things (formerly Android IoT).

There are a few things (such as limitations) that you need to know before delving into the material. First of all, this chapter provides a cursory introduction to VR. If you plan to acquire a deeper knowledge of VR, the last part of the VR section makes a recommendation based on a high-level comparison between Google VR and Unity.

In addition, some code samples require Android 7 (Nougat), and the screenshots for those code samples are from a Google Pixel phone. Since the Pixel phone is designed to work with the DayDream headset, we've used a Pixel to generate screenshots in this chapter. In addition, you will only be able to see the full VR effects and the 360-degree panorama of Macchu Picchu, Peru on a Pixel phone (or one with comparable power).

Moreover, the Google VR code samples require a Google "certified" phone, and the setup with the Pixel phone is straightforward. However, if you don't have a Pixel phone, it's possible to use a Nexus 6P (see the online documentation for the setup steps) with Android VR, as well as Android-based simulators to view the code samples.

The first part of this chapter provides a modest overview of some features of Android VR (Virtual Reality), which you can view on Google Cardboard (about USD 35) and also with the Google DayDream headset (about USD 80). This section also discusses portions of an Android VR application that is available in a Github repository. The companion disc for this chapter contains several video files running on a Pixel phone, including one of Macchu Picchu in Peru, which illustrates a 360-degree panoramic view.

The second part of this chapter discusses Android TV, along with a code sample that you can create in Android Studio. As you will see, Android TV applications make significant use of Android Fragments (which are discussed in Chapter 3). The code sample for Android TV can be rendered on an Android device by installing a simulator, which is an Android apk that is part of the Android SDK.

The third part of this chapter discusses how to create Android Auto applications in Android Studio. Android Auto applications can be created for music and also for messaging, and this section contains code samples for both types. Furthermore, the code samples can also be rendered on an Android device by installing a simulator, which is another Android apk in the Android SDK.

The fourth part of this chapter discusses Android Things, which is a successor to Brillo. The code sample in this section consists of a template that is based on a Github repository, and there is no emulation involved for this code sample.

The fifth (optional) portion of this chapter introduces you to TensorFlow, which is an open-source tool from Google or machine learning. You will see where to download the TensorFlow code, how to build an Android apk, and then how to deploy TensorFlow to an Android device. (An iOS version for TensorFlow is available as well.)

Android VR (Virtual Reality)

One of the goals of this section is to provide information for configuring a Pixel phone with Daydream and Cardboard, along with some screenshots of VR applications, and also discuss a section of code in a VR application.

If you are new to Virtual Reality, you can learn about the concepts by reading an article such as this Wikipedia article: *https://en.wikipedia.org/wiki/Virtual_reality*.

In brief, Google Daydream is an Android-powered VR platform that involves hardware and software. Daydream is more advanced than Cardboard (released two years earlier), which consists of a very inexpensive headset.

The `Daydream` headset (made of lightweight fabric) is paired with a controller, along with a Pixel phone (other options are possible) that is mounted in the `Daydream` headset. You launch a VR application on the phone, and the controller enables you to navigate around the available menu options that are displayed in the headset.

If you are able to view the Google VR applications in a `DayDream` headset, you will immediately notice that they move slightly whenever you hover over any of them with the controller: this behavior is called a parallax effect. The VR applications in the Play Store will provide motion intensity ratings.

`DayDream`-compatible phones have low persistence display, no "ghosting" effects, low latency, the ability to render at 60fps, and high quality sensors. Android 7.x utilizes the sensors on a Pixel phone with head-tracking algorithms.

Incidentally, Google services such as YouTube, Street View, Play Movies, Play Store, and Google Photos will be available through dedicated VR applications.

Android VR SDK

The Android VR SDK supports both `Daydream` and `Cardboard`, with an API to create applications. A more complex API is available that supports `Daydream`-ready phones and the `Daydream` controller. The Android VR SDK can handle various VR development tasks such as:

- Lens distortion correction
- Spatial audio
- Head tracking
- 3D calibration
- Side-by-side rendering
- Stereo geometry configuration
- User input event handling

The Google VR NDK for Android provides a C/C++ API for developers writing native code (not covered in this chapter). After creating such applications, deploy them to a Pixel phone and then insert the phone into the `DayDream` headset or the `Cardboard` viewer.

Configuring Android `DayDream` and `Cardboard`

First navigate to the Google Play Store and install the Google `DayDream` application on an Android Pixel phone. Next, pair the `DayDream` application with the `DayDream` headset by following the prompts of the set-up program. You also need to pair the remote control with the `DayDream` headset. In both cases, the built-in software provides prompts for you to follow during the setup process.

Similar setup steps are required for `Cardboard`: navigate to the Google Play Store and install the Google `Cardboard` application on an Android device. In fact, most `Cardboard` devices have a `QRcode` that takes you to the correct location in the Google Play Store. Pair the `Cardboard` application with `Cardboard`; note that no setup is necessary for a remote control device, such as the one that accompanies `DayDream`.

The Android VR Sample Applications

Download the Google VR SDK and NDK by cloning the following repository: *https://github.com/googlevr/gvr-android-sdk.git*.

The SDK libraries of the repository are `.aar` files in the `libraries` directory.

The sample projects are in the `samples` directory as `Gradle` projects ready for Android Studio. Currently the following projects are available (the `ndk`-based samples involve C++ code):

ndk-controllerpaint
ndk-treasurehunt
sdk-controllerclient
sdk-simplepanowidget
sdk-simplevideowidget
sdk-treasurehunt
sdk-videoplayer

Two sample applications demonstrate the VR View functionality in the SDK: `simplepanowidget` and `simplevideowidget`. Both samples are single-activity applications that display an embedded panoramic image or video using `VrPanoramaView` and `VrVideoView`, respectively.

Pixel Phone and Android VR Screenshots

The screenshots in this section are from the Android VR projects in the `gvr-android-sdk-master` directory that you downloaded from Github

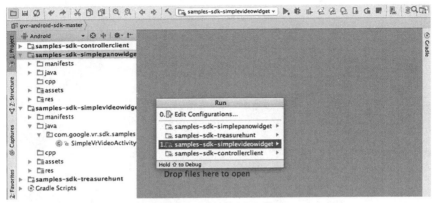

FIGURE 9.1 Android Studio launch options for the VR projects.

in the previous section. The screenshots were taken via `Vysor`, which is a Chrome extension that allows you to "mirror" the contents of an Android device on a MacBook (and vice versa). As you navigate around your Android device, you will see the contents updated on your MacBook (and vice versa).

FIGURE 9.2 Pixel Phone and the `simplepanowidget` VR project.

The code samples in previous chapters contain single Android Studio projects. By contrast, the VR code samples in this section are in the top-level directory `gvr-android-sdk-master`, and you can launch different projects at runtime in Android Studio. For your convenience, Figure 9.1 displays a screenshot of a section of Android Studio that displays the list of the VR projects after you navigate to `Run > Run`.

Figure 9.2 displays a screenshot with the `simplepanowidget` project rendered on a Pixel phone.

Figure 9.3 displays a screenshot with the `treasurehunt` project rendered on a Pixel phone.

Figure 9.4 displays a screenshot with the `simplevideowidget` VR project rendered on a Pixel phone.

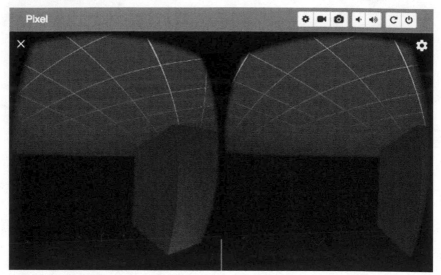

FIGURE 9.3 Pixel Phone and the `treasurehunt` VR project.

Figure 9.5 displays a screenshot with the `controllerclient` VR project rendered on a Pixel phone.

The next section discusses some of the code samples associated with the screenshots in this section.

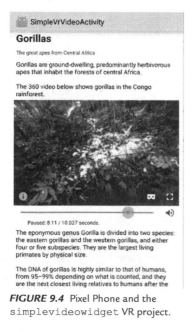

FIGURE 9.4 Pixel Phone and the `simplevideowidget` VR project.

FIGURE 9.5 Pixel Phone and the `controllerclient` VR project.

Android VR Code Samples

This section contains code blocks from some of the VR projects whose screenshots are shown in the previous section.

Important: In Android Studio make sure that you open the top-level directory gvr-android-sdk-master and not the individual projects. The top-level directory contains a build.gradle file that specifies various resources that are required for the sample projects, whereas the build.gradle file in each project contains project-specific information.

The Android VR sample projects allow users to view different parts of the panorama by rotating their phone. The simplevideowidget sample also allows users to pause and play their video by tapping on the VR View, and seek through the video using the slider. The samples expose the fullscreen mode and Cardboard mode buttons in the VR View that allow users to change modes.

Listing 9.1 displays the contents of the onCreate() method from the Java file SimpleVrVideoActivity.java that is included in the project.

LISTING 9.1 SimpleVrVideoActivity.java

```
public void onCreate(Bundle savedInstanceState)
{
  super.onCreate(savedInstanceState);
  setContentView(R.layout.main_layout);

  seekBar = (SeekBar) findViewById(R.id.seek_bar);
  seekBar.setOnSeekBarChangeListener(new SeekBarListener());
  statusText = (TextView) findViewById(R.id.status_text);

  // Make the source link clickable.
  TextView sourceText = (TextView) findViewById(R.id.source);
  sourceText.setText(Html.fromHtml(getString(R.
                                   string.source)));
  sourceText.setMovementMethod(LinkMovementMethod.
                                   getInstance());

  // Bind input and output objects for the view.
  videoWidgetView = (VrVideoView) findViewById(R.
                                   id.video_view);
  videoWidgetView.setEventListener(new
                                   ActivityEventListener());

  volumeToggle = (ImageButton) findViewById(R.
                                   id.volume_toggle);
  volumeToggle.setOnClickListener(new View.OnClickListener() {
    public void onClick(View v) {
```

```
        setIsMuted(!isMuted);
    }
});

loadVideoStatus = LOAD_VIDEO_STATUS_UNKNOWN;

// Initial launch of the app or an
// Activity recreation due to rotation
handleIntent(getIntent());
}
```

Listing 9.1 displays the onCreate() method that simply references the UI components in the main XML layout file, and also defines relevant listeners. For example, the TextView component has a motion-associated listener, whereas the VrVideoView component has an associated event listener.

Listing 9.2 displays a portion of the contents of main_layout.xml, which is associated with this VR project.

LISTING 9.2 main_layout.xml

```xml
<?xml version="1.0" encoding="utf-8"?>
<ScrollView xmlns:android="http://schemas.android.com/
                                        apk/res/android"
    android:layout_width="fill_parent"
    android:layout_height="wrap_content"
    android:background="@android:color/white">

    <LinearLayout
        android:layout_width="match_parent"
        android:layout_height="match_parent"
        android:id="@+id/main_layout"
        android:padding="10dip"
        android:orientation="vertical" >

        <TextView
          android:id="@+id/title"
          style="@style/ContentText"
          android:textSize="@dimen/title_text_size"
          android:textStyle="bold"
          android:textColor="@color/textDark"
          android:text="@string/title" />

        <com.google.vr.sdk.widgets.video.VrVideoView
            android:id="@+id/video_view"
            android:layout_width="match_parent"
            android:scrollbars="@null"
            android:layout_height="250dip"/>
```

```
<LinearLayout
    android:layout_width="match_parent"
    android:layout_height="wrap_content"
    android:orientation="horizontal" >
    <!-- Seeking UI & progress indicator.-->
    <SeekBar
        android:id="@+id/seek_bar"
        style="?android:attr/progressBarStyleHorizontal"
        android:layout_height="32dp"
        android:layout_weight="8"
        android:layout_width="0dp"/>
    <ImageButton
        android:background="@android:color/transparent"
        android:id="@+id/volume_toggle"
        android:paddingTop="4dp"
        android:paddingStart="0dp"
        android:layout_width="0dp"
        android:layout_height="wrap_content"
        android:layout_weight="1"
        android:src="@drawable/volume_on"/>
</LinearLayout>
// omitted elements are on the companion disc
  </LinearLayout>
</ScrollView>
```

Listing 9.2 contains a top-level <ScrollView> element that contains several child elements, including a <LinearLayout> element (the other elements are not shown). The <LinearLayout> element contains a <TextView> element and a <VrVideoView> element (shown in bold) and then another <LinearLayout> element.

You can also create VR applications in Android Studio, which involves updating the contents of build.gradle, creating modules, and importing library files. Detailed instructions are here: *https://developers.google.com/vr/android/get-started#start_your_own_project.*

Android VR SDK and OpenGL versus Unity/Unreal

Now that you have read about Android VR and have seen some examples, this section provides information that will help you decide how to delve further into VR.

First, the Android VR SDK provides a number of Java interfaces and classes that deal mostly with stereoscopic rendering and head tracking. However, this SDK does not provide any functionality for building 3D applications. One alternative involves the use of OpenGL directly (which is a complicated technology, especially for beginners), and another alternative is to use a game engine (such as jMonkey).

The Android VR SDK for Android provides access to Android (Nougat) native-level OS APIs for VR. These APIs will be available in Android Nougat phones (such as the Pixel phone) to provide Daydream-ready capability. Developers who use the Android VR NDK will use a C/C++ API to write native code. In addition, developers who are familiar with OpenGL can quickly create VR applications using the Android VR SDK. The development kit simplifies a number of common tasks, such as lens distortion correction, spatial audio, head tracking, 3D calibration, and so forth.

The Android VR SDK for Unity provides access to the API that plugs in with the Unity game engine, which is an extremely powerful 3D graphics engine with strong mobile support. Developers who use the Google VR SDK can do the following:

1) "prefab" a new VR Unity project from scratch
2) adapt existing Unity 3D apps to VR
3) create apps that can easily swap in and out of VR mode

The SDK also has many additional features specific to the Unity engine, such as simulating head movement with a mouse, controlling approximate field-of-view, and so forth.

By contrast, the Unity SDK is a plugin for the Unity 3D game engine, which is fully featured for creating 3D applications. Developers who currently use Unity can create Cardboard applications simply by attaching one script to the main camera. The Unity plugin "sits" on top of the Android SDK and basically translates it from Java to C# in Unity, and also adds some extra features such as gaze control.

Conclusion: Developing VR applications with Unity will be considerably easier for most new developers.

Useful Links

The following link shows you how to create a VR video: *http://mashable.com/2016/04/20/lg-360-cam-camera-review/#GCsZJ0DfAuqp*.

Play the VR in an Android VR video viewer in an Activity, as described here: *https://developers.google.com/vr/concepts/vrview*.

A Reddit link with additional information about VR: *https://www.reddit.com/r/GoogleCardboard/comments/39jnyo/new_to_vr_development_what_is_the_difference/*.

The next section gives you an overview of Android TV, along with instructions for creating Android TV applications in Android Studio.

Android TV

Android Studio enables you to create Android TV applications, which rely on Android Fragments and Lists. Fragments are very useful in these applications, especially for reducing the amount of time to load different videos in a section of an `Activity` (i.e., for performance reasons).

Google released the TV Input Framework (TIF), which is an easier alternative for creating Android applications for Android TV. The TIF provides an API for creating TV Input Modules and live TV search and recommendations, where the latter facilitates meeting regional digital TV broadcast standards.

The TIF provides implementations of various TV input service features, along with various components, such as HDMI-CEC, TV Input, and TV Input HAL. For more information about building Android TV applications, navigate to the website developer.android.com and search for "Building Apps for TV."

Useful Links

A video for Android TV: *https://developer.android.com/training/tv/index.html*.

Android TV documentation: *https://developer.android.com/training/tv/tif/tvinput.html*.

A sample Android TV application on Github: *https://github.com/googlesamples/androidtv-sample-inputs*.

Android TV Applications

Before we look at a code block in an Android TV application, this section provides a condensed description of what you will encounter when you create Android TV applications. Android TV applications that are created in Android Studio consist of the following thirteen Java files:

- BrowseErrorActivity.java
- CardPresenter.java
- DetailsActivity.java
- DetailsDescriptionPresenter.java
- ErrorFragment.java
- MainActivity.java
- MainFragment.java
- Movie.java
- MovieList.java
- PlaybackOverlayActivity.java
- PlaybackOverlayFragment.java
- Utils.java
- VideoDetailsFragment.java

The preceding list of Java files contain a total of nearly 1800 lines of code (which does not include any custom code), so obviously this section is limited to a cursory description of their contents.

Four of those Java classes contain Android Fragments, and another four Java classes contain Android Activitys. The class `MainActivity.java` contains pure boilerplate code that is automatically generated during the creation of the project. The `onCreate()` method sets the content to the layout file `activity_main.xml` that "defers" to `MainFragment.java`, which contains UI initialization code.

The class `VideoDetailsFragment.java` creates an instance of the class `PlaybackOverlayActivity` for video playback that handles user events and sets the content to the `playback_controls.xml` layout file.

The layout file `playback_controls.xml` contains a `VideoView` component (an example of this component is discussed in Chapter 6) and a `Fragment` component (Fragments are discussed in Chapter 3) in order to play a selected video.

The remaining Java classes contain an assortment of functionality, such as handling errors and displaying lists of movies. Now let's take a look at how to create an Android TV application, which is discussed in the next section.

Creating Android TV Applications

Launch Android Studio and create an Android TV application and select only the option for TV, which will generate the project files that you saw in an earlier section.

When you create a new Android TV application in Android Studio, make sure that you select only the option for TV (i.e., deselect tablet).

Alternatively, copy the directory AndroidTV from the companion disc to a convenient location. Listing 9.3 displays some of the methods in MainFragment.java. Keep in mind that the code below will only give you a flavor of one section of the code sample.

LISTING 9.3 MainFragment.java

```
@Override
public void onActivityCreated(Bundle savedInstanceState)
{
    Log.i(TAG, "onCreate");
    super.onActivityCreated(savedInstanceState);

    prepareBackgroundManager();
    setupUIElements();
    loadRows();
    setupEventListeners();
}

private void loadRows()
{
    List<Movie> list = MovieList.setupMovies();

    mRowsAdapter = new ArrayObjectAdapter(new
                                    ListRowPresenter());
    CardPresenter cardPresenter = new CardPresenter();

    int i;
    for (i = 0; i < NUM_ROWS; i++) {
        if (i != 0) {
            Collections.shuffle(list);
        }

        ArrayObjectAdapter listRowAdapter =
                new ArrayObjectAdapter(cardPresenter);

        for (int j = 0; j < NUM_COLS; j++) {
```

```
            listRowAdapter.add(list.get(j % 5));
        }

        HeaderItem header =
                new HeaderItem(i, MovieList.MOVIE_CATEGORY[i]);

        mRowsAdapter.add(new ListRow(header, listRowAdapter));
    }

    HeaderItem gridHeader = new HeaderItem(i, "PREFERENCES");

    GridItemPresenter mGridPresenter = new GridItemPresenter();

    ArrayObjectAdapter gridRowAdapter =
                new ArrayObjectAdapter(mGridPresenter);

    gridRowAdapter.add(
            getResources().getString(R.string.grid_view));

    gridRowAdapter.add(getString(R.string.error_fragment));

    gridRowAdapter.add(
            getResources().getString(R.string.personal_settings));

    mRowsAdapter.add(new ListRow(gridHeader, gridRowAdapter));

    setAdapter(mRowsAdapter);
}
```

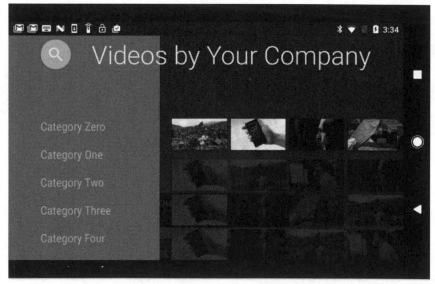

FIGURE 9.6 An Android TV app on a Pixel phone with Android 7.1.

Listing 9.3 contains the `onActivityCreated()` method that acts as an "initializer" by invoking several other methods to set up a manager, UI components, initialize lists, and set up event listeners.

Next, the `loadRows()` method starts by initializing the `list` variable with a set of movies, followed by an adapter called `mRowsAdapter` for the list of movies. The next part of `loadRows()` contains a loop that in essence constructs a displayable list of movies based on the category of each movie. There is a considerable amount of additional code in this sample project that has not been discussed here, which you need to read if you want a more thorough understanding of the inner workings of this sample application.

Figure 9.6 displays the result of launching the `AndroidTV` project on a Pixel phone with Android 7.1.

Android Auto Applications

Android Auto applications involve `<service>` elements (discussed in Chapter 8), `<receiver>` elements (also discussed in Chapter 8), and also a `Thread/Handler` class (see Appendix C). Review the appropriate sections of Chapter 8 and Appendix C before you delve into the code details of Android Auto Applications.

In addition, before you can use the Simulator for Android Auto applications, you need to install the Desktop Head Unit (DHU), which is discussed in the next section.

You can create two types of Android Auto applications in Android Studio: one type is for music and the other type is for messaging. Subsequent sections briefly discuss both types of applications, including portions of the code for both types.

Useful Links

https://codelabs.developers.google.com/codelabs/androidauto-messaging/index.html

A free Android Auto course is offered by Udacity: *https://www.udacity. com/course/android-auto-development--ud875C.*

An Android Auto book is available here: *http://www.apress.com/us/ book/9781484217832.*

The Github repository for the Android Auto book is here: *https://github. com/apress/android-tv-apps-dev.*

Android Auto Setup and Testing

You need to install the Desktop Head Unit (DHU) in order to test your Android Auto applications. The complete set of steps is listed here: *https:// developer.android.com/training/auto/testing/index.html.*

After completing the DHU setup steps, you can run and test audio applications on an Android device. The required steps are listed here:

* install the Android Media Browser simulator
* enable developer options on the test device
* install your application on that device
* launch the Android Media Browser simulator

Go to the `<sdk>/extras/google/simulators/` directory and install the Android Media Browser simulator `media-browser-simulator.apk` on an Android test device. Next, enable developer options on the test device, and then install your application on that device.

Now launch the Android Media Browser simulator to see how your audio application appears in Auto. If your app does not appear, stop the simulator from `Settings > Apps` and restart it.

Go here to install Android Auto application on an Android device: *https:// play.google.com/store/apps/details?id=com.google.android.projection. gearhead&hl=en.*

In case you're interested, the directory `<sdk>/extras/google/auto/ voice` contains a good collection of sound files for common voice commands.

Android Auto Music Applications

Create an Android Auto application for music in Android Studio. The file `MainActivity.java` contains only boilerplate code: the `onCreate()` method contains but two lines of code, so it won't be displayed here. Listing 9.4 displays some of the methods in `MyMusicService.java`.

LISTING 9.4 MyMusicService.java

```
public class MyMusicService extends MediaBrowserService
{
    private MediaSession mSession;

    @Override
```

```
public void onCreate() {
    super.onCreate();

    mSession = new MediaSession(this, "MyMusicService");

    setSessionToken(mSession.getSessionToken());

    mSession.setCallback(new MediaSessionCallback());

    mSession.setFlags(
        MediaSession.FLAG_HANDLES_MEDIA_BUTTONS |
        MediaSession.FLAG_HANDLES_TRANSPORT_CONTROLS);
}

@Override
public void onDestroy() {
    mSession.release();
}

// code omitted
}
```

Listing 9.4 is straightforward: the onCreate() method that initializes mSession as an instance of the MediaSession object, and also sets the callback method. The last portion of the onCreate() method sets two flags for buttons and controls.

Android Auto Messaging Applications

Create an Android Auto application for messaging in Android Studio. The file MainActivity.java contains just boilerplate code (the same as the previous example).

Listing 9.5 displays the contents of MessageReceiver.java.

LISTING 9.5 MessageReceiver.java

```
package com.example.oswaldcampesato2.myandroid2auto;

import android.content.BroadcastReceiver;
import android.content.Context;
import android.content.Intent;
import android.support.v4.app.NotificationManagerCompat;
import android.util.Log;

public class MessageReadReceiver extends BroadcastReceiver
{
    private static final String TAG =
```

```
                MessageReadReceiver.class.getSimpleName();

        @Override
        public void onReceive(Context context, Intent intent)
        {
            if(MyMessagingService.READ_ACTION.
                                    equals(intent.getAction()))
            {
                int conversationId =
                    intent.getIntExtra(
                    MyMessagingService.CONVERSATION_ID, -1);

                if (conversationId != -1) {
                    Log.d(TAG,
                        "Conversation " +conversationId+" was read");

                    NotificationManagerCompat notificationManager =
                            NotificationManagerCompat.from(context);

                    notificationManager.cancel(conversationId);
                }
            }
        }
    }
}
```

Listing 9.5 contains boilerplate code, followed by the contents of the custom class `MessageReadReceiver` that extends the `BroadcastReceiver` class. As you know from Chapter 8, a `Broadcast Receiver` must implement the `onReceive()` method that is invoked when the associated event occurs.

The code compares the action specified in the intent that is the second argument of the `onReceive()` method with the value of `MyMessaging.READ_ACTION` (not shown here). If they match, then the extra data of the same intent is retrieved: if this value differs from `-1`, then the current notification is cancelled.

Getting Started with Android Things (IoT)

Android Things is a "rebranding" of Android `Brillo`, which is the codename for a developer preview of an Android-based embedded operating system platform by Google, announced at GIO 2015, to be used with low-power and memory-constrained IoT devices. One key difference: `Brillo` used C++ as the primary development environment, whereas Android Things targets Java developers.

Android Things is integrated with `Weave`, the communication platform for IoT devices. Keep in mind that Android Things OS supports a subset of the original Android SDK, and can also be integrated with Firebase. Android Things enables you to develop Android applications for various boards that are listed here: *https://developer.android.com/things/hardware/developer-kits.html*.

Supported devices include Intel Edison `Arduino`, Intel Edison `Sparkfun`, `NXPixo`, and Raspberry PI. You must use API Level 24 or higher and a device with Android 7.x. When you create an application (discussed later) you must update `build.gradle` as follows:

```
dependencies {
    ...
    provided 'com.google.android.
                        things:androidthings:0.1-devpreview'
}
```

You must also add the `things` shared library entry in `AndroidManifest.xml`:

```
<application ...>
    <uses-library android:name="com.google.android.things"/>
    ...
</application>
```

The supported boards and the `GPIO` pins are assumed on each board.

Environment Setup and Samples

The Android Things SDK is downloadable here: *https://developer.android.com/things/sdk/index.html*.

Setting up your environment is described here: *https://developer.android.com/things/preview/index.html*.

Some Android Things code samples are downloadable here: *https://developer.android.com/things/sdk/samples.html*.

Additional code samples are here: *https://github.com/androidthings*.

The following link contains the details for building your first device: *https://developer.android.com/things/training/first-device/index.html*.

Important Caveats for Android Things

Although Android Things applications use the same tools, there are some important differences between "regular" Android applications and Android Things applications.

Permissions and Notifications

Runtime Permissions are not supported because embedded devices aren't guaranteed to have a UI to accept the runtime dialog. Declare permissions that you need in the manifest file. All normal and dangerous permissions declared in the manifest file are granted at install time.

Since there is no system-wide status bar and window shade in Android Things, notifications are not supported. Hence, avoid calling the `NotificationManager` APIs in applications.

Content Providers

Android Things does not include the standard suite of system applications and content providers. In particular, avoid using common intents as well as the following content provider APIs in applications:

- CalendarContract
- ContactsContract
- DocumentsContract
- DownloadManager
- MediaStore
- Settings
- Telephony
- UserDictionary
- VoicemailContract

Peripheral I/O API and User Driver API

The Peripheral I/O APIs enable applications to communicate with sensors and actuators using industry standard protocols and interfaces. The following interfaces are supported: `GPIO`, `PWM`, `I2C`, `SPI`, and `UART`.

User drivers extend existing Android framework services and allow applications to inject hardware events into the framework that other apps can access using the standard Android APIs.

Android Things expects one application to expose a "home activity" in its manifest as the main entry point for the system to automatically launch on boot. This activity must contain an intent filter that includes both `CATEGORY_DEFAULT` and `IOT_LAUNCHER`.

For ease of development, this same activity should include the intent filter `CATEGORY_LAUNCHER` so Android Studio can launch it as the default `Activity` when deploying or debugging.

Listing 9.6 displays a portion of `AndroidManifest.xml`.

LISTING 9.6 AndroidManifest.xml

```
<application
    android:label="@string/app_name">
    <activity android:name=".HomeActivity">
        <!-- Launch activity as default from Android Studio -->
        <intent-filter>
            <action android:name="android.intent.action.MAIN"/>
            <category android:name="android.intent.
                                      category.LAUNCHER"/>
        </intent-filter>

        <!-- Launch activity automatically on boot -->
        <intent-filter>
            <action android:name="android.intent.action.MAIN"/>
            <category
              android:name="android.intent.category.
                                      IOT_LAUNCHER"/>
            <category android:name="android.intent.
                                      category.DEFAULT"/>
        </intent-filter>
    </activity>
</application>
```

Listing 9.6 contains a standard `Intent Filter` that launches `HomeActivity` as the default `Activity` when the application is launched from Android Studio. The second `Intent Filter` is for launching the `Activity` during boot-up time of the device.

Android Things Sample-Button Project

Navigate to the following link and download the `sample-button` project: *https://github.com/androidthings/sample-button*.

Listing 9.7 displays part of the contents of `ButtonActivity.java` in this project.

LISTING 9.7 ButtonActivity.java

```
@Override
protected void onCreate(Bundle savedInstanceState)
{
    super.onCreate(savedInstanceState);
    Log.i(TAG, "Starting ButtonActivity");

    PeripheralManagerService pioService =
                    new PeripheralManagerService();
```

```
try {
    Log.i(TAG, "Configuring GPIO pins");
    mLedGpio = pioService.openGpio(BoardDefaults.
                                   getGPIOForLED());
    mLedGpio.setDirection(Gpio.
                          DIRECTION_OUT_INITIALLY_LOW);

    Log.i(TAG, "Registering button driver");

    // Initialize and register the InputDriver that
    // will emit SPACE key events on GPIO state changes.
    mButtonInputDriver = new ButtonInputDriver(
        BoardDefaults.getGPIOForButton(),
        Button.LogicState.PRESSED_WHEN_LOW,
        KeyEvent.KEYCODE_SPACE);

    mButtonInputDriver.register();
} catch (IOException e) {
    Log.e(TAG, "Error configuring GPIO pins", e);
}
}
```

Listing 9.7 contains an onCreate() method that starts by initializing the variable pioService as an instance of the PeripheralManagerService class. Next, a try/catch block contains code to initialize the GPIO (General Purpose Input Output) pins on the attached device.

The next section of code in the onCreate() method is for the button input UserDriver that listens to GPIO pin changes and key events, and then changes the state of an LED accordingly.

The next section discusses some aspects of the Android Things template.

Android Things Project Template

The following Github repository contains a minimalistic Android application that provides a template for an Android Things application: *https://github.com/androidthings/new-project-template*.

Listing 9.8 displays the contents of MainActivity.java in this project template.

LISTING 9.8 MainActivity.java

```
/*
 * Copyright 2016, The Android Open Source Project
 *
 * Licensed under the Apache License, Version 2.0 (the "License");
```

```
 * you may not use this file except in compliance with
   the License.
 * You may obtain a copy of the License at
 *
 *       http://www.apache.org/licenses/LICENSE-2.0
 *
 * Unless required by applicable law or agreed to in
   writing, software
 * distributed under the License is distributed on an
   "AS IS" BASIS,
 * WITHOUT WARRANTIES OR CONDITIONS OF ANY KIND, either
   express or implied.
 * See the License for the specific language governing
   permissions and
 * limitations under the License.
 */

package com.example.androidthings.myproject;

import android.app.Activity;
import android.os.Bundle;import android.util.Log;

/**
 * Skeleton of the main Android Things activity.
   Implement your
 * device's logic in this class.
 *
 * Android Things peripheral APIs are accessible
   through the class
 * PeripheralManagerService. For example, the snippet
   below will
 * open a GPIO pin and set it to HIGH:
 *
 * <pre>{@code
 * PeripheralManagerService service = new
   PeripheralManagerService();
 * mLedGpio = service.openGpio("BCM6");
 * mLedGpio.setDirection(Gpio.DIRECTION_OUT_
   INITIALLY_LOW);
 * mLedGpio.setValue(true);
 * }</pre>
 *
 * For more complex peripherals, look for an existing
   user-space driver, or implement one if none
 * is available.
 *
 */
public class MainActivity extends Activity
{
    private static final String TAG =
                    MainActivity.class.getSimpleName();
```

```
@Override
protected void onCreate(Bundle savedInstanceState)
{
    super.onCreate(savedInstanceState);
    Log.d(TAG, "onCreate");
}

@Override
protected void onDestroy() {
    super.onDestroy();
    Log.d(TAG, "onDestroy");
}
}
```

Listing 9.8 contains the standard onCreate() method and the onDestroy() method, both of which simply invoke their corresponding method in the parent class.

Notice that the initial portion of Listing 9.6 contains a comment section with the following code block:

```
PeripheralManagerService service =
                    new PeripheralManagerService();
mLedGpio = service.openGpio("BCM6");
mLedGpio.setDirection(Gpio.DIRECTION_OUT_INITIALLY_LOW);
mLedGpio.setValue(true);
```

The preceding code block opens a GPIO (General Purpose Input Output) pin of an attached device and sets it to HIGH.

Useful Links

The IoT Starter is a sample Android application for interacting with the IBM Watson IoT Platform, and you can download the code from this Github repository: *https://github.com/ibm-messaging/iot-starter-for-android.*

More information regarding the Watson IoT Platform is here: *https://docs.internetofthings.ibmcloud.com/index.html.*

Google TensorFlow (optional)

TensorFlow is an open source software library for numerical computation using data flow graphs. Nodes in the graph represent mathematical operations, while the graph edges represent the multidimensional data arrays (tensors) communicated between them.

The flexible architecture allows you to deploy computation to one or more CPUs or GPUs in a desktop, server, or mobile device with a single API. Researchers and engineers working on the Google Brain Team developed TensorFlow in order to conduct machine learning and deep neural networks research. However, the system is general enough to be applicable in a wide variety of other domains as well.

TensorFlow provides a framework that enables you to create Deep Learning Neural Networks. Other similar frameworks (prior to TensorFlow) include Theano, Torch, Caffe, Nervana, H2O, DL4J and many other variations. TensorFlow also provides greater flexibility in deploying to distributed environments.

TensorFlow supports a Python-based REPL. In addition, you can deploy TensorFlow to Android devices as well as iOS devices (the latter is not discussed in this chapter).

Simple Examples of TensorFlow

TensorFlow programs use a tensor data structure to represent all data: only tensors are passed between operations in the computation graph. You can think of a TensorFlow tensor as an n-dimensional array or list. A tensor has a static type, a rank, and a shape.

After you have installed TensorFlow and Python (the latter is preconfigured on MacBooks), type python from a command shell to launch the Python REPL. Next, enter the following Python commands to access TensorFlow functionality in order to display a text string:

```
>>> import tensorflow as tf
>>> hello = tf.constant('Hello, TensorFlow')
>>> sess = tf.Session()
>>> sess.run(hello)
Hello, TensorFlow
```

If you see the preceding text string on the screen, then TensorFlow is installed correctly on your machine.

The following Python commands access TensorFlow in order to add two numbers:

```
>>> a = tf.constant(10)
>>> b = tf.constant(32)
>>> sess.run(a+b)
42
```

The following code block shows you how to define two matrices and compute their product:

```
>>> import tensorflow as tf

>>> matrix1 = tf.constant([[3., 3.]])
>>> matrix2 = tf.constant([[2.],[2.]])
>>> product = tf.matmul(matrix1, matrix2)
>>> sess = tf.Session()
>>> result = sess.run(product)
>>> print(result)
[[ 12.]]
>>> sess.close()
```

The preceding code block can be rewritten in the following manner:

```
>>> import tensorflow as tf
>>>    with tf.Session() as sess:
>>>    matrix1 = tf.constant([[3., 3.]])
>>>    matrix2 = tf.constant([[2.],[2.]])
>>>    product = tf.matmul(matrix1, matrix2)
>>>    result = sess.run([product])
>>>    print(result)
[array([[ 12.]], dtype=float32)]
```

If you have more than one GPU available on your machine, you can assign specific GPU beyond the first, and you must assign a value to it explicitly. Devices are specified with strings, and the currently supported devices are:

```
"/cpu:0": The CPU of your machine
"/gpu:0": The GPU of your machine (if one exists)
"/gpu:1": The second GPU of your machine
```

Use with...Device statements to specify which CPU or GPU to use for operations, as shown here for the CPU:

```
>>> import tensorflow as tf
>>> with tf.Session() as sess:
...     with tf.device("/cpu:0"):
...         matrix1 = tf.constant([[1., 2.]])
...         matrix2 = tf.constant([[3.],[4.]])
...         product = tf.matmul(matrix1, matrix2)
...         result = sess.run(product)
...         print(result)
...
[[ 11.]]
```

The following code block specifies a GPU, followed by an error message if the GPU does not exist:

```
with tf.Session() as sess:
  with tf.device("/gpu:0"):
    matrix1 = tf.constant([[1., 2.]])
    matrix2 = tf.constant([[3.],[4.]])
    product = tf.matmul(matrix1, matrix2)
    result = sess.run(product)
    print(result)
```

Here is the error message:

```
tensorflow.python.framework.errors.InvalidArgumentError: Cannot
assign a device to node 'MatMul_2': Could not satisfy explicit
device specification '/device:GPU:1' because no devices
matching that specification are registered in this process;
available devices: /job:localhost/replica:0/task:0/cpu:0
```

Launching the Graph in a Distributed Session

To create a `TensorFlow` cluster, launch a `TensorFlow` server on each of the machines in the cluster. When you instantiate a `Session` in your client, you pass it the network location of one of the machines in the cluster:

```
with tf.Session("grpc://example.org:2222") as sess:
  # Calls to sess.run(...) will be executed on the cluster.
  ...
```

This machine becomes the master for the session. The master distributes the graph across other machines in the cluster (workers), much as the local implementation distributes the graph across available computer resources within a machine.

You can use `with tf.device()`: statements to directly specify workers for particular parts of the graph:

```
with tf.device("/job:ps/task:0"):
  weights = tf.Variable(...)
  biases = tf.Variable(...)
```

See the `Distributed TensorFlow` "How To" for more information about distributed sessions and clusters.

Deploying TensorFlow to an Android Device

Install one of the `TensorFlow` binary packages, as described here: *https:// github.com/tensorflow/tensorflow.*

NOTE

The companion disc contains ten-sorflow_demo.apk *that was created from the* TensorFlow *source code and deployed to a Nexus 7 2 tablet with Android 6.0.1.*

If you prefer to compile the source code to generate an apk file, the necessary steps are described here: *https://github.com/tensorflow/tensorflow/tree/master/tensorflow/examples/android/*.

After you have completed the preceding steps, you can deploy the generated Android apk to Android devices and then launch TensorFlow.

Figure 9.7 displays the screen of a Nexus 7 2 tablet with Android 6.0.1 that is running TensorFlow.

FIGURE 9.7 Google TensorFlow on a Nexus 7 2 tablet with Android 6.0.1.

Summary

This chapter started with a brief introduction to Android VR, with sample videos of VR on a Pixel phone, and a discussion of how to use Cardboard, the DayDream headset, and a Pixel phone for viewing Android VR applications. You also saw some Java classes that are part of Android VR applications.

Then you learned about Android TV applications, which make heavy use of Fragments and Lists. Next you saw how to create two types of Android Auto applications: music-based and messaging-based applications. Then you learned about Android Things (IoT) applications.

Finally, you got an introduction to TensorFlow, along with information for installing the TensorFlow apk to an Android device.

CHAPTER 10

FUNCTIONAL REACTIVE
PROGRAMMING

his chapter discusses Functional Reactive Programming (FRP) as
a segue for RxAndroid for Android applications. If you are new to
FRP, you might be surprised to discover that it originated almost
twenty years ago. In fact, Microsoft has been involved in FRP since 2009
(more or less), and early contributors to ReactiveX are current or former
Microsoft employees.

Moreover, FRP is available not only as RxAndroid for Android, but also
for fifteen or more programming languages, including JavaScript (RxJS),
Java (RxJava2), Scala (RxScala), and even Swift (RxSwift). FRP has
undergone a sort of "resurgence" recently, perhaps popularized through
the use of FRP in Angular 2 and (to a lesser extent) ReactJS. FRP arguably has the potential to become a significant technology in the near future,
which is the rationale for this chapter.

If you plan to use FRP in Android mobile applications, the good news
is that RxAndroid is an Android-specific extension of RxJava2, so the
knowledge that you gain from the RxJava2 material in this chapter will
serve you well. If you are already familiar with the material in any of the
preliminary sections, feel free to skim those sections.

The first part of this chapter provides a very brief (and equally fast) "dive"
into operators and then an analogy to help you understand Observables.
The purpose of this section is for readers who have never worked with an
Observable, and there's a decent chance that the other portions of this
chapter will become easier to understand.

The second part of this chapter briefly discusses Lambda expressions in Java8, why they are supported in Java8, and some basic examples of how to define Lambda expressions.

The third part of this chapter discusses Java Streams, along with some basic examples. This chapter discusses Java8 Streams because a) Android supports Java8 and b) the preponderance of the code that you will encounter is based on Java8 instead of Java9 (or Java10). Recall that in Chapter 4 you saw how to use some Java classes in the java.io package, such as InputStreamReader and DataInputStreamReader. However, the Stream-related functionality in this chapter is based on Java classes that belong to the java.util.stream package.

One other important point to keep mind: in Java8 Streams are processed synchronously and Java8 provides support for Parallel Streams. On the other hand, Java9 provides the Flow API that supports asynchronous processing of data streams: *https://community. oracle.com/docs/DOC-1006738.*

The fourth part of this chapter discusses RxJava2, which provides support for FRP by means of Observables. You will see Java code samples that use Observables, along with some of the operators that are available in RxJava2. The final portion of this chapter discusses RxAndroid, along with some code samples.

As you will soon discover, this lengthy chapter contains a *lot* of information, and if you are new to FRP, don't be surprised if you find your head "swimming" in some sections of this chapter. Hence, some concepts (e.g., Java8 Streams versus Observables) are mentioned multiple times in this chapter in order to reinforce them, but ultimately the recommendation is to re-read sections to raise your comprehension level of the plethora of topics in this chapter.

A Fast Dive into Observables: An Analogy

If you are new to Observables, or if you struggle with code samples that contain Observables, please read this section about intermediate operators, and then the next section that contains a humorous analogy by Venkat Subramanian with a clever insight into the world of Observables.

Let's start discussing core aspects about Observables: there are intermediate operators (such as map(), filter(), and so forth) that you can chain together, and there are terminal operators (such as subscribe() or forEach) that you can invoke in order to "make stuff happen" (which will become clearer in the analogy). In other words, an `Observable` comprises one or more intermediate operators that transform a stream of data, followed by a terminal operator that actually "kicks off" the `Observable` in order to generate a stream of data.

Intermediate Operators are Passive

Skipping the syntax-related details for the moment, consider the following pair of Observables in JavaScript that involve the intermediate operators `map()` and `filter()`:

```
var source = [0,1,2,3,4,5,6];

var result1 = source.map(x => 3*x)
                    .filter(x => x % 4 == 0);
console.log("result1: "+result1);

var result2 = source.map(x => 3*x)
                    .filter(x => x % 4 == 0)
                    .subscribe();
console.log("result2: "+result2);
```

Question: What is the difference between **result1** and **result2**?

Answer: Only `result2` contains the terminal operator `subscribe()`, so only `result2` will contain any output.

Both observables start with the numbers 0 through 6, which are multiplied by 3 because of the `map()` operator, and then only the numbers that are multiples of 4 will be displayed. Thus, the output consists of the numbers 0 and 12.

Terminal Operators are Active

Venkat Subramanian explains the difference between intermediate operators and terminal operators in Observables by recounting a story of his wife and two teenaged sons (paraphrased below), all of whom are watching television in their living room:

```
Mother: "It's time to switch off the TV."
Sons:   [No response.]
Mother: "It's time to take out the trash."
Sons:   [Nobody moves.]
Mother: "You need to start working on your homework."
Sons:   [Still nothing.]
```

```
Some time passes . . .
Mother: "I'm going to get your father."
Sons:   [Leaping into action . . .]
```

If this analogy has triggered a "lightbulb moment" for you regarding intermediate operators and terminal operators, the good news is that many of the
code samples in this chapter will be *much* simpler to understand. If you still
aren't sure, think of the first three "requests" (by the mother) as analogous
to intermediate operators. The mother's final statement acts like a terminal
operator, which then results in the execution of the first three "requests."

With these observations in mind, let's rewind to the beginning with
Lambda Expressions in Java8, which is the topic of the next section.

Lambda Expressions in Java8

Lambda Expressions are included in this chapter because such expressions appear in Java classes that use RxJava2. The examples involving
Lambda Expressions will give you enough knowledge to understand
basic expressions, and you can find online material that delves more
deeply into Lambda Expressions if you are interested in doing so.

In essence, Java8 Lambda Expressions are a replacement for anonymous inner classes in Java. As you know, a method must belong to a Java
class, whereas a Lambda Expression can exist outside of a Java class.
Hence, you will sometimes see a Lambda Expression described as an
"anonymous function."

Here are some other properties of Lambda Expressions:

- single as well as multi-line code for the "body"
- the body can throw exceptions
- an explicit return statement is not required
- round brackets represent a no-argument list
- curly braces are not required for single-line body

Java8 supports Lambda Expressions that enable you to replace anonymous inner classes. As a simple example, the following code block illustrates how to start an instance of the Java Thread class via an anonymous
inner class:

```
new Thread(new Runnable() {
    public void run() {
```

```
      showName();
   }
}).start();
```

The preceding code block is very compact: the `new` operator creates an instance of the `Thread` class, and the `run()` method invokes the `showName()` method (defined elsewhere), after which the `start()` method is invoked in order to execute the `Thread`.

In Java8 you can replace the preceding code block with this code snippet:

```
new Thread(() -> showName()).start();
```

The preceding code snippet uses the new Java8 syntax for `Lambda Expressions` and, as you can see, the code is much shorter and simpler than the first code block that contains an anonymous inner class. In addition, the Java compiler performs the necessary code generation and compilation "behind the scenes."

Notice that both code blocks reference a method `showName()` that is defined elsewhere. In fact, Listing 10.1 displays the contents of the class `Lambda1.java` that contains both of the preceding code blocks and also an example of the `showName()` method.

LISTING 10.1 Lambda1.java

```
public class Lambda1
{
    private String fname = "John";
    private String lname = "Smith";

    public void showName()
    {
        System.out.println("Name: "+fname+" "+lname);
    }

    public Lambda1() {}

    public void performTest()
    {
        System.out.println("Old style invocation...");
        new Thread(new Runnable() {
            public void run() {
                showName();
            }
        }).start();
```

```
        System.out.println("New style invocation...");
        new Thread(() -> showName()).start();
    }

    public static void main(String[] args)
    {
        Lambda1 l1 = new Lambda1();
        l1.performTest();
    }
}
```

Listing 10.1 contains two code blocks, both of which were discussed earlier in this section (please read them if you have not already done so).

Other Aspects of Lambda Expressions

This section contains an overview of the following topics that are discussed in subsections:

- Functional Interfaces
- Type Inferencing
- Method References

Functional Interfaces

A functional interface is a Java interface that contains a single abstract method. For example, the `Runnable` interface consists only of the `run()` method. In case you are new to Java programming, Java8 introduced default methods (which are not abstract) in Java8 interface definitions, and also introduced interfaces with static methods.

In addition, Java8 and higher support the `@FunctionalInterface` annotation (in order to support `Lambda Expressions`), an example of which is here:

```
@FunctionalInterface
public interface MyInterface {
    int doSomething();
}
```

The preceding annotation (shown in bold) indicates that `MyInterface` is a functional interface, which is clearly true because this interface contains only the `doSomething()` method.

Type Inferencing

Java8 and higher also support type inferencing, which means that the compiler can often infer the parameter types in an expression. Java8 supports type inferencing for `Lambda Expressions`, an example of which is here:

```
T void sort(List<T> l, Comparator<? Super T> c);
```

The preceding method sorts an array of objects based on the order induced by the specified comparator. All array elements must be mutually comparable by the specified comparator. Specifically, `c.compare(e1, e2)` must not throw a `ClassCastException` for any elements e1 and e2 in the array.

Method References

Method references enable the reuse of a method as a `Lambda Expression`. Method references use a double colon ("::") instead of an arrow ("->") syntax that you see in definitions of `Lambda Expressions` (an example is given later in the chapter).

There are three types of method references in Java8:

- a static method
- an instance method of an existing type
- an instance method of an arbitrary type

As an illustration of a defining a static method reference, suppose that you want to convert a given string to an integer. The latter can be accomplished via the `parseInt()` method of the `Integer` class. The `Lambda Expression` for the conversion has a very simple definition, as shown here:

```
(String str) -> Integer.parse(int(str)
```

This concludes the material regarding `Lambda Expressions`, and the next section discusses Streams in Java8.

Working with Streams

A `Stream` is an abstraction that is a layer above actual data and objects. A `Stream` involves the flow of data and operators that can be "applied" to a `Stream`. Examples of data streams include: a Twitter stream, a Netflix movie that is streaming through a browser (or other device), a live stream of a remote presentation, a stock market stream, and so forth.

NOTE *The goal is to realize that everything is a stream.*

A `Stream` is evaluated "lazily," which means evaluation is delayed as long as possible. The types of operators that you can use to evaluate data items in a `Stream` are discussed in the next section.

Stream Operators

A `Stream` supports two types of operators: intermediate ("eager") operators and terminal ("lazy") operators. Terminal operators minimize memory consumption, so they are well-suited for large data streams. On the other hand, intermediate operators are well-suited for performance, but they also consume large amounts of memory. An intermediate operator manipulates the data in the stream, after which subsequent operators (if any) can perform additional data manipulation.

For example, suppose that a data stream consists of positive integers. The `filter()` operator enables you to "extract" only the numbers that meet some criteria that is expressed via conditional logic. Simple examples of conditional logic include determining whether or not a number is an even number, or a multiple of 7, or a multiple of 3 that is also a multiple of 10, and so forth. The conditional logic can be placed in a single `filter()` operator, or split into multiple `filter()` invocations.

NOTE *Intermediate operators are executed after a terminal operator is invoked.*

The following stream illustrates how to define a `filter()` operator to retrieve only even numbers:

```
Arrays.stream(new int[] {1, 2, 3, 4})
    .filter(n -> n % 2 == 0)
    .forEach(System.out::println);
```

In the preceding code snippet, the `stream()` operator and the `filter()` operator are intermediate operators, and the `forEach()` operator is the terminal operator. When we discuss Observables, you will see that the `filter()` operator is also available, and the `subscribe()` method is the terminal operator instead of the `forEach()` operator.

Marble Diagrams

"Marble diagrams" are popular because of their visually oriented representation of the execution sequence of intermediate operators in FRP. An example of a marble diagram involving the filter() operator is here: *http://rxmarbles.com/#filter.*

If you prefer marble diagrams, then by all means study them for the other operators that are co-located in the preceding link.

Order of Data Evaluation

By way of analogy, Unix enables you to combine multiple commands via the Unix pipe ("|") symbol, whereby the output of one "stage" becomes the input of the next "stage." Some Unix commands reduce the output between successive stages, whereas other Unix commands create a new set of data. Here is a simple example:

```
find . -print | grep "\.java$" |xargs grep Observable >mylist.
txt
```

However, the preceding comparison between Unix pipes and Streams (or Observables) is imprecise. On one hand, each executable in a Unix pipe performs its entire operation before sending its output to the next command. On the other hand, each object in a Stream (or Observable) "winds its way" through all the operators that are included in the Stream, and then the next object is similarly processed, and so on until every object has been processed. This difference has implications regarding the impact on performance due to the order of operators. In general, specify the filter() operators (if any) before any map() operators, provided that you do not change the output (more about this later).

Collections versus Streams

In very brief terms, a Collection is a number of objects defined at one point in time, and they occupy storage in memory. By contrast, streams process on-demand data and do not store data. One analogy is to compare a DOM-based XML parser versus a SAX-based parser. An even simpler analogy: a Collection is like a set of cars in a parking lot, whereas a Stream is like sitting on the side of a road and watching cars drive past you.

Another important difference is that a Stream can represent an infinite number of data elements, such as data retrieved from periodically making `HTTP` requests from an external data source. Although Streams and Collections iterate on a number of elements, Streams use internal iteration while Collections use external iteration.

Infinite Streams

Infinite Streams are streams that do not "impose" a terminal value. An example of such a stream is here:

```
System.out.println(
  Stream.iterate(1, e -> e+1)
        .filter(e -> e > 40)
        .findFirst()
        .orElse(3));
```

The preceding stream contains the `iterate()` operator that starts from the integer 1 and then "maps" each integer to its successor (i.e., the integer incremented by 1). The `filter()` operator returns a given integer only if its value is greater than 40.

Next the `findFirst()` operator returns the first value if one exists, which in this case is the integer 41. If a first value does not exist, the `orElse()` operator returns the integer 3.

The interesting point to notice is that the `iterate()` method can start with initial value and return all the numbers that are greater than that initial value (which is an infinite stream).

Java Streams and Operators

The material in this section is included in this chapter because this material will greatly facilitate your understanding of Observables (so you only need to "struggle" once). However, keep in mind that while a `Stream` is very similar to an `Observable`, there is a key difference: a Java8 `Stream` is processed synchronously whereas an `Observable` is processed asynchronously. Moreover, a Java8 `Stream` is pull-based whereas an `Observable` is push-based.

The previous sections described Streams and the types of `Stream` operators, and also how Streams are evaluated. This section discusses some of the details regarding Streams in Java8.

A Java `Stream` is a source of objects, where the objects are produced at different points in time. Java Streams support a diverse set of operators, such as `filter()`, `map()`, `merge()`, `range()`, `sorted()`, `findFirst()`, `ifPresent()`, `anyMatch()`, `noneMatch()`, and numeric operators such as `sum()`, `max()`, and `min()`.

The preceding operators have intuitive names, whereas some other operators have similar-sounding names with non-intuitive differences in behavior. For example, the map-related operators `flatMap()`, `flatMapLatest()`, `mergeMap()`, `concatMap()`, `switchMap()`, and `flatten()` have different semantics. This chapter contains code samples that illustrate some of those differences (and some of them are left as an exercise). As pointed out earlier, marble diagrams provide a very nice visual illustration of how operators are executed.

Java Stream Classes

The Java package `java.util.stream` contains `Stream`-related classes and interfaces. For example, the `StreamsFilter1.java` class (shown later in this chapter) contains the following `import` statements:

```
import java.util.Arrays;
import java.util.List;
import java.util.stream.*;
```

As a quick preview, this Java class contains the following stream definition:

```
Stream.of("d2", "a2", "b1", "b3", "c")
    .filter(s -> {
        System.out.println("filter1: " + s);
        return true;
    });
```

As you will see in the Java class `Streams2.java` (discussed later in this chapter), `Streams` can be obtained from a range of numbers, as shown here:

```
IntStream.range(1,4).forEach(System.out::println);
```

A `Stream` can be applied to any collection, which obviates the necessity of `for` loops in functional programming. A `Stream` can also be obtained from a Java `Array`, as shown here (notice the absence of `for` loops):

```
Arrays.stream(new int[] {1, 2, 3, 4})
    .map(n -> 3*n)
    .average()
    .ifPresent(System.out::println);
```

Although the preceding code snippets might not be 100% clear, you can probably get a sense of what they do, and you can see how to chain operators together.

Java8 and Parallel Streams

Java 8 provides Parallel Streams for parallel programming. A `Stream` can process a `Collection`, and any `Collection.stream()` can be "parallelized" by replacing it with the `Collection.parallelStream()` method.

As an exercise, replace the `stream()` method with the `parallelStream()` method in the code samples that involve a `Collection`: doing so will utilize all the available cores on your machine.

A Java Stream Example (1)

Before you can work with the code samples in this section, download `rxjava.jar` here: *http://mvnrepository.com/artifact/io.reactivex/rxjava/1.1.5.*

Next, include `rxjava.jar` in the CLASSPATH environment variable in order to create Java programs with Observables.

Listing 10.2 displays the contents of the `Streams1.java` that illustrates how to create a simple `Stream` in a Java program. Notice that the code invokes the `stream()` method in the `Arrays` class in order to convert a `List` of items into a `Stream`.

LISTING 10.2 Streams1.java

```
import java.util.Arrays;
import java.util.List;

public class Streams1
{
    public static void main(String[] args)
    {
        List<String> myList =
            Arrays.asList("a1", "a2", "b2", "b1", "b3");

        // output: B1 B2 B3 (on separate lines)
        myList
          .stream()
          .filter(s -> s.startsWith("b"))
          .map(String::toUpperCase)
```

```
        .sorted()
        .forEach(System.out::println);

    // output: a1
    Arrays.asList("a1", "a2", "a3")
          .stream()
          .findFirst()
          .ifPresent(System.out::println);
  }
}
```

Listing 10.2 contains a `main()` method that starts by initializing the variable `myList` as a list of strings. The next code block creates a `Stream` from the `myList` array by invoking the `stream()` method. Next, the `Stream` chains the intermediate operators `filter()`, `map()`, and `sort()` that retrieve the strings which start with lowercase "b," then converts those strings to uppercase, and then sorts the matching strings. The terminal operator `forEach()` causes the result set to be printed. The third code block in Listing 10.2 uses the `findFirst()` operator to extract the first data item from a stream of strings and then prints that data item (if it exists).

Compile and launch the code in Listing 10.2 (make sure `CLASSPATH` is set correctly) and you will see the following output:

```
B1
B2
R3
a1
```

A Java Stream Example (2)

Listing 10.3 displays the contents of the `Streams2.java` that illustrates how to use Streams in a Java program. Unlike the code in Listing 10.1, this code sample uses the `Stream` class and the `IntStream` class in the `java.util.stream` package in order to create Streams.

LISTING 10.3 Streams2.java

```
import java.util.Arrays;
import java.util.List;
import java.util.stream.*;

public class Streams2
{
    public static void main(String[] args)
    {
```

```
// #1 output: a1
Stream.of("a1", "a2", "a3")
      .findFirst()
      .ifPresent(System.out::println);

// #2 output: 1 2 3 4 (on separate lines)
IntStream.range(1, 4)
         .forEach(System.out::println);

// #3 output: 7.5
Arrays.stream(new int[] {1, 2, 3, 4})
      .map(n -> 3*n)
      .average()
      .ifPresent(System.out::println);

// #4 output: 3
Stream.of("a1", "a2", "a3")
      .map(s -> s.substring(1))
      .mapToInt(Integer::parseInt)
      .max()
      .ifPresent(System.out::println);

// #5 output: Z1 Z2 Z3 Z4 Z5 (on separate lines)
IntStream.range(1, 5)
         .mapToObj(i -> "Z" + i)
         .forEach(System.out::println);

// #6 output: X1 X2 X3 X4 (on separate lines)
Stream.of(1.0, 2.0, 3.0, 4.0)
      .mapToInt(Double::intValue)
      .mapToObj(i -> "X" + i)
      .forEach(System.out::println);
    }
}
```

Listing 10.3 contains a main() method that defines six Streams, and each stream is preceded with a comment line that displays the output of that stream. For instance, stream #4 is a stream consisting of the strings a1, a2, and a3, followed by the map() operator that "extracts" the character in the second position of each string via the substring() function. When the first element of the stream reaches the map() operator, the *string* 1 is passed to the mapToInt() operator that returns the *integer* 1, which is assigned the current maximum via the max() operator.

In a similar manner, the string a2 is processed, after which the number 2 (from the string a2) becomes the new maximum value, and then the number 3 becomes the new (and final) maximum value after the third stream element a3 is processed.

Compile and launch the code in Listing 10.3 and you will see the output that is listed in the comments in Listing 10.3.

How Stream Items Are Processed

The "intuitive" (and incorrect) thought is that the strings a1, a2, a3 in Listing 10.3 are passed "in bulk" to the map() operator, after which the numbers 1, 2, and 3 are passed "in bulk" to the mapToInt() operator, and so forth.

However, each element in a Stream is processed from "top to bottom" and *not* in a "bulk" manner. Consequently, the first item a1 is processed all the way down to the max() operator before the second item a2 is processed (and then a3 is processed).

Thus, Streams—and Observables—are different from Unix pipe commands that send *all* the output of one command in the pipe as the "full" input to the next command in the pipe.

Why is this point important? Consider a Collection class, such as an array, that needs to allocate memory for a set of items. In an (albeit extreme) case where the array contains 1,000,000,000 items, a large amount of memory is required for those items, which could cause in an out-of-memory error. On the other hand, Streams and Observables do not need to pre-allocate memory for all the items in the Stream because the items appear over a period of time instead of "all at once."

NOTE *Intermediate operators in Observables process stream elements in a "depth-first" manner, not in a "breadth-first" manner.*

A Java Stream Example (3)

Listing 10.4 displays the contents of the StreamsFilter1.java that illustrates how to use Streams in a Java program.

LISTING 10.4 StreamsFilter1.java

```
import java.util.Arrays;
import java.util.List;
import java.util.stream.*;

public class StreamsFilter1
{
   public static void main(String[] args)
   {
      // #1 output: nothing
      Stream.of("d2", "a2", "b1", "b3", "c")
            .filter(s -> {
                System.out.println("filter1: " + s);
                return true;
            });
```

```
// #2 output: (on separate lines)
Stream.of("d2", "a2", "b1", "b3", "c")
    .filter(s -> {
        System.out.println("filter2: " + s);
        return true;
    })
    .forEach(s -> System.out.println("forEach:
                                        " + s));


// #3 output: (on separate lines)
Stream.of("d2", "a2", "b1", "b3", "c")
    .map(s -> {
        System.out.println("map: " + s);
        return s.toUpperCase()+s;
      //return s.toUpperCase();
    })
    .anyMatch(s -> {
        System.out.println("anyMatch: " + s);
        return s.startsWith("A");
    });
    }
}
```

Listing 10.4 contains three Streams that are preceded with a comment line that indicates the output of each Stream. Compile and launch the code in Listing 10.4 and you will see that the output is the concatenation of the output listed in the comment lines.

So far you have seen examples of chaining intermediate operators together. Due to their simplicity, performance was not an issue. However, performance can become an important consideration in more complex Streams, and the following article (along with its accompanying code) provides some insight regarding filters and streams:

> *https://dzone.com/articles/*
> *single-filter-perform-better-than-multiple-one-in*
>
> *https://github.com/rokon12/stream-filter-benchmark*

As you learned earlier, Java8 Streams are processed synchronously. However, the JDK9 Flow API processes streams asynchronously, which makes it well-suited for reactive programming, and also provides methods such as Flow.Publisher and Flow.Subscription. In case you are interested in a comparison of JDK9 Flow API versus RxJava Observables in order to see the differences, the following link is useful: *http://stackoverflow.com/questions/30216979/difference-between-java-8-streams-and-rxjava-observables*.

This concludes the section in this chapter regarding Java Streams. Hopefully you have a reasonable understanding of a `Stream`, which will serve you well in the discussion regarding Observables in the next section.

What Is Functional Reactive Programming (FRP)?

There are various definitions of FRP that you can find on the Web. For our purposes, FRP is based on a combination of the `Observer` pattern, the `Iterator` pattern, and functional programming. Also navigate to the Reactive home page: *http://reactivex.io/*.

If you're really impatient to get started with FRP, here is a very good starting point: *https://gist.github.com/staltz/868e7e9bc2a7b8c1f754*.

Conal Elliott created the Functional Reactive Programming paradigm, and his definition has very specific semantics, some of which is described here: *https://stackoverflow.com/questions/1028250/ what-is-functional-reactive-programming*.

A looser definition of FRP involves a combination of two other concepts:

1) Reactive Programming focuses on asynchronous data streams, which you can listen to and react to accordingly
2) Functional Programming emphasizes calculations via mathematical-style functions, immutability and expressiveness, and minimizes the use of variables and state

Reactive Programming supports a number of operators that provide powerful functionality when working with asynchronous streams. The Reactive Programming paradigm avoids "callback hell" that can occur in other environments, which is arguably an important consideration. Moreover, Observables provide greater flexibility than working with Promise-based toolkits and libraries.

Regarding the use of functional programming: this style of programming can reduce the amount of state in a program, which in turn can help you reduce the number of bugs in your code. Hence, the combination of Reactive Programming and functional programming enables you to write more succinct yet powerful code.

According to the Reactive home page, FRP handles errors properly in asynchronous streams and also avoid the necessity of writing custom code to deal with threads, synchronization, and concurrency. From another (perhaps more familiar) perspective, FRP is the "culmination" of the progression that starts from Collections, then to Streams, and finally to asynchronous Streams.

The previous part of this chapter showed you how to create Java Streams from Java Collections. The next section introduces you to `RxJava2`, along with code samples that illustrate how to use `Observables` and various operators that are available in `RxJava2`.

The `Observer` Pattern

The `Observer` pattern is a powerful pattern that is implemented in many programming languages. In simplified terms, the `Observer` pattern involves an `Observable` (i.e., something that is observed or "watched") and one or more `Observer` objects. An `Observer` (also called a subscriber) "watches" for changes in data or the occurrence of events in another object. In general, an `Observable` is "tracked" by one or more `Observer` objects. When a state change or an event occurs, the `Observable` notifies those `Observer` objects.

What Is RxJava2?

`RxJava2` is a library of APIs for asynchronous and event-based programs using observable sequences for the Java VM. `RxJava` was created as a port from Netflix and is available with an Apache 2.0 License, and its home page is here: *https://github.com/ReactiveX/RxJava/tree/2.x.*

Note that the preceding link is the Github repository for `RxJava2`, which supersedes `RxJava 1.x`. If you are using an older version of `RxJava`, it's probably a good idea to plan on updating your code. Fortunately, support for version `1.x` will be available for several years, according to the `RxJava2` documentation.

`RxJava2` is a Java VM implementation of Reactive Extensions, which is a library for composing asynchronous and event-based programs by using observable sequences.

The relevant code snippet for `build.gradle` is here:

```
compile 'io.reactivex.rxjava2:rxjava:x.y.z'
```

RxJava2 and Observables

`RxJava2` extends the observer pattern to support sequences of data/events and adds operators that allow you to compose sequences together declaratively while abstracting away concerns about things like low-level threading, synchronization, thread-safety and concurrent data structures.

RxJava2 supports Observables and Subscribers. Observables notify Subscribers when Observables emit data or events. In addition, Subscribers are notified about an "end of data" event (onCompleted) or about any errors (onError). The three scenarios involving events, an error, and an end of data event have corresponding functions called onNext, onError, and onCompleted() that are included in the Observer interface. A Subscriber also has an unsubscribe() method that "breaks" the connection between an Observer and a Subscriber. The support for this method is one important way in which FRP differs from IPC (Inter Process Communication).

Operators

Observables support various operators that can be chained together in order to transform data that is emitted by an Observable, and the destination of the transformed data is a subscriber. Operators are methods in Observables that enable you to compose new observables and also to create custom operators based on RxJS operators. Examples of intermediate operators include filter(), map(), reduce(), merge(), and flatMap(), and you will see code samples involving these operators later in this chapter.

RxJava with Observables

Make sure that you update the CLASSPATH environment variable to include the appropriate JAR file (mentioned earlier in this chapter), otherwise the Java code samples referencing an Observable class will not compile correctly.

Listing 10.5 displays the contents of RxObservable1.java that illustrates how to use an Observable to print a message in a Java program.

LISTING 10.5 RxObservable1.java

```
import java.util.Arrays;
import java.util.List;

import rx.Observable;
import rx.Observer;

public class RxJavaObservable1
{
```

```
public static void main(String[] args)
{
   List<String> list = Arrays.asList("one", "two",
                                                 "three");
   Observable<List<String>> listObservable =
                                   Observable.just(list);

   listObservable.subscribe(new
                            Observer<List<String>>() {
       @Override
       public void onCompleted() {}

       @Override
       public void onError(Throwable e) {}

       @Override
       public void onNext(List<String> list) {
                       System.out.println(list);
       }
   });
}
}
```

Listing 10.5 initializes the `list` variable as a `List` of the 3 strings `one`, `two`, and `three`, followed by the `listObservable` variable that is an `Observable` created from the `list` variable.

The next section in Listing 10.5 implements the `subscribe()` operator by defining the methods `onCompleted()`, `onError()`, and `onNext()` that are invoked when the `Observable` is complete, when an error occurs, or when the next item in the `Observable` is available, respectively.

Compile and launch the code in Listing 10.5 and you will see the 3 strings `one`, `two`, and `three` displayed on separate output lines.

A Simple Observable with the map() Function

Listing 10.6 displays the contents of the `MyObservableMapJ.java` that illustrates how to use Observables in a Java program.

LISTING 10.6 MyObservableMapJ.java

```
import rx.Observable;
import rx.functions.Func1;
import java.util.List;
import rx.functions.Action1;
import rx.Subscriber;
import java.util.concurrent.TimeUnit;

public class MyObservableMapJ
```

```
{
  public static void main(String[] args)
  {
     Observable
        .interval(200, TimeUnit.MILLISECONDS)
        .take(10)
        .map(new Func1<Long, String>() {
           @Override
           public String call(Long x) {
              return "x = "+x+" "+x+"*10 = "+(x*10);
           }
        })
        .toBlocking()
        .forEach(new Action1<String>() {
           @Override
           public void call(String s) {
              System.out.println(s);
           }
        });
  }
}
```

Listing 10.6 defines an `Observable` that starts when 200 milliseconds have elapsed, and after each "clock tick" of duration `TimeUnit.` `MILLISECONDS` an integer is emitted. The integers start from 0, and only the first 10 integers are "taken" via the `take()` operator.

Each integer is supplied to the `map()` operator, which generates an output of the following form (x is replaced successively by the integers 0 through 10):

```
"x = "+x+" "+x+"*10 = "+(x*10);
```

Next, the `toBlocking()` method in the main method of a Java program prevents the program from exiting prematurely: comment out this line of code to confirm that no output is displayed.

Finally, the `forEach()` operator (which is a terminal operator) displays the output, which is shown below:

```
x = 0 0*10 = 0
x = 1 1*10 = 10
x = 2 2*10 = 20
x = 3 3*10 = 30
x = 4 4*10 = 40
x = 5 5*10 = 50
x = 6 6*10 = 60
x = 7 7*10 = 70
x = 8 8*10 = 80
x = 9 9*10 = 90
```

The next section contains another example of an `Observable` and the `map()` function in a Java program.

Another Observable with the map() Function

Listing 10.7 displays the contents of the `MyObservableMapJ.java` that illustrates how to use Observables in a Java program.

LISTING 10.7 MyObservableMap2J.java

```
import rx.Observable;
import rx.functions.Func1;
import java.util.List;
import rx.functions.Action1;
import rx.Subscriber;
import java.util.concurrent.TimeUnit;

public class MyObservable2J
{
    public static void main(String[] args)
    {
        Observable
          .interval(200, TimeUnit.MILLISECONDS)
          .take(10)
          .map(new Func1<Long, String>() {
              @Override
              public String call(Long x) {
                  if (x % 3 == 0) {
                      return x+": Multiple of 3";
                  } else if (x % 5 == 0) {
                      return x+": Multiple of 5";
                  } else {
                      return x+": NEITHER";
                  }
              }
          })
          .toBlocking()
          .forEach(new Action1<String>() {
              @Override
              public void call(String s) {
                  System.out.println(s);
              }
          });
    }
}
```

Listing 10.7 contains the operators `interval()`, `take()`, `map()`, `toBlocking()`, and `forEach()` that you saw in the previous section. The difference is the conditional logic in the `call()` method, which checks whether or not a number is a multiple of 3, a multiple of 5, or neither.

Compile and launch the code in Listing 10.6 and you will see the following output:

```
0: Multiple of 3
1: NEITHER
2: NEITHER
3: Multiple of 3
4: NEITHER
5: Multiple of 5
6: Multiple of 3
7: NEITHER
8: NEITHER
9: Multiple of 3
```

Exercise: Change Listing 10.7 to take 30 numbers and to display the numbers that are multiples of 3 *and* 5 before the numbers that are multiple of 3 *or* 5.

An Observable with Multiple Operators

Listing 10.8 displays the contents of the RxJavaOperators1.java that illustrates how to use Observables in a Java program.

LISTING 10.8 RxJavaOperators1.java

```java
import java.util.Arrays;
import java.util.List;

import rx.Observable;

public class RxJavaOperators1
{
    public static void main(String[] args)
    {
        List<String> list = Arrays.asList("Hello",
                                "World", "RxJava");

        Observable.from(list)
                .filter(s -> s.contains("e"))
                .map(s -> s.toUpperCase())
                .reduce(new StringBuilder(),
                                StringBuilder::append)
                .subscribe(System.out::print,
                        e -> {},
                        () -> System.out.println("!")
                );
    }
}
```

Listing 10.8 creates an `Observable` from a list of three strings, and then invokes several intermediate operators. The `from()` operator converts other objects and data types into Observables, which in this example creates an `Observable` from the variable `list`. Next, the `filter()` operator returns a string if it contains the letter e, followed by the `map()` operator that returns the result of converting the string to uppercase letters.

Next the `reduce()` operator uses an instance of the Java `StringBuilder` class and invokes its `append()` method in order to concatenate the strings that it "receives." Finally, the `subscribe()` operator invokes the `print()` method of the Java `System.out` class in order to display the result, which is shown here:

```
HELLOWORLDRXJAVA!
```

Cold versus Hot Observables

A *cold* observable is comparable to watching a recorded movie (e.g., viewed in a browser). Although users navigate to the same URL at different times, all of them see the entire contents of the movie, from the start of the movie until the end of the movie (or whenever they navigate away from the website). In the case of cold observables, a new producer (movie instance) is created for each consumer (which is analogous to a person watching the movie).

By contrast, a *hot* observable is comparable to watching a live online presentation. Users navigate to a website at different times, and instead of seeing the entire presentation, they only see the portion from the point in time that they launched the presentation. In the case of cold observables, the same producer (streaming presentation) is used for each consumer (person watching the presentation).

What Is Back Pressure?

Back pressure refers to the situation in which an `Observable` emits items faster than an operator or observer can consume them. For example, the `zip` operator combines data from two (or more) Observables. If the first `Observer` emits items faster than the second `Observer`, this will result in back pressure.

RxJava 1.1 supports the `onBackpressureBuffer` operator that keeps a buffer of all unobserved emissions from the source `Observable`. You can specify the capacity of the buffer, and an `Observable` will terminate with an error in the event of a buffer overflow.

More information is here: *http://reactivex.io/RxJava/javadoc/rx/Observable.html#onBackpressureBuffer(long,%20rx.functions.Action0)*.

An `RxMarbles` diagram is here: *http://rxmarbles.com/#pausable Buffered*.

The key point to understand is that an `Observer` controls the rate (and stop/start points) at which cold Observables can produce items.

By contrast, hot Observables generate items immediately and at their own pace, which can result in back pressure. For instance, a simple example of a hot `Observable` involves mouse-related events, which are generated by users (and can be extremely rapid), and hence are not under the control of any Observers. As an additional point, note that the hot `Observable` for a live online presentation (discussed in the previous section) does not create back pressure.

This concludes the portion of the chapter regarding Observables. There are many other intermediate operators available (such as `flatMap`, `merge`, and `concat`) that you can read about in the online documentation.

What Is RxBinding?

`RxBinding` is a set of libraries for handling UI events in a fashion that is similar to RxJava. By way of comparison, consider the following code block, which is a typical way to handle a button-click event:

```
Button btn = (Button)findViewById(R.id.button);
btn.setOnClickListener(new View.OnClickListener() {
        @Override
        public void onClick(View v) {
          // do something
        }
    });
```

The following code block illustrates how to rewrite the preceding code block using `RxBinding`:

```
Button btn = (Button)findViewById(R.id.button);
Subscription buttonSub =
            RxView.clicks(btn).subscribe(new
                            Action1<Void>() {
```

```
                    @Override
                    public void call(Void aVoid) {
                        // do something
                    }
                });
// make sure to unsubscribe the subscription
```

Keep in mind the following points. First, avoid the use of weak references (read the documentation for a detailed explanation). Second, the packages and classes in each RxBinding library have a corresponding counterpart in Android. For example, the package android.widget.* contains views and widgets, and their RxBinding counterparts are located in the package com.jakewharton.rxbinding.widget.*.

Finally, RxBinding also provides libraries for the support libraries, an example of which is shown here:

```
compile 'com.jakewharton.rxbinding:rxbinding:0.4.0'
compile 'com.jakewharton.
                        rxbinding:rxbinding-design:0.4.0'
```

An Android Code Sample with RxBinding

Listing 10.9 displays the contents of MyRxBinding.java, which illustrates how to use the RxBinding library.

LISTING 10.9 MyRxBinding.java

```
package com.example.oswaldcampesato2.myrxbinding;

import android.os.Bundle;
import android.support.v7.app.AppCompatActivity;
import android.util.Log;
import android.widget.Button;
import com.jakewharton.rxbinding.view.RxView;
import rx.Subscription;
import rx.functions.Action1;

public class MyRxBinding extends AppCompatActivity
{
    private String TAG = "MyRxBinding";

    @Override
    protected void onCreate(Bundle savedInstanceState)
    {
        super.onCreate(savedInstanceState);
        setContentView(R.layout.activity_my_rx_binding);

        Button btn = (Button)findViewById(R.id.button);
```

```
Subscription buttonSub =
  RxView.clicks(btn).subscribe(new
                                Action1<Void>() {
    @Override
    public void call(Void aVoid) {
        Log.i(TAG, "Inside call method");
    }
  });

  // remember to unsubscribe the subscription
  }
}
```

Listing 10.9 contains boilerplate code and RxBinding-related import statements. Next the onCreate() method initializes btn as a reference to a Button component defined in the layout file, which is shown below:

```
<Button
    android:text="Button"
    android:layout_width="wrap_content"
    android:layout_height="wrap_content"
    android:id="@+id/button"
    app:layout_constraintBottom_toTopOf="@+id/textView"
    android:layout_marginStart="16dp"
    app:layout_constraintLeft_toLeftOf="@+id/activity_
                                my_rx_binding" />
```

Next the buttonSub variable in Listing 10.9 is an instance of the Subscription class, which subscribes to click events on the Button element. Whenever users click on the Button, the Log.i() method displays a message in the console.

Before you compile the preceding code, make sure to include the following snippet in build.gradle:

```
compile 'com.jakewharton.rxbinding:rxbinding:0.4.0'
```

An "alternative" to RxBinding is Butterknife (not discussed in this book), whose home page is here: *http://jakewharton.github.io/butterknife/*.

Butterknife uses annotations and might be more intuitive for people who have not made the transition to FRP.

What Is RxAndroid?

RxAndroid is an extension of RxJava that provides additional functionality, and its home page is here: *https://github.com/ReactiveX/RxAndroid.*

RxAndroid adds a Scheduler that schedules on the main thread or any given Looper. Download the JAR files that are required for RxAndroid from this website: *https://jar-download.com/*.

Enter the string rxandroid into the search box of the preceding link, and after a few moments the website will return a clickable link to download a zip file called jar_files.zip. Unzip the downloaded zip file, and you will see something like this:

```
jar xvf jar_files.zip
inflated: rxjava-1.0.12.jar
inflated: rxandroid-framework-0.25.0.jar
inflated: rxandroid-0.25.0.jar
```

As this book goes to print the latest version for the RxAndroid JAR files is 0.25, which might be different when you download this zip file.

After uncompressing jar_files.zip, *add the* JAR *files to the* CLASSPATH *environment variables in order to compile the code samples that are presented later in this chapter.*

Use FRP in Android for the scenario in which users rotate their Android device from portrait to landscape mode while a currently running Android application is executing a long-running task.

Examples of RxAndroid Operators

Create a project in Android Studio and then add the following lines to build.gradle:

```
compile 'io.reactivex:rxandroid:1.1.0'
compile 'io.reactivex:rxjava:1.1.0'
```

The preceding additions to build.gradle will handle the download of the required RxAndroid classes that are imported in Android mobile applications that use RxAndroid. Two common import statements are here:

```
import rx.Observable;
import rx.functions.Action1;
```

The following subsections show you how to use the RxAndroid operators just(), filter(), and map() in an Android application. For your convenience, the stand-alone Java class RxOperators.java contains the Observables (with Log.i() replaced with System.out.println()) that you will see in the following subsections, which you can launch from the command line.

Using the just() Operator

Listing 10.10 displays the contents of MainActivity.java, which illustrates how to use the just() operator.

LISTING 10.10 MainActivity.java

```
package com.example.rxandroid1;

import android.os.Bundle;
import android.support.v7.app.AppCompatActivity;
import android.util.Log;

import rx.Observable;
import rx.functions.Action1;

public class MainActivity extends AppCompatActivity
{
    private String TAG = "RxAndroid";

    @Override
    protected void onCreate(Bundle savedInstanceState)
    {
        super.onCreate(savedInstanceState);
        setContentView(R.layout.activity_main);

        Observable<String> myObservable =
                        Observable.just("Hello");

        myObservable.subscribe(new Action1<String>() {
            @Override
            public void call(String s) {
                Log.i(TAG, "s = "+s);
            }
        });
    }
}
```

Listing 10.10 contains boilerplate code and an onCreate() method that initializes the variable mObservable so that it emits "just" the string Hello. Next, the Action1 interface contains a single method named `call`. Simply pass an instance of `Action1` to the `subscribe` method, and the `call` method is invoked whenever the `Observable` emits data.

However, you can also pass an instance of the `Observer` class, which enables you to invoke its other methods called `onCompleted` and `onError`. You will see an example of doing so later in this section.

Launch the Android application and you will see the following output in `logcat`:

```
07-20 21:11:35.089 21465-21465/com.example.oswaldcampesato2.
rxandroid1 I/RxAndroid: s = Hello
```

Using the `from()` Operator

Replace the code for `MyObservable` in Listing 10.10 with the following code block:

```
//Log.i(TAG, "The from operator:");
Observable<Integer> myObservable2 =
    Observable.from(new Integer[]{1,2,3,4,5,6});

myObservable2.subscribe(new Action1<Integer>() {
    @Override
    public void call(Integer i) {
        Log.i(TAG, "i = "+String.valueOf(i));
    }
});
```

Compile the modified code and launch the application, and you will see the following output in `logcat`:

```
07-20 21:33:24.747 7209-7209/com.example.rxandroid1 D/
                              RxAndroid: i = 1
07-20 21:33:24.747 7209-7209/com.example.rxandroid1 D/
                              RxAndroid: i = 2
07-20 21:33:24.747 7209-7209/com.example.rxandroid1 D/
                              RxAndroid: i = 3
07-20 21:33:24.747 7209-7209/com.example.rxandroid1 D/
                              RxAndroid: i = 4
07-20 21:33:24.747 7209-7209/com.example.rxandroid1 D/
                              RxAndroid: i = 5
07-20 21:33:24.747 7209-7209/com.example.rxandroid1 D/
                              RxAndroid: i = 6
```

Using the `skip()` and `filter()` Operators

Replace the code for `MyObservable` in Listing 10.10 with the following code block:

```
import rx.functions.Func1;

//Log.i(TAG, "The skip/filter operators:");
Observable<Integer> myObservable3 =
    Observable.from(new Integer[]{1,2,3,4,5,6});

myObservable3
    .skip(2) // Skip the first two items
    .filter(new Func1<Integer, Boolean>() {
        @Override
        public Boolean call(Integer num ) {
            return num % 2 == 0;
        }
    })
    .subscribe(new Action1<Integer>() {
        @Override
        public void call(Integer i) {
            Log.i(TAG, "i = "+String.valueOf(i));
        }
    });
```

Compile the modified code and launch the application, and you will see the following output in logcat:

```
07-20 21:33:24.747 7209-7209/com.example.rxandroid1 D/
                                        RxAndroid: i = 2
07-20 21:33:24.747 7209-7209/com.example.rxandroid1 D/
                                        RxAndroid: i = 4
07-20 21:33:24.747 7209-7209/com.example.rxandroid1 D/
                                        RxAndroid: i = 6
```

Using the `from()` and `map()` Operators

Replace the code for `MyObservable` in Listing 10.10 with the following code block:

```
//Log.i(TAG, "The from/map operators:");
Observable<Integer> myObservable4 =
  Observable.from(new Integer[]{1,2,3,4,5,6});

myObservable4
```

```
.map(new Func1<Integer, Integer>() {
  @Override
  public Integer call(Integer num) {
    return num*num;
  }
})
.subscribe(new Action1<Integer>() {
  @Override
  public void call(Integer i) {
    Log.i(TAG, "i = "+String.valueOf(i));
  }
});
```

Compile the modified code and launch the application, and you will see the following output in `logcat`:

```
07-20 21:33:24.747 7209-7209/com.example.rxandroid1 D/
                                               RxAndroid: 1
07-20 21:33:24.747 7209-7209/com.example.rxandroid1 D/
                                               RxAndroid: 4
07-20 21:33:24.747 7209-7209/com.example.rxandroid1 D/
                                               RxAndroid: 9
07-20 21:33:24.747 7209-7209/com.example.rxandroid1 D/
                                               RxAndroid: 16
07-20 21:33:24.747 7209-7209/com.example.rxandroid1 D/
                                               RxAndroid: 25
07-20 21:33:24.747 7209-7209/com.example.rxandroid1 D/
                                               RxAndroid: 49
```

An `Observable` with RxAndroid

For your convenience, the Java code sample in this section can be compiled and launched from the command line. The Java code contains an `Observable`, and you can modify the code to specify other operators. Then when you create an Android project, just copy the relevant portions of code from Listing 10.10 into the main `Activity` class of that new Android project. Keep in mind that whenever you need to test actual functionality (such as user input from an Android text field), you need to create an Android application.

Listing 10.11 displays the contents of `RxObservable1.java`, which illustrates how to use an `Observable` in a Java class.

Note that the code sample in this section requires the inclusion of the `RxAndroid` JAR file in the `CLASSPATH` environment variable (described below).

LISTING 10.11 RxObservable1.java

```java
import java.util.ArrayList;
import java.util.List;

import rx.Observable;
import rx.Observer;

public class RxObservable1
{
   public static void main(String[] args)
   {
      ArrayList<String> names = new ArrayList<>();
      names.add("Sally");
      names.add("Dave");
      names.add("Sarah");
      names.add("John");
      names.add("Edward");

      Observable<List<String>> listObservable =
                                Observable.just(names);

      listObservable.subscribe(new
                             Observer<List<String>>() {
         @Override
         public void onCompleted() {
           System.out.println("Inside onCompleted");
         }

         @Override
         public void onError(Throwable e) {
           System.out.println("Inside onError");
         }

         @Override
         public void onNext(List<String> names) {
           System.out.println("Inside onNext names =
                                                "+names);
         }
      });
   }
}
```

Listing 10.11 contains boilerplate code and then initializes the variable names (which is an instance of the Java ArrayList class) and populates its contents with five user names. The next portion of Listing 10.11 initializes the the listObservable variable that is an Observable created from the list variable.

The next section in Listing 10.11 implements the `subscribe()` operator by defining the methods `onCompleted()`, `onError()`, and `onNext()` that are invoked when the `Observable` is complete, when an error occurs, or when the next item in the `Observable` is available, respectively.

Now add the `JAR` file `rxjava-1.1.5.jar` to the `CLASSPATH` environment variable, compile the Java code, and then launch the class in Listing 10.11. The output is shown here:

```
Inside onNext names = [Sally, Dave, Sarah, John, Edward]
Inside onCompleted
```

What about RxJS?

`RxJS` code and `RxAndroid` are very similar: after you learn one, the other is much simpler to learn. However, there are some code differences between `RxJS` code and `RxAndroid` code. For example, the following code block is for `RxJS`:

```
RxTextView.textChanges(textInput)
        .filter(text -> text.length() >= 3)
        .debounce(150, TimeUnit.MILLISECONDS)
        .subscribe(this::updateSearchResults);
```

On the other hand, the corresponding code block for `RxAndroid` is here:

```
final EditText textInput =
        (EditText)findViewById(R.id.text_input);

RxTextView.textChanges(textInput)
        .filter(text -> text.length() >= 3)
        .debounce(150, TimeUnit.MILLISECONDS)
        .observeOn(AndroidSchedulers.mainThread())
        .subscribe(this::updateSearchResults);
```

Notice the extra `Thread`-related line of code (shown in bold) in the preceding code block.

Working with RxKotlin

Kotlin provides various extensions to the Java language that you can use in Android applications, and its home page is here: *https://kotlinlang.org/*.

Since Kotlin has gained traction in Android development, this section shows you how to create a basic Kotlin application for Android in Android

Studio (which requires the Kotlin plugin) and also how to convert an existing Android application to a Kotlin application.

In case Kotlin is not already installed in Android Studio on your machine, launch Android Studio, navigate to `Configure > Plugins > Browse` repositories, and search for Kotlin. Install the Kotlin plugin (which also installs its dependencies) and then perform the following steps:

- create a new Android project
- open the MainActivity.java file
- click on the "Help" menu
- enter "Convert Java file to Kotlin file"

More information about Kotlin is here:

http://blog.gouline.net/2014/08/31/kotlin-the-swift-of-android/

http://kotlinlang.org/docs/tutorials/kotlin-android.html

https://github.com/ahmedrizwan/RxRealmRetroKotlin/tree/master

An RxKotlin Code Sample is here:

https://github.com/ReactiveX/RxKotlin.

Miscellaneous Topics

This section contains an assortment of links that might be helpful for learning about Observables

Examples of Observables and Click Events are here:

http://stackoverflow.com/questions/25457737/
how-to-create-an-observable-from-onclick-event-android

http://fernandocejas.com/2015/07/18/architecting-android-the-evolution/

Working with SQLite, Android, and RxJava:

http://java.dzone.com/articles/easy-sqlite-android-rxjava

http://blog.danlew.net/2015/09/01/how-to-upgrade-to-rxandroid-10/

`Reductor` is essentially `Redux` for Android, an example of which is here:

http://yarikx.github.io/Reductor-prologue

https://github.com/Polidea/RxAndroidBle

The following Github repository contains an Android application that creates animation effects with RxAnimation: *https://github.com/0ximDigital/* RxAnimations.

Summary

This chapter provided an introduction to FRP (Functional Reactive Programming). Then you learned about RxJava, which is a port from Netflix, along with some Java code samples that use FRP.

Next you learned about RxAndroid, which is an extension of RxJava. You saw some Java code samples that rely on an RxAndroid JAR file to use the Observable class. These code samples are convenient because they can be launched from the command line, and you can easily "blend" the RxAndroid-related code into your Android applications.

In addition, you learned about various operators that are supported by Observables, such as map(), filter(), reduce(), and also how to use Observables in RxAndroid.

INDEX